MARKETING TO THE FORTUNE 500

and other corporations

MARKETING TO THE FORTUNE 500

and other corporations

Jeffrey P. Davidson, CMC

DOW JONES-IRWIN
Homewood, Illinois   60430

This publication is designed to provide accurate and
authoritative information in regard to the subject matter
covered. It is sold with the understanding that the copyright
holder is not engaged in rendering legal, accounting, or
other professional service. If legal advice or other expert
assistance is required, the services of a competent
professional person should be sought.

*From a Declaration of Principles jointly adopted by a Committee
of the American Bar Association and a Committee of Publishers.*

ISBN 0-87094-984-5

Library of Congress Catalog Card No. 86–51669

Printed in the United States of America

1 2 3 4 5 6 7 8 9 0 K 4 3 2 1 0 9 8 7

This book is dedicated to Nancy and Richard who both always have had the entrepreneurial spirit, to Joseph V. Casamento, a champion in the cause of small business, and to the nation's business entrepreneur's—America's present-day pioneers.

PREFACE

Less than 135,000 small business suppliers currently serve the nation's largest corporations—the Fortune 500. This represents only 1 percent of all small businesses. Millions of entrepreneurs want to know how to market to major corporations.

The importance of small business to the nation's economy is well documented. The president's annual *Report to Congress on the State of Small Business* indicates that small business contributes more than 80 percent of all new jobs and a sizable portion of all research and development and gross business receipts. The small business entrepreneur has been hailed as America's contemporary pioneer and has spawned the growth of such publications as *Inc., Venture, In Business, Business Owner, Entrepreneur,* and *Enterprise.*

Margaret Hickey, Reference Librarian of the U.S. Small Business Administration, reports that over the past four years the same types of questions have come up over and over: Where can I find market research information? Where can I get addresses of corporations? Who manufacturers or distributes this product?

This is a significant information gap because the nation's Fortune 500 corporations and other major corporations have vast procurement needs, are constantly seeking new and better sources of supply, and often can't find qualified vendors.

Marketing to the Fortune 500 provides step-by-step, detailed information on how small business entrepreneurs can successfully market their goods or services to the nation's largest buyers. The material in this book embodies the results of a three-year project that the author initiated, managed, and directed. The project involved surveying 100 Fortune 500 purchasing agents, visiting on-site with 10 purchasing agents, reviewing successful corporate-sponsored small business procurement programs, and examining marketing techniques used by entrepreneurs who successfully sell to Fortune 500 firms.

The latest figures from the Small Business Administration indicates that there are now over 14 million small businesses in the United States.

Among these small businesses are firms that presently market to major corporations but wish to improve their technique, firms that would like to venture forth but have not done so, and firms that don't even realize that their products or services may be of interest to Fortune 500 corporations. Such firms will find this book useful.

ACKNOWLEDGMENTS

A partial forerunner of *Marketing to the Fortune 500* was a study directed by its author to pinpoint and determine how small and small disadvantaged businesses could effectively market to Fortune 500 and other major corporations. Accordingly, the input expertise and editorial contributions of several individuals must be recognized. Victor G. Morris was instrumental in conceptualizing and outlining many of the steps in the study. Leslie M. Rhatican's ability to develop and expand upon concepts and source material represented a crucial input. William J. Holleran ably researched, diagnosed, and synthesized the role of the modern purchasing manager and, with Dianne L. Walbrecker, performed excellent fieldwork in gathering primary research and engaged in writing and editing.

In addition, I would like to thank Joseph V. Casamento for his staunch and continuing support of my work and of the nation's small business entrepreneurs. Thanks are also offered to Louis P. Baron, Robert G. Bird, Glenn Juman, and Ziad Baradi for research and office assistance and to Judy Dubler for word processing support.

Jeffrey P. Davidson

CONTENTS

Company Approaches Market Planning: *Marketing Philosophy. Types of Individuals Employed. Long-Term Marketing Effort. Marketing Research Capabilities.* Getting Started on Your Plan

Periodical Indexes. Directories of Corporations: *Specific
Industry Directories. International Corporations. Additional
Industry Data.* Information From Uncle Sam. State
Information Sources. Newsletters. Local Resources.
Research through Networking. Using Data Bases to Reduce
Your Research Efforts. In Summary.

Who They Are. What They Do. The Changing Picture of
Purchasing. What They Look For. The Purchasing
Hierarchy: *Vice President or Director of Purchasing.
Manager of Purchasing. Procurement Engineer. Purchasing
Analyst. Expediter. Traffic Manager. Buyer. Buyer
Categories.* Getting "Inside" Purchasing: Information
Sources Abound: *Purchasing Periodicals. Purchasing
Handbooks. Local "Inside" Information.*

Calling on Purchasing Agents: *Preparation. Professionalism.
Presentation. Proof. Performance.* Calling on Technical
Personnel: *Know the Corporation Purchasing Department
Type. Know the Corporation's Purchasing Policy. Discover
Technical Needs. Play Both Ends against the Middle.*

*Cost Reduction Program. Conformance Standards and
Innovation. Security—A Growing Concern. Emergency
Contingency Planning. Quality Control Program.* Quality
Control and Assurance for Manufacturers and Distributors:
Components of the Quality Assurance Plan. Quality Control
and Assurance for Service Firms: *Developing an Overall
Quality Assurance Program.*

Directories Available. Key Periodicals. Association
Convention Information. Federal and State Agency

Information: *Regional Purchasing Magazines.* Exhibiting at
Trade Shows. A Modern-Day Phenomenon. A Low-Cost
Alternative.

Exhibits, Charts, Boxes, Lists

Introduction

*Get all the education you
can, but then, by God,* do
*something! Don't just
stand there; make something
happen.*

LEE IACOCCA

Since the start of 1980, the index of small business optimism, as compiled by the National Federation of Independent Business, indicates an upward, if uneven, trend. According to Dun & Bradstreet, a business research firm, over 650,000 new businesses are started each year and there are now some 14 million small businesses across the nation.

THE IMPORTANCE OF SMALL BUSINESS

The importance of the role played by small business in the nation's economy cannot be overemphasized. Small firms employ nearly 50 percent of the private work force, contribute over 40 percent of total revenues, and account for 38 percent of the gross national product. The 80s have been called by some the "age of the entrepreneur." The small business entrepreneur has been hailed as America's contemporary pioneer and has spawned the growth of such publications as *Inc., Venture, In Business, Business Owner, Entrepreneur,* and *Enterprise.* In 1985, *Venture* magazine boldly stated, "By almost any measure, the 1980s are shaping up as the most entrepreneurial decade in U.S. history." The word *entrepreneur* has been analyzed, headlined, and examined "more than at any other time since this nation first dreamed the American dream." With a renewed emphasis on competition, achieving excellence, and "making it on your own," this trend should continue throughout the 90s.

The biggest and best market for the products and services of small to medium-size business vendors is our nation's major industrial corporations, literally and symbolically identified as the Fortune 500—so named from the annual rankings that *Fortune* magazine bestows on private and industrial firms. These rankings are based on 14 measures: sales, assets, net income, sales change from previous year, profit change from previous year, stockholders' equity, number of employees, net income as a percentage of sales, net income as a percentage of stockholders' equity, 10-year growth in earnings per share, total return to investors—10-year average, total return to investors for previous year, assets per employee, and sales per employee.

The corporations listed in the Fortune 500 are grouped into 26 industrial categories:

Aerospace	Mining, Crude Oil Production
Apparel	Motor Vehicles and Parts
Beverages	Petroleum Refining
Building Materials	Pharmaceuticals
Chemicals	Publishing, Printing
Computers, Office Equipment	Rubber Products
Electronics	Scientific and Photographic
Food	Equipment
Forest Products	Soaps, Cosmetics
Furniture	Textiles
Industrial and Farm Equipment	Tobacco
Jewelry, Silverware	Toys, Sporting Goods
Metal Products	Transportation Equipment
Metals	

SALES IN THE BILLIONS

Since the ranking of Fortune 500 companies was initiated in 1954, General Motors has been ranked number one 22 times and Exxon Corporation 10 times. No other corporations have held the top spot. General Motors sales of $96.4 billion in 1985 represent an all-time high for sales by a single corporation. To fully appreciate their magnitude, consider that this sales total exceeds the gross national product of more than 125 countries. Quite a feat for a company that was founded less than 80 years ago.

On the lower end of the scale, but still an industrial giant, is Winnebago Industries, headquartered in Forest City, Iowa, with 1985 sales of $424 million. Firms ranked 466 to 308 obtained sales of between $500 million and $1 billion in 1985. Firms ranked between 307 and 183 had $1 billion to $2 billion in sales. Firms ranked 182 to 135 earned $2 billion to $3 billion, with the $4 billion mark being achieved at Fortune 99. Eastman Kodak (33),* headquartered in Rochester, New York, stepped over the $10 billion mark; Shell Oil (14), of Houston, Texas, tipped the $20 billion mark; and AT&T (8), headquartered in New York City, hit $34.9 billion. Here are the seven heavyweights:

General Motors (Detroit)	$96.3 billion
Exxon (New York City)	86.7 billion
Mobil (New York City)	55.9 billion
Ford Motor Company (Dearborn, Michigan)	52.8 billion
IBM (Armonk, New York)	51.1 billion
Texaco (White Plains, New York)	46.3 billion
Chevron (San Francisco)	41.7 billion

The Fortune 500 are major corporations with major purchasing needs. These needs remain constant in some areas, while changing in others. One hundred years ago Edison and Swan formed a partnership to commercially produce the first electric lamps, H. W. Goodwin invented celluloid film, Nikola Tesla constructed an electric motor that was later manufactured by Westinghouse, J. B. Dunlop invented the pneumatic tire, and George Eastman perfected the Kodak box camera. Time marches on, and the Fortune 500 corporations purchase and consume larger and larger quantities of raw materials, products, and services, providing incalculable opportunities for product and service vendors.

CALLING SMALL BUSINESS!

Yet a strange paradox exists—less than 1 percent of the nation's 14 million small businesses regularly serve as product and service vendors to the Fortune 500.

Why?

Joseph V. Casamento, former associate district director for management assistance in the Washington, D.C., district office of the U.S. Small Business Administration, believes that the reason is *fear,* or more specifically, "fear of the unknown." "Many small businesses rely on other small businesses or the federal government as their chief customers." Casamento, a 29-year veteran with the Small Business Administration, carved out a reputation as a champion of small business development

---

*Note: Number in parentheses following corporate name indicates the 1986 Fortune 500 ranking.

throughout his career. He observed entrepreneur after entrepreneur who didn't know how to get started in marketing to large corporations simply because the corporations were so large. Others, who had obtained supplier or vendor guides and knew whom to call on, failed to follow through because they were intimidated—a sad situation indeed.

If you've been considering "upping" your marketing efforts to include major corporations, now is as good a time as any. Theodore Roosevelt once said, "Do what you can, with what you have, where you are."

Small business entrepreneurs face recurring problems in their attempts to market to major private sector corporations, such as finding the time and money to market effectively, finding the right marketing contact within the corporate maze, obtaining marketing leads by geographic and product/service areas, and being able to effectively follow up on the initial contacts that have been made. Many entrepreneurs are looking for what Richard A. Connor, Jr., calls "the blue and pink pill to swallow" to immediately generate success or, in this case, contracts with major corporate buyers.

Today's society, unfortunately, is often geared toward quick results. Images of unobtainable material wealth thrown daily in our faces by Madison Avenue and Hollywood undermine our resolve to stick to a concentrated program of planning, implementation, and follow-up. There are no quick or easy solutions to the challenging task of successfully marketing to Fortune 500 and other major corporations. The lead time between the time when the potential customer is first identified and the time when the sale is actually consummated averages 18 months. For start-up firms and first-time entrepreneurs, this lead time can be crushing. For those already in business, the need to contact many buyers, make many presentations, and have many irons in the fire becomes abundantly clear. The way to get many irons in the fire is to start now!

THE CRUCIAL FACTOR

The most important component in successfully marketing to large companies, or to anyone else for that matter, is *you*, the entrepreneur. Purchasing agents first "buy" you, or your marketing representative, and then they buy the products or services of your company. Your track record, your professionalism, your integrity, and your ability to pinpoint and satisfy needs are the foundation upon which fruitful, continuing industrial relationships can be developed. The long-term reputation that you build as a vendor of integrity becomes your company's greatest asset.

CHAPTER ONE

Why Fortune 500 Corporations Want to Do Business with You

All men dream . . . but not equally,
They who dream by night in the
dusty recesses of their minds
wake in the day to find that it
is vanity; but the dreamers of
the day are dangerous men, for
they act their dream with open
eyes, to make it possible

T. E. LAWRENCE

General Motors (1), Honeywell (56), and Control Data (106) are looking for you! Why? The reasons are many. Benefits accrue to a corporation that operates a small purchasing program from numerous perspectives—business, economic, and social. Increasingly, social responsibility is a demand placed on large organizations.

The development of a small business purchasing program demonstrates an awareness of and a commitment to varied segments of our society. Major corporations have the capability to take the lead in increasing growth and marketing opportunities for small businesses. To ensure maximum economic return, these businesses must participate in capital formation and productivity. The free enterprise system can provide the stimulus for expanded participation by small business owners in the economic system. Fostering the relationship between major corporations and small businesses will develop competent entrepreneurs who provide quality, competitive products and services. The revenues produced in this way—sales, personal income, business property, and profits—will contribute to an expanded tax base.

Activities of large corporations directly affect their respective business communities. Business communities with small vendor purchasing programs have experienced additional investment opportunities for community residents, new construction and renovation of commercial property, increased purchasing and leasing of equipment, increased employment opportunities, and expansion of the local tax base. Not to be overlooked, using small business suppliers can be a boon to a corporation's public relations and help offset negative attitudes that the public may have regarding the corporation.

Organizations employing an aggressive small business procurement program reap additional benefits. A broadened pool of suppliers can increase competitiveness and result in improved goods and services and lower prices in the long run. It may provide increased leverage and flexibility with suppliers, and better service through improvement of lead times and scheduling. Many corporations have also experienced lower overhead and labor costs, as well as decreased transportation charges due to the proximity of suppliers. However, about one third of corporations prefer to use fewer vendors to a greater degree.

New suppliers are often very eager to please, and they may offer startling new services and benefits that previously had not been known by or offered to large corporations. More and more purchasing agents are realizing the contributions that vendors make to value analysis and actively seeking close vendor relations.

Major corporations that serve as prime contractors to the federal government, such as Martin Marietta (85) and Northrop (71), must, by law, submit summaries of their subcontracting activity to the U.S. Small Business Administration. A *Small Business Contracting Directory* is published annually (see accompanying box).

FEDERAL REQUIREMENT TO USE SMALL VENDORS

The *Small Business Contracting Directory* is published by the U.S. Small Business Administration, Office of Procurement Assistance, primarily for use by small business concerns as an aid in marketing. Pursuant to the Small Business Act, as amended by Public Law 95–507, a contractor's subcontracting activity under federal contracts is subject to review by the federal agency awarding the prime contract and by the Small Business Administration. The SBA has selected the major prime contractors to the federal government as those offering the greatest potential for subcontracting to small business concerns. On that basis, these companies have been selected as the SBA portfolio of prime contractors whose subcontracting activities under federal contracts, and subcontracts under those contracts, will be monitored for compliance on a regular basis under the SBA Subcontracting Assistance Program.

In the directory, companies are listed alphabetically by name (corporation, division, or company) within each of the 10 SBA regions. A sample page from the 1985 directory follows.

Small Business Subcontracting Directory

Region: 09

Company	Small Business Representative	Type of Business
Teledyne Inc Teledyne Camera Teledyne Camera Systems 131 North 5th Ave Arcadia CA 91006	Richard Herbert Small Business Administrator (818) 359-6691 Ext	Electronic Systems
Tenneco Inc Tenneco West 201 New Stine Road Bakersfield CA 93389	Earle Cooper Director of Purchasing (805) 835-6390 Ext	Processed & Fresh Foods Land Management
Textron Inc Dalmo Victor Operations Bell Aerospace Division 1515 Industrial Way Belmont CA 94002	Michal Stephens Small Business Liaison Officer (415) 594-1414 Ext 587	Antennas, TV Systems, Com- munications Systems
Textron Inc Hydraulic Research and Man- ufacturing 25200 West Rye Canyon Road Valencia CA 91355	Dudley S Averill S/B Administrator (805) 259-4030 Ext 577	Hydraulic Systems and Com- ponents
The Rand Corporation 1700 Main St Santa Monica CA 90401	C C Coy SBLO (213) 393-0411 Ext	Research Institute
Todd Shipyards 20th & Illinois Sts San Francisco CA 94120	Chuck Driskill Purchasing Agent (415) 621-8633 Ext 281	Ship Conversion and Repair
Todd Shipyards Corporation Todd Pacific Shipyards Cor- poration Los Angeles Division 710 North Front Street San Pedro CA 90733	Judy Leach Small Business Liaison Officer (213) 832-3361 Ext	Shipbuilding and Repair
Towne Realty Inc Pacific Division Offices 96-1173 Waihona Street Pearl City HI 96782	Joseph L Belin Regional Vice President (808) 455-9065 Ext	General Construction Family Housing Electrical Re- pair Marine Corps Air Station

IT STARTS AT THE TOP

The success of any purchasing program is directly related to the endorsement and level of commitment of the chief executive officer. Veteran consultant Victor G. Morris, who has had extensive experience working with and for corporate purchasing departments and to whom frequent reference will be made, points out that it is the chief executive who makes it clear that the small business purchasing program will become an integral part of the normal business operation. This is how it's done at Control Data Corporation (106), McDonnell Douglas (29), Hewlett-Packard (58), and General Motors (1), for example. Thus *your* decision to call on a major corporation is often supported from their top!

Even if the CEO endorses the small business purchasing program, for an effective program of this kind to occur, there must be a coordinated effort throughout the organization. To facilitate such an effort, there is usually one individual—clearly identified both within and outside the organization—with responsibility for developing, guiding, and monitoring the program. This is the case with Fortune 500 corporations such as International Paper (83), Philip Morris (27), Pfizer (99), and Varian Associates (311).

A TYPICAL MESSAGE TO SUPPLIERS

President's Message

This booklet will serve as a guide for prospective suppliers to us. In it they will find the policies and procedures we believe best enable us to work effectively with them.

Suppliers are a very important part of our organization. Our ability to satisfy customer needs depends on the quality of the products and services that our vendors supply and on the timeliness of their delivery. For that reason, our goal is to establish relationships with suppliers based on mutual benefit, understanding, and trust. Such relationships can only flourish in an atmosphere of honesty, fairness, and high ethical standards. These prerequisites we are pledged to provide.

Introduction

Over the years, our corporation has gained a worldwide reputation as a manufacturer of quality products. Our suppliers have played a key role in our success, and their cooperation and dependability in providing quality materials, services, and ideas have contributed greatly.

We view the contribution of our suppliers in an atmosphere of mutual respect and understanding, in which honesty and fairness are ever-present guidelines. Some of the principles underlying this philosophy will be described in succeeding pages.

The overall purpose of this pamphlet is to introduce first-time (new) suppliers to us, and to supply them with enough information to begin the process. It is only through evaluating new suppliers and their products and services that we can remain competitive.

So, we welcome you and hope that this booklet is helpful in getting you started.

The coordinator functions primarily as a central information source and contact point for company buyers and small vendors, and therefore maintains familiarity with the purchasing activities of the firm. The coordinator's duties include identifying potential suppliers and soliciting information from them, conducting seminars and workshops for purchasing personnel and small vendors, and monitoring the program's performance.

"When dealing with small suppliers, a distinction must be made between qualified and qualifiable," points out a purchasing officer with FMC (120) in Chicago. Many potential vendors will be qualifiable—with some assistance they will become qualified. Few, however, will meet the standard requirements for vendors initially. This book will help you greatly in this area.

To bring potential vendors up to standards requires an effort that goes beyond normal purchasing department procedures. Most corporations are not prepared to make this effort (for a profile of one that does, see Chapter 12). Here are a few of the ways in which purchasing coordinators have assisted small vendors:

- Provide technical, managerial, and financial assistance.
- Allow longer lead times.
- Arrange special payment terms.
- Broaden product specifications.
- Supply information on pricing practices, bid preparation, production, sales, and servicing.
- Assist in the development of a quality control program.

The accompanying chart highlights how 24 progressive Fortune 500 corporations facilitate the use of small vendors. Ten broad program areas are covered:

- Has corporate small business vendors policy.
- Has separate small/minority business office/program.
- Uses external small business vendor directories.
- Provides information on goods and services purchased.
- Provides names and phone numbers of plant purchasing agents.
- Provides specialized assistance (management, financial, technical) to small business vendors.
- Maintains directory or file on small business vendor supplier capabilities.
- Sets goals for small business vendor utilization (dollars or percentage of total purchases).

WHAT IS A SMALL BUSINESS?

The set of definitions of small business established by the U.S. Small Business Administration (SBA) is the most widely used and recognized by small business entrepreneurs, prime contractors, and government agencies.

The SBA body of definition, called "size standards," can be found in Title 13 of the *Code of Federal Regulations* (CFR), part 121. Small business is defined using different size categories for different categories of business enterprises, including agricultural production, communications, manufacturing, retailing, service, transportation and warehousing, and wholesaling.

The definitions also include subcategories under each of the categories named above. Size is usually determined by the amount of gross annual receipts. For example, service businesses in general have a size standard of $2 million for loans, meaning that a business is "small" and therefore eligible for loans if its gross annual receipts are under $2 million. There are numerous exceptions.

For some industries, the number of employees is used as a size standard. A mining firm is considered "small" if it has fewer than 500 employees.

The body of definitions for size standards is complex, and you'll need help to determine which definitions are applicable in a particular case. For more information, contact the Size Standards Division, Small Business Administration, (202) 653-6229.

- Provides incentives to purchasing personnel regarding small business vendor utilization.
- Participates in Regional Minority Purchasing Council activities.

Goals are an essential feature of the more successful procurement programs. Some progressive corporations, such as Todd Shipyards (462) and Honeywell (56), have established aggressive small vendor procurement goals. They provide a target for expected performance as well as an indicator of actual performance. Corporate goals can be based on:

- Percentage of purchases.
- Dollar value of contracts.
- Number of contracts.
- Number of small vendors used.

Others goals include number of visits to vendor sites, number of new vendors used, and number of contracts over a certain size let to small vendors. Todd Shipyards (462) publishes the efforts of its individual purchasing agents!

How Progressive Fortune 500 Corporations Facilitate Use of Small Vendors

	Amdahl (348)	Boise Cascade (105)	Control Data (106)	Crouse/Hinds–Cooper Industries (129)	Dow Corning (336)	Economics Laboratories (376)	FMC Corporation (120)	Harris (163)	Inland Steel (126)	International Paper (83)	Kaiser Aluminum (143)	Martin Marietta (85)	McDonnell Douglas (29)	Minnesota Mining (47)	Northrop (71)	Norton (277)	Owens-Illinois (108)	Penwalt (299)	Pfizer (99)	Philip Morris (27)	Todd Shipyards (462)	Upjohn (176)	Varian (311)	Zenith (225)
Has corporate SBV policy.	●	●	●	●	●	●	●	●	●	●	●	●	●	●	●	●	●	●	●	●	●	●	●	●
Has separate small/minority business office/program.		●			●	●	●	●	●	●	●	●	●	●		●		●	●	●		●	●	●
Uses external SBV directories.	●	●	●	●	●	●	●	●	●	●	●	●	●	●		●	●	●	●	●	●	●	●	●
Provides information on goods and services purchased.	●	●	●	●	●	●	●	●	●	●	●	●	●	●	●	●	●	●	●	●	●	●	●	●
Provides names and phone numbers of plant purchasing agents.	●	●	●	●	●	●	●	●	●	●	●	●	●	●	●	●	●	●	●	●	●	●	●	●
Provides specialized assistance (management, financial, technical) to SBVs.	●	●		●				●	●		●		●	●			●		●	●	●	●		
Maintains directory or file on SBV supplier capabilities.	●	●	●		●	●	●			●	●	●	●	●	●	●	●	●	●	●	●	●	●	●
Sets goals for SBV utilization ($ or % of total purchases).		●	●		●						●	●	●	●	●				●	●	●		●	●
Provides incentives to purchasing personnel re SBV utilization.		●				●	●		●			●	●	●					●	●	●			
Participates in Regional Minority Purchasing Council activities.	●	●			●				●	●	●	●	●	●	●	●		●	●	●		●		

SBV = Small business vendor.

FINDING YOUR NICHE

While many corporations are actively seeking new qualified sources of goods and services, unfortunately many small business owners, including manufacturers, but particularly nonmanufacturers such as construction contractors and professional service providers, don't recognize the varied marketing opportunities that are available. Some small business entrepreneurs, when considering their marketing potential with a particular corporation, focus only on that corporation's end product. "If Corporation X makes widgets, then all it is buying must be widget parts." This narrow focus may lead the contractor or professional service provider to believe that he or she has nothing to offer the corporation.

Although corporate purchasing departments do an excellent job of staying on stop of the wide-ranging buying needs of their firms, they are sometimes unaware of contracting and professional service needs in other divisions or departments. At Polaroid (257), for example, there is need for small service vendors in such diverse areas as transportation, construction, data entry, and even snow removal. Polaroid also seeks vendors of office furniture, electronic equipment, chemicals, and fuels. Chesebrough-Ponds (136) has used diverse small vendors, from a manufacturer of hoses and gaskets to a pharmaceuticals laboratory.

After making initial contact with the purchasing office and after being careful to "work through the system," as will be explained later, the entrepreneur can call on the key technical people who may have a need for his or her professional or contractor services.

No small contractor or professional service provider should be discouraged just because one office, department, or purchasing agent of a corporation says, "We can't use your product or service," or is otherwise discouraging. There may be great need for your product or service elsewhere in the corporation.

WHAT DO CORPORATIONS NEED?

What, then, are some of the wide-ranging needs of major corporations? The *brief* listing below indicates just some of the opportunity areas:

> *Accounting services.* At a recent conference, several corporate purchasing directors stated that there were numerous professional service opportunities throughout their corporations. Accounting services were one of the many areas cited.

Advertising. Large corporations traditionally spend millions of dollars yearly promoting their various products and employ a wide variety of services in advertising and public relations.

Architecture. Continuous additions, renovations, and remodeling of internal and external corporate facilities create the opportunity to provide architectural services.

Audiovisual Production. Corporations often require these services—but not often enough to have in-house capability. Therefore, opportunities are available in this field.

Building Management. This category includes such services as energy audits, emergency equipment, and maintenance.

Clipping Services. Large corporations are always interested in reviewing how they are portrayed in the print media and may need to concentrate on specific geographic areas.

Computer Software. Corporate data processing departments may need custom-designed software for specialized applications.

Construction. Most corporations are continuously in the process of constructing roadways, parking lots, or new buildings. Many corporations have massive construction projects under way that require use of small contractors.

Data Processing. Data entry and conversion are best handled by firms that specialize in this service, reducing the error rate and eliminating the start-up time required by in-house staff to "learn the system."

Demolition/Disposal. The demolition/disposal needs of major corporations can rival those of any municipality or city-based developer.

Electrical Contracting. As more computers, terminals, and peripherals invade the workplace, the need for rewiring and restructuring existing facilities increases. In addition, electrical contractors are needed whenever a company renovates, redesigns, or adds to its facilities.

Engineering Services. All types of engineering—civil, mechanical, chemical, biochemical, stress analysis, and structural—may be used by corporations in the development stage of new products or in the design stage of new structures.

Environmental Services. The impact of corporate operations on the environment has been under examination for more than 15 years. Specific expertise in various aspects of environmental protection and impact analysis are of interest to many corporations.

Food Services. Large corporations have tens of thousands of employees to feed each day.

Graphics. Often the best way to achieve a fresh approach in graphic design is to use new sources of talent. A major corporate account would be a real asset in a small business's marketing portfolio.

Health Services Planning. Many corporations, recognizing that a healthy and fit employee is more productive, actively seek health service planners and programs to assist with corporate human resource development.

Industrial Design/Exhibit. The marketing divisions of major corporations frequently send staff to trade shows and exhibits. Imaginative and creative exhibits are always in demand.

Landscaping. Corporations need landscape contracting services for the very same reasons that commercial developers and government agencies need them—maintaining the appearance of facilities.

Legal Services. As society grows more complex, a wider variety of legal services are needed by corporations, some of which may not be provided by their legal departments.

Management Consulting. Virtually all of the top 1,000 corporations in the United States have employed the services of one or more management consultants in the past 12 months. Consulting engagements may range from feasibility studies to placement services.

Noise Impact Studies. Noise impact, particularly within the office, is another area offering potential opportunities.

Office Furniture and Supplies. Corporations require desks, lamps, tables, computer furniture, fixtures, dividers, cabinets, shelves, and chairs; plus pens, paper, and so forth.

Printing. Printed materials used by corporations are proliferating, and the need for printing services continues unabated. Electronic mail and similar technologies have not yet had an adverse impact on the printing industry.

Repair Services. While much of the equipment and machinery used by corporations is under warranty or service contract, general repair services are always in demand.

Research. This is a broad category. However, depending on the type of research and/or testing provided, there can be many opportunities within different product lines of the same corporation.

Security.   Major corporations, particularly their CEOs and presidents, recognize the growing need for corporate and personal security and want reliable services and systems.

Storage.   Many plant sites with fixed plant capacity and storage availability must seek nearby facilities to relieve the need for heavy plant-related expenditures.

Transportation.   Most corporations need trucking companies to deliver their supplies and transport their products to the marketplace. For its own fleet of vehicles, a corporation will need equipment and maintenance, security and protection services, and mobile communication equipment and services.

Videotape Production.   This service is especially needed by human resource departments for in-house training programs.

Word Processing.   Technical projects and "onetime" projects are more cost-effective if they are done by an outside firm—eliminating the need for a massive increase in corporate personnel.

Don't assume that a company cannot use your service just because it may not be directly related to the corporation's end products. Contractors, professional service companies, and manufacturers that cannot recognize the wide-ranging opportunities with major corporations are limiting their potential. It will take some prospecting to identify the right corporate contacts, but the potential rewards certainly justify the effort!

Now let's look at the case of an entrepreneur who knew that what he had to offer was in demand but never took the first step because he felt like an outsider.

THERE ARE NO INSIDERS: OR, EVERYONE STARTS AS A STRANGER

Marvin Reeves, a Decatur, Illinois, small business entrepreneur, goes to a trade show in Chicago and sees one of his competitors laughing and joking with the corporate purchasing agent of a firm he wants to sell to. A few days later he reads a press release in his local newspaper that details how a small firm in the next county was able to grow 23 percent in one year due to its acquisition of several large clients. Marvin's mental receptors are set to see, hear, and receive messages indicating that everyone knows everyone else and that efforts on his part to win new business with major corporations would be fruitless because he is not known.

Marvin is not alone. A common myth that seems to pervade humanity is that on an individual level we each have a deck stacked against us because of the unfair advantages that others maintain over us. Do others have inside connections that enable them to obtain superior marketing results?

Yes and no.

No from the standpoint that everyone in this world starts out as a stranger to everyone else. Even your own parents were strangers to you until you got to know them. If we look at the question from this perspective, it is easier for us to see that the people we know in this world and the connections we have made are largely the results of our own choices and our own actions.

But do some of your competitors maintain an advantage over you because of whom they know? Most assuredly. Returning to Marvin's situation, the competitor he saw laughing and joking with a corporate purchasing agent must have spent time calling on, meeting, and getting to know that purchasing agent. Along the way, luck could have certainly played a part in the success of Marvin's competitor. In the long run, however, those who are "wired" or who have the inside connection usually worked for it by allocating time, energy, and money toward the cultivation of key introductions, presentations, and follow-ups.

When I was a freshman at Bloomfield High School, in Bloomfield, Connecticut, the junior varsity soccer coach accepted everyone for the team who showed up at tryouts. We often had many more bodies at practice in the early weeks of the season than we would need during the season, but the coach knew that the development of the team was largely a self-selection process. Those who wanted to play stuck it out all the way. The only players who were cut were those who cut themselves—they stopped coming to practice.

Making key connections with corporate purchasing agents is also largely a self-selection process. They can't possibly get to know you if, as Earl Nightengale says, "you're one of the timid feeders in the lagoon who never ventures out into the broad deep sea." And they can't possibly get to know you unless you show up—show up at their plant, show up at trade shows, show up by mailing them appropriate information, and show up by calling. That great observer of business, Peter Drucker, says, "Business has only two basic functions—marketing and innovation." And that great observer of life, Woody Allen, says, "Just showing up is 85 percent of everything."

Last year I attended a regional meeting of the second White House Conference on Small Business. In one session numerous small business entrepreneurs were commenting on how difficult it was for them to effectively market their firms. This ''line'' was quite popular among the majority of those present who were also small business entrepreneurs.

Risking unpopularity for the balance of the session, I posed this question to the group: ''How many of you, right now, can tell me the name of at least one purchasing agent from a Fortune 500 corporation?'' Everyone in the room was silent. For an extremely long three or four seconds, no one said a thing. Risking even greater unpopularity, I said, ''Then you are going to have a very difficult time ever selling to large firms.''

At this point I expected a verbal free-for-all against me. It didn't happen. Surprisingly, the issue was not dealt with at all. The next person to speak brought up another topic. The moderator followed his lead, and my carefully crafted ''gem,'' which I thought would represent a turning point in the meeting and would help participants to realize unless they *knew* purchasing agents they weren't ever going to sell to them, was quickly lost in the shuffle.

Look around. If everybody else appears to be maintaining competitive advantages based on key connections, why not ask yourself, ''Have I cut myself from the team, or will I stick it out and play this season?''

A SAMPLING OF THE BEST

Here now is a list of 100 of the nation's largest industrial corporations, in alphabetical order by industry, ranked by several measures:

**A Sampling of Fortune 500 Corporations
(Alphabetical by Industry, 1986)**

	Fortune Ranking	Sales ($ billions)	Assets ($ billions)	Net Income ($ billions)
Aerospace				
Allied-Signal	37	$ 9.1	$13.3	$(0.3)
Boeing	21	13.6	9.2	0.6
Fairchild Industries	329	0.9	0.7	(0.2)
General Dynamics	42	8.4	4.4	0.4
Grumman	131	3.0	1.6	<0.1
Martin Marietta	85	4.4	2.3	0.2

( ) = Net loss.
NA = Not available.
< = Under.
© *Fortune*, April 28, 1986. Reprinted with permission.

A Sampling of Fortune 500 Corporations *(continued)*
(Alphabetical by Industry, 1986)

	Fortune Ranking	Sales ($ billions)	Assets ($ billions)	Net Income ($ billions)
McDonnell Douglas	29	$11.5	$ 7.3	$ 0.3
Northrop	71	5.1	2.3	0.2
Rockwell International	30	11.3	7.3	0.6
United Technologies	16	15.7	10.5	0.3
Apparel				
Levi Strauss	148	2.6	2.1	NA
Beverages				
Anheuser-Busch	51	7.0	5.1	0.4
PepsiCo	41	8.5	5.9	0.5
Seagram (Joseph E.) & Sons	218	1.7	5.0	0.3
Building Materials				
Anchor Hocking	378	0.7	0.5	<0.1
Corning Glass Works	217	1.7	2.0	0.1
Norton	277	1.2	1.0	(0.1)
Owens-Corning Fiberglas	118	3.3	2.4	0.1
PPG Industries	88	4.3	4.1	0.3
Chemicals				
Air Products & Chemicals	205	1.8	2.6	0.1
BASF	149	2.6	2.3	<0.1
Celanese	132	3.0	2.8	0.2
Dow Chemical	28	11.5	11.8	0.1
Dow Corning	336	0.9	1.0	<0.1
Du Pont (E. I.) de Nemours	9	29.5	25.1	1.1
FMC	120	3.3	2.7	0.2
Monsanto	53	6.7	8.9	(0.1)
Olin	195	1.9	1.6	(0.2)
Computers (includes Office Equipment)				
Amdahl	348	0.9	0.9	<0.1
Burroughs*	72	5.0	4.6	0.2
Control Data	106	3.7	3.1	(0.6)
Digital Equipment	55	6.7	6.4	0.4
Hewlett-Packard	58	6.5	5.7	0.5
Honeywell	›56	6.6	5.0	0.3
IBM	5	50.0	52.6	6.6
Sperry*	63	5.7	5.8	0.3
Wang Laboratories	161	2.4	2.4	<0.1
Electronics				
American Telephone & Telegraph	8	34.9	40.5	1.6
Eaton	107	3.7	2.8	0.2
General Electric	10	28.3	26.4	2.3
Motorola	66	5.4	4.4	<0.1

* Recently merged to form UNISYS.

A Sampling of Fortune 500 Corporations *(continued)*
(Alphabetical by Industry, 1986)

	Fortune Ranking	Sales ($ billions)	Assets ($ billions)	Net Income ($ billions)
National Semiconductor	209	$ 1.8	$ 1.4	<$0.1
Singer	156	2.4	1.4	0.1
Texas Instruments	75	4.9	3.1	(0.1)
Varian Associates	311	1.0	0.7	< 0.1
Westinghouse Electric	32	10.7	9.7	0.6
Zenith Electronics	225	1.6	0.9	<(0.1)
Food				
Borden	77	4.7	2.9	0.2
Campbell Soup	100	4.0	2.4	0.2
ConAgra	65	5.5	1.5	<0.1
General Foods	38	9.0	4.6	0.3
Hormel (George A.)	235	1.5	0.6	<0.1
Pillsbury	80	4.7	2.8	0.2
Forest Products				
Bemis	362	0.8	0.4	<0.1
Boise Cascade	105	3.7	3.3	0.1
Champion International	62	5.8	6.1	0.2
International Paper	83	4.5	6.0	0.1
Westvaco	215	1.7	1.9	0.1
Furniture				
Mohasco	370	0.8	0.4	<0.1
Industrial and Farm Equipment				
Allis-Chalmers	315	1.0	0.7	(0.2)
Black & Decker	212	1.7	1.5	(0.2)
Cincinnati Milacron	373	0.7	0.7	<(0.1)
Combustion Engineering	127	3.1	2.2	(0.1)
Cummins Engine	174	2.1	1.7	<0.1
Figgie International Holdings	359	0.8	0.6	<0.1
Metal Products				
Gillette	158	2.4	2.4	0.2
Stanley Works	275	1.2	0.8	<0.1
Metals				
Aluminum Company of America	69	5.2	6.4	<(0.1)
Inland Steel	126	3.1	2.6	(0.2)
Mining, Crude-Oil Production				
AMAX	183	2.0	3.6	(0.6)
Occidental Petroleum	19	14.5	11.6	0.7
Motor Vehicles and Parts				
Borg-Warner	101	4.0	2.8	0.2
Chrysler	13	21.3	12.6	1.6

A Sampling of Fortune 500 Corporations *(concluded)*
(Alphabetical by Industry, 1986)

	Fortune Ranking	Sales ($ billions)	Assets ($ billions)	Net Income ($ billions)
Ford Motor	4	$52.8	$31.6	$ 2.5
General Motors	1	96.4	63.8	4.0
Petroleum Refining				
Amoco	11	27.2	25.2	2.0
Exxon	2	86.7	69.2	4.9
Mobil	3	56.0	41.8	1.0
Texaco	6	46.3	37.7	1.2
U.S. Steel	15	18.4	18.4	0.4
Pharmaceuticals				
Bristol-Myers	84	4.4	3.7	0.5
Johnson & Johnson	59	6.4	5.1	0.6
Pfizer	99	4.0	4.5	0.6
Publishing, Printing				
Dow Jones	303	1.0	1.2	0.1
Harcourt Brace Jovanovich	356	0.8	0.8	0.1
Knight-Ridder Newspapers	213	1.7	1.4	0.1
Rubber Products				
Uniroyal	175	2.1	1.5	NA
Scientific and Photographic				
Bell & Howell	371	0.8	0.7	<0.1
Eastman Kodak	33	10.6	12.1	0.3
Minnesota Mining & Manufacturing	47	7.8	6.6	0.7
Polaroid	257	1.3	1.4	<0.1
Xerox	40	8.9	9.8	0.5
Soaps, Cosmetics				
Chesebrough-Pond's	136	2.9	3.0	<0.1
Economics Laboratory	376	0.7	0.4	<0.1
Procter & Gamble	22	13.6	9.7	0.6
Textiles				
Burlington Industries	141	2.8	2.1	<0.1
Fieldcrest Mills	425	0.6	0.4	<0.1
Toys, Sporting Goods				
Mattel	300	1.1	0.7	<0.1
Transportation Equipment				
Todd Shipyards	462	0.5	0.4	<0.1
Winnebago Industries	500	0.4	0.2	<0.1

Allocating Time for Marketing, Creating a Clearing, Maintaining Visibility

This time, like all times,
is a good one if we but
know what to do with it.

RALPH WALDO EMERSON

When asked, many entrepreneurs report that they would like to have a few Fortune 500 firms under contract but that it would take substantial effort to achieve this. "I don't have time to get involved in long-term marketing right now," or "We'll get around to designing a company brochure sometime in the next few months," or "I'd like to call on major corporations, but I am just not prepared."

The list of excuses is endless. Entrepreneurs report that they don't have enough leads, money, or time. There are literally millions of small vendors who could serve as suppliers to the Fortune 500 but who continue to do nothing to further their opportunities or expose themselves to this market.

Marketing is much more than thinking about or even knowing where your next contract is coming from. Marketing is planning ahead and taking time each week to sow the seed from which contracts will spring over the next few years. "Marketing is . . . much broader than selling," according to Peter Drucker. "It encompasses the entire business . . . seen from the point of its final result, that is, from the customer's point of view."

BUSINESS PLANS, MARKETING PLANS

Ideally, the start of a business should commence with a business plan; however, few entrepreneurs ever produce a complete business plan. A business plan is a document that you produce for yourself to guide you in your thinking. It focuses on marketing, financing, and human resources—all of the elements that make your business successful. Unfortunately, most business plans are only produced when the entrepreneur has to persuade a banker, the SBA, or some financial institution to supply start-up capital.

Often the terms *business plan* and *marketing plan* are erroneously used interchangeably. The marketing plan is a subset or component of the business plan, the most important subset. If you can't describe what markets you will serve and how you're going to generate revenue, then all the other information in your business plan is meaningless. Preparing a marketing plan and revenue forecasting are discussed in Chapter 3.

An 18-Month Cycle

Underestimating the effort and time required to market to the Fortune 500 is a *classic* mistake that entrepreneurs repeatedly make. From the time you first make contact, it takes *18 months* or more, on the average, to close a contract with a major corporation!

If you're going to be calling on the "big boys," you'll need a realistic perspective and approach. *Eighteen months is realistic.* Embracing reality also means recognizing that you'll never have all the time or money you need to take the big leap. Consequently, the time will never be exactly right. To put it another way, a good time to start is right *now*.

How's Your Marketing Staff?

If your company employs more than 12 people, you should probably have at least one full-time marketing person. If you have a small staff and no marketing help, at least 20–25 percent of your time should be spent on marketing and you should delegate marketing support activities such as researching and organizing. If you spend 20 percent of your time on marketing, you must give marketing *at least* 8 hours per week, 400 hours per year; 12–15 hours per week is better still, regardless of your other responsibilities.

Delegating responsibility is unnatural: it is natural to want to do the work yourself. However, the easiest way to increase your marketing effectiveness is to free your time by not handling what can be delegated.

Here are 20 questions offered by Dr. Donald W. Huffmire, an associate professor at the School of Business Administration of the University of Connecticut. Huffmire conducts frequent seminars for businesspeople

MARKETING NEW TECHNOLOGY

If you think the 18-month cycle for marketing to the Fortune 500 is long, it's much worse for marketing new technology. On June 18, 1976, a *New York Times* article by Stephen Rosen provided this information on the year in which the following products were conceived and the year in which these products became marketable.

Innovation	Conception	Realization	Interval (years)
Automatic transmission	1930	1946	16
Ballpoint pen	1938	1945	7
Fluorescent lighting	1901	1934	33
Frozen foods	1908	1923	15
Heart pacemaker	1928	1960	32
Helicopter	1904	1941	37
Long-playing records	1945	1948	3
Minute rice	1931	1949	18
Nylon	1927	1939	12
Photography	1782	1838	56
Radar	1904	1939	35
Radio	1890	1914	24
Roll-on deodorant	1948	1955	7
Silicone	1904	1942	38
Stainless steel	1904	1920	16
Telegraph	1820	1838	18
Television	1884	1947	63
Transistor	1940	1956	16
Videotape recorder	1950	1956	6
Photocopying	1935	1950	15
Zipper	1883	1913	30

Yet, as you'll read later, project managers can be very receptive to new technology when you can demonstrate a time or cost savings.

on delegation, and his articles on the subject have appeared in many publications.

1. Do you frequently take work home?
2. Do you work longer hours than the people you manage?
3. Are your people slow or reluctant to make decisions?
4. Are you frequently interrupted by others coming to you for advice or decisions?
5. Are you doing work that others are paid to do?

6. Do you have trouble meeting deadlines?
7. Do unfinished jobs build up so that you're always "one behind"?
8. Do you spend more time working than planning?
9. Do you lack time to think out future assignments?
10. Are many sudden daily and weekly unexpected emergencies and crises common in your operation?
11. Do you work at details that are low priority to your main objective?
12. Are details your headache because you don't have employees who are capable of handling them?
13. Are simple routine jobs delegated but not promptly done, with much follow-up required?
14. Do you lack confidence in the abilities of your subordinates?
15. Do you keep details of your job secret from others?
16. Do you feel that you're doing more to earn your keep when you're rushed?
17. Do you feel compelled to keep close tabs on everything that is going on in your operation?
18. Do things get fouled up when you are not on the job?
19. Do you and your subordinates usually disagree on what results are expected from them?
20. Do your people feel that they do not have enough authority to achieve their objectives?

The effective delegator can answer each of these questions with a no. If you answer yes to even a few of them, you are probably not delegating properly. In the long run, your marketing effectiveness will live or die with your ability to delegate.

Huffmire, who has worked with such corporations as Westinghouse (32) and IBM (5), says "Don't make negative assumptions about your people. If you assume that your people don't want more responsibility, don't want to think for themselves, resist change, or must be watched closely, you won't delegate much to them." Instead, you will do more of the work than you should and you will overcontrol your people. This will result in "low motivation, low teamwork, low risk-taking, low creative problem-solving, and low marketing effectiveness."

Delegation means trusting your staff to handle the job, stepping in only when it is clear they do not understand what you want. Consultant and author Dianne Walbrecker, president of Getting It Write, advises that you "explain exactly what the task involves and how you want it accomplished." She believes that writing down clear, concise instructions will also be helpful. Asking staff members to "verbally capsulize your instructions" will disclose possible misunderstandings immediately. If your staff members can't do the job, or if they display an exanimate approach to the assigned task, you may need new people.

CREATE A CLEARING

Take time at the end of the current week to organize your time for the coming week. Examine the tasks that you have chosen for yourself and the relative importance of each. Then prepare a written schedule. Schedule everything—staff meetings, time for marketing telephone calls and visits, even time for questions from your staff. Post this information on a wall calendar where it will be visible at all times. You may even want to make another copy of your schedule to post outside your door for your staff.

Organizing your desk or office efficiently will leave you more time to market. If you're weak in this area, read *The Organized Executive* by Stephanie Winston. Resolve to handle each piece of paper just once. Decide immediately whether you need to throw the paper away, file it for future reference, do something with it at some specific time, or delegate responsibility for it to a staff member.

If you can't figure out what to do with something, follow the advice of Edwin C. Bliss in his short classic *Getting Things Done*. Bliss says, "When in doubt, throw it out!"

A tickler file can help you organize papers that you need for future reference. Have a tickler file for each month. Use separate folders for each day of the month if necessary. Then check your file every day to see whether there is anything special you must do on that day. Making notes on a large calendar serves the same purpose as a tickler file.

Write down the names of all prospective customers, and plan to contact them at least once a month by a personal visit, telephone call, or letter. Entrepreneur and millionaire Michael O'Harro says that he regularly goes through his stack of business cards and calls people he hasn't spoken to recently, just to maintain the contact. Use the monthly calendar as a reminder of the date each month on which you will make a contact. One call, visit, or letter per day will provide you with at least 20 continuing new business exposures each month.

A Week in the Life of an Effective Marketer

	M	T	W	T	F
8 AM		REVIEW WEEKLY, MONTHLY SALES FIGURES			
9 AM		WRITE FOLLOW-UP LETTERS	MAKE 6 CALLS TO NEW PROSPECTS	BRIEF STAFF ON TELEPHONE PROCEDURES	
10 AM		SEND STAFFER TO RESEARCH MORE ON		REVIEW VIDEO-TAPE OF PRACTICE SALES PRESENTATION	
11 AM		3 NEW PROSPECTS			
NOON					
1 PM					
2 PM	CALL ON COMPANY A				PLAN SALES CALLS FOR NEXT WEEK
3 PM	AND BY 4 PM CALL ON NEARBY				REVIEW PRESENTATION STRATEGY
4 PM	COMPANY B				
5 PM			REVIEW COMPETITOR LITERATURE		
6 PM	REVIEW RESULTS OF CALLS. PLAN FOLLOW-UP				
7 PM					

"12 TO 15 HOURS PER WEEK MINIMUM DEVOTED TO MARKETING EVEN IF YOU'RE THE ENTIRE MANAGEMENT TEAM"

Know Your Optimal Schedule

Dianne Walbrecker points out that "everyone has differing levels of energy during the day and even during the week." These levels usually fall into patterns. For instance, some people have high levels of energy most mornings along with a midafternoon slump. If you fit this pattern, you should perform difficult tasks in the morning and easier ones in the afternoon.

If you find it difficult to compose letters but easy to make telephone calls, you could schedule your days to write letters in the morning and make all of your calls during the midafternoon slump. Publicist Jack

Wynn of Jack Wynn & Co. saves up 10 or 15 calls at a time and then mows them all down. Some people find that they are more productive late in the day.

The variations in your energy levels should also be considered in your weekly schedule. Some people work better at the beginning of the week than later in the week, while other people do not reach their peak efficiency until the second or third day of the week.

Realizing what your optimal schedule is and organizing your time to take advantage of it will increase your productivity. Read about "supervising cycles of productivity" in *Checklist Management: The Eight-Hour Manager* (Bethesda, Md.: National Press, 1986). Discuss this schedule with your staff, and instruct its members on ways in which they can help you maintain it. For instance, you may want all of your calls held until the afternoon. When you respect your own time, others will also.

Plan for the Long Range

The purpose of marketing is to plan for your company's long-range future. It is all too easy to do the tasks that bring immediate satisfaction or reward and to ignore those that can be put off.

Remember, it takes *an average of 18 months* from initial contact with a purchasing manager to establishment of a solid contractural arrangement. Lever Brothers (177), with decentralized purchasing, is interested in hearing from new vendors, but many vendors regard its response time as very slow. However, slowness in responding is normal for large corporations. It therefore behooves any small vendor to plan far ahead and to keep on track with potential customers. Plant seeds now and keep them watered.

Plan where you want your company to be in one year, three years, and five years. All 500 of the Fortune 500 corporations do this, and with good reason. Include in your long-range planning the products and services that you want to offer and the number of employees and amount of space that you will need. Make your plans realistic, but do not let them limit your growth. Then map out and follow specific strategies to reach your goals, revising both the strategies and the goals as necessary.

The Power of Setting Goals

The importance of setting goals and writing them down can be seen from the following true story told by Zig Ziglar, a well-known sales trainer and motivational speaker:

In 1954, Yale University studied goal setting as a determinant of future performance. Yale seniors were asked whether they had identified their goals for future financial worth. Of these students, 3 percent had written goals clearly identifying a dollar value, 11 percent had formulated goals in mind, and the remainder had no definite financial goals.

A follow-up was conducted in 1974, with astonishing results. The 3 percent with clearly defined written financial goals had a net worth that exceeded the net worth of the remaining 97 percent.

Setting marketing goals will not guarantee success, but there is strong evidence that the attainment of goals is far more likely if they are clearly identified and if they serve as a focus for effort. Chapter 3 explores goal setting further and provides examples of goal statements.

MAINTAINING ACCESSIBILITY: HOW TO MAKE SURE "THEY" CAN FIND YOU

Virtually all small businesses find it necessary to relocate in the first several years. This is a fact of business life—face it, and accept responsibility for maintaining accessibility.

Consider this scenario. A purchasing agent for Penwalt (299) or Harris (163) is sitting at his desk, considering whom to call for a printed circuit board that his company needs. He thinks back to the last trade fair he attended and remembers four small vendors who might be able to supply the part. He opens a file drawer, looking for the literature that they gave him. Searching through folders, he finds brochures provided by three of the vendors.

"That phone number has been disconnected," says the operator in response to two of his calls. One vendor is left, and that's the one who gets the appointment.

Whether you have recently moved or whether you have been in the same location since you started in business, it is vital to make it easy for callers to find you.

Keep a stack of mailing labels on hand with your company name and address. Walbrecker says, "You could hire a student for a few hours to type these or have an address stamp made." If you have a computer or word processor there are dozens of simple software labeling programs. Include one of your mailing labels with each letter you send out. The corporate employee receiving your mailing label can then peel it off and use it on an envelope of any size. You'll make a good impression by saving the corporation time and you'll make sure they have your correct address at all times.

When *answering* an inquiry by mail, be sure to indicate on the envelope that the enclosed information was requested. Otherwise, your reply runs the risk of being thrown out during screening. For example, you might state on the envelope, "Here is the information you requested."

Jeffrey P. Davidson CMC

3709 So. George Mason Dr., #315E
Falls Church, Virginia 22041

HERE IS THE INFORMATION
THAT YOU REQUESTED!

Every time you meet a potential customer, ask for his or her business card. Jot down any important information on the back of the card. For instance, note any special product or service needs that may not be immediately apparent from the name of the potential customer's corporation.

Want to accelerate your ability to file new leads whom you meet personally? While you're still on the road, phone home (your home office, that is) and dictate to your secretary the names, addresses, and marketing habits that you pick up. By the time you get back to the office, your follow-up letter could be ready for your signature. I used this technique for years. Blew prospects right off their feet when they received a letter the day after meeting me.

Keep the business cards you obtain in a file at your office. And put the names and addresses on a mailing list as soon as possible. Updating the mailing list frequently will allow you to avoid the last-minute headache of composing one when you need it.

Mail Forwarding

When moving, as soon as you know your new address, get a change of address form from your local post office. If you fill out and turn in this form, your mail will be forwarded at no charge for 18 months. In addition, the manager of your local post office has the authority to extend the duration of the change of address notice. It is certainly worth a phone call or visit to see whether that can be done in your case.

Send a second, or even a third, letter announcing your new address with an updated address label to those companies that continue to use your old address. Use something eye-catching, such as red ink.

Also, make sure that you list your firm's new or proper address in the directories appropriate to your product or service:

- Service directories.
- Industry directories.
- Small and minority business regional directories.
- Local business directories.
- Regional business directories.

Rolodex Cards

With your initial written communication to a corporation, include a standard-size Rolodex card with your name, address, and phone number and a few words describing your product or service. If you have many types of products, you may want to describe one or two that meet that particular corporation's needs.

It may even be useful to include two such cards in each mailing—one for the desk of the purchasing agent and one for the desk of his or her secretary or assistant. Patricia Fripp, a San Francisco–based corporate and association trainer, uses laminated preprinted Rolodex cards as her business card and sends two at a time. The tab on one card reads "Fripp, Patricia." The tab on the other card reads "Speaker." "That way," says Fripp, "if they forget my name, they can still find me." Making it easy for purchasing agents to find you makes it more likely that they will.

Post-Office Boxes

If you anticipate the need to change office and production space due to fluctuations in the volume of business, you may want to consider renting a post-office box. The sizes of such boxes are fairly standard across the country. A small box is 3 inches wide and 5 inches high; a medium box is 5 inches wide and 5 inches high; and a large box is 12 inches wide and 5 inches high. These boxes are generally 12 to 18 inches deep.

The rentals for post-office boxes vary according to the revenue generated at the local post office, but a moderate rental is $30 a year for a small box, $45 a year for a medium box, and $75 a year for a large box. You may find that the disadvantage of picking your mail up at the post office is largely offset by the consistency in your address. This consistency means you will not have to change your business cards or stationery when you move. Be sure to include your street address along with your post-office box when possible. Author and consultant Howard Shenson notes that "outside of New England" people may be wary of a company that supplies only a post-office box address with no street information.

Is Your Company Telephone-Responsive?

How does your company look to outsiders? According to supermanager Robert Townsend, former head of Avis Rent-A-Car, one way you can easily find out is by phoning in anonymously from time to time and pretending to be a customer who needs help. "You'll find some real horror shows." Worse, try to phone yourself. If you do so, says Townsend, you'll see clearly what "indignities your defenses inflict on callers."

Consider adding an extra phone line. The cacophony of a busy signal affects all callers. Progressive vendors recognize the need to facilitate the ability of callers to "get right in touch."

Joe Stumpf, co-owner of Automated Sales Training, North Hollywood, California, managed a project that involved randomly calling 5,000 yellow pages advertisers throughout the United States, each of which had spent more than $200 per month on its ads, to test reactions to phone inquiries.

Each advertiser was asked this question: "I saw your ad in the yellow pages. How much does your product (or service) cost?"

Here are the results of this survey, as reported by Stumpf. (The figures add up to more than 100 percent because the responses elicited from many firms fell into more than one of the categories listed.) Of the 5,000 advertisers questioned:

- 3,918 (78.4 percent) never asked for our name.
- 2,791 (55.8 percent) took more than eight rings to answer.

- 2,117 (42.3 percent) gave the price, then, without hesitation, gave us a list of other products or services, but never asked for any action (to buy or make an appointment).
- 1,711 (34.2 percent) gave the price and, with no further comment, hung up.
- 573 (11.5 percent) said that they didn't know and asked us to call back when the boss was in.
- 414 (8.2 percent) put us on hold for more than two minutes.

On the positive side:

- 42 (0.8 percent) introduced themselves.
- 77 (1.5 percent) asked us for our phone number.
- 385 (7.7 percent) said that they owned the company.
- 414 (8.2 percent) had a professional planned presentation and made us feel that they wanted our business.

These amazing results point to a widespread need among all businesses to improve telephone response. One purchasing agent at Fieldcrest Mills (425) was aghast when a small vendor asked how much Fieldcrest was paying for the product that the vendor was attempting to sell.

Since the first impression of your company may be disseminated by phone, it pays to have the phone answered in a professional manner—or not at all! "After seeing these results," Stumpf said, "AST developed 29 telephone techniques for turning phone inquiries into sales, and demonstrated and explained them in an audiotape." The tape is called, "It's for You . . . Your Most Important Call."

Make Your Phone Number Work

Most telephone companies will allow you to reserve a special number, as long as it is not in use by another customer. For instance, if you manufacture paint, you might reserve the number 87P-AINT; if you manufacture microchips, you might reserve 27C-HIPS; or if you are a therapist, you might reserve 9AD-VICE. My own phone number, chosen in 1981, is 931–1984. After 1984 passed, I sought to get 1987, 1988, or 1989, but, alas, they were all taken for my exchange.

Having a telephone number that makes a marketing point for you will make you more noticeable among competitors and will make it easier for the purchasing agent to remember your number without having to look it up. Most telephone companies charge no extra fee for providing you with such a number, but check with the local company.

SMALL INVESTMENT, BIG PAYOFF

This chapter has explored methods that will enable you to plan realistically, make your time more effective, and let purchasing agents know who or where you are and make it easy for them to reach you. The effort needed to make these methods work can pay off if, as a result of that effort, even *one* purchasing agent ready to do business finds you who might have given up looking for you otherwise.

CHAPTER THREE

The Marketing Plan

*If we all did the things
we are capable of doing,
we would literally astound
ourselves.*

THOMAS A. EDISON

The answer to the question "Who needs a marketing plan?" is a resounding "Everyone." Whether you're a manufacturer, a distributor, or a service provider, you need a marketing plan to sell products, services, ideas, yourself. A marketing plan defines what is offered, to whom, and through what methods. A concise marketing plan will allow you to focus your time and energy in one direction, thereby increasing your effectiveness. If you lack a marketing plan, you are apt to keep jousting with windmills.

KEY TERMINOLOGY

Market planning has been defined as a systematic process that involves assessing opportunities and organizational resources, determining objectives, and developing a plan for implementation and control. A marketing plan is an organized written communications tool that is usually prepared annually and updated as needed. It describes your present business situation—opportunities and problems facing your business—and it establishes specific and realistic business objectives. A marketing plan also outlines the specific actions that are required to accomplish these objectives, including the assignment of responsibility for the execution of marketing programs.

One of your chief responsibilities as an entrepreneur is anticipating changes in the marketplace so that you will have enough time to act decisively in response to them. Since your company's plans must be changed as the environment and the company itself change, market planning is a continuous process.

In examining ways to expand your present market, you could consider new users of your product or service, displacement of competitors, increased use of your product or service, new applications of your product or service, variations of your product or service, additions to your product or service, and diversification into new product and service areas.

Marketing strategy represents the key decisions required to reach an objective or a set of objectives. Marketing strategy encompasses selecting and analyzing a target market and creating and maintaining a marketing mix, a product, prices, distribution, and promotion that will satisfy the target market. The target market is the buyers for whom your product or service is specifically tailored.

Procrastinating and preparing a marketing plan seem to go hand in hand. Excuses for not developing a marketing plan range from "It takes too long" to "This is how we've been doing it" to "We don't have one, and it really hasn't hurt us so far."

Various courses of study, ranging from intensive two-hour classes on marketing your business to masters in business administration programs at top universities, offer formulas for developing marketing plans. Some of the plans I've seen have been so complete and complex that they would daunt any sensible person. Moreover, busy entrepreneurs simply do not have the time or patience to deal with inordinately long outlines and voluminous plans. A good marketing plan can be followed!

To get started, we'll first review methods for defining your business setting goals, and forecasting revenue.

WHAT BUSINESS ARE YOU IN?

I suggest developing a one-sentence, one-minute definition of what business you're in—a one-sentence "marketing plan." But how will a one-sentence, one-minute marketing plan work for you?

One sentence, carefully thought out, will point you in the right direction and help focus all of your efforts. Here is my own one sentence: "I'm in the business of providing marketing and management assistance to businesses and organizations in the United States, Western Europe, and Japan through books, speaking engagements, and consulting assignments." That one sentence describes the services I provide, for whom, and how.

Years ago, Waldenbooks defined itself as being "in the bookselling business." That was how it had started as a company. However, an examination of its product and service line revealed that, in addition to books, it was offering cassettes, training guides, video programs, work-books, calendars, magazines, and notions. Defining itself as being in the "bookselling business" no longer sufficed. The definition was re-worked to: Waldenbooks is in the business of providing general reference, nonfictional, fictional, educational reading, audiovisual, and related mate-rials through retail bookstores nationwide.

Waldenbooks added geography to its definition and expanded the scope of the products/services offered. It's easy to understand the power of the dynamics that take place when a large corporation commits time, money, and energy to a marketing plan; following formulation of the reworked marketing plan, Waldenbooks' sales and marketing effective-ness rose dramatically.

Preparing the one-sentence marketing definition can prove just as effec-tive for a small product or service vendor. Your one sentence should be realistic, acknowledging your current position while focusing on your goals.

Suppose you are the owner or manager of a biochemical research firm with 18 employees. Your sentence might be: "We're in the business of providing Fortune 500 and other organizations with state-of-the-art procedures for dramatically increasing their ability to use biochemical engineering to achieve greater productivity." It's a mouthful, but it does the job and it serves as an excellent starting point for developing the marketing plan.

The principles that apply to marketing plans for companies also apply to marketing plans for individuals. Try transforming your company's one-sentence, one-minute marketing definition into your own. This will give you a sharper personal focus immediately. It will help you and your company to focus energy in the right direction. For example, "My company is in the business of ABC . . ." on the individual level might translate to "My role in support of the company's marketing plan is to DEF."

What about the situation where a vendor offers various products or services? A classic entrepreneurial faux pas that I've frequently observed is the effort to be all things to all customers. Have you ever heard it said of someone that "he jumped on his horse and rode off in all direc-tions"? Or, have you ever been told, "If you don't know where you're going, any road will take you there"? Ubiquity may be useful in a political campaign, but it has little application to your marketing plan. You *must* establish a market niche. The immediate reason is that you simply don't have the time or the resources to scatter your efforts all over creation. You may be able to offer X, Y, and Z, but start only with the one that's best. If product X or service X is best (that is, the most profitable, the easiest to provide, the most challenging—whatever the criteria), then market that for openers.

If you analyze markets A, B, C, and D, and they *all* look lucrative and there are reasons for promoting your product or service in all four markets, the best strategy, still, is to attack the market that you can *most readily penetrate,* either because it costs less to do so (perhaps because you're geographically close) or because you have some kind of competitive advantage. Fully exploit the product or service that is your forte, and penetrate the key market area.

Nothing will work faster or enable you to reach your goals sooner.

SELECTING GOALS

In sports, observes Leslie M. Rhatican, goals are clearly established and understood by all players. Rhatican, an MBA and manager–marketing support with GTE Telenet Communications, asks, "How would a football, hockey, soccer, or basketball game be played if one were to remove the goalposts or nets?" The answer is obvious—without the goal there is no game. This premise also applies to marketing—without a goal there is no method of measurement, no way to keep score.

A marketing objective or marketing goal is a statement of what is to be accomplished through marketing activities. Your goal statement should be written in clear, simple terms; it should be specific as to time frame; and it should be consistent with your company's long-term objectives. Of most importance, it should be measureable. For example, "Our company will market two new products by August 1, 1990." Or: "Our company will increase its gross sales this year by 12 percent over gross sales last year." Or: "Our company will generate $350,000 in contracts with new customers from the ranks of Fortune 500 corporations by June 30, 1989."

Corporate managers have long understood the necessity of determining objectives for their companies and of setting goals as a means of measuring the attainment of those objectives. You won't find a single CEO among the Fortune 500, or among any other successful ventures for that matter, who hasn't developed goals for the corporation. Yet many small business vendors, for reasons that are still a mystery to me, operate without written, quantified goals.

What kinds of goals can you establish?

- Revenue, per year or by December 31, 19XX. (*Note:* The time element is an integral part of any goal.)
- Number of contracts won.
- Number of bids made.
- Size of contract backlog.
- Number of full-time marketing people on staff.
- Number of contacts with specified companies.
- Percentage increase in after-tax profits.
- Average dollar size of contracts.
- Equity dollars raised.
- On the cover of *Venture* magazine.
- Listed among the *Inc.* 100.

The list is endless.

METHODS USED IN FORECASTING

One of your probable goals is "to earn $X in revenue this year." But is the revenue figure you've chosen realistic? Forecasting can help you make this determination.

There are many methods used in forecasting, several of which are discussed briefly:

Questionnaires. By surveying customers and prospective customers, some entrepreneurs are able to generate a rough 12-month revenue estimate.

Delphi Method. Using a group of experts—perhaps key members of your management staff, your board of directors, or an advisory board—to give their "best guess" as to what revenue will be. This method derives its name from the oracle of Delphi, who, according to the ancient Greeks, could foretell the future!

Regression Analysis. Plotting the change, hopefully upward, of your sales (the dependent variable) in relation to an independent variable, such as the number of bids made or product improvement, or to a combination of several independent variables.

Sales Force Estimates. Summing the individual projections of what each member of your sales staff thinks he or she can sell. This is an excellent way to establish a revenue forecast.

Forecasting Services. Using the industrial forecasts, by Standard Industrial Classification (SIC) codes, that are available from such firms as Predicasts and Dun & Bradstreet. However, a forecast

for growth within an industry must be applied cautiously when forecasting revenue for an individual firm within the industry.
Other Industry Forecasts. Finding other forecasts within your industry. Such forecasts may be prepared by trade associations or research or advocacy groups.

If possible, use more than one forecasting technique to determine revenue. The figure you develop using several techniques will be "stronger," perhaps closer to reality. Achieving the amount of revenue forecast for the coming 12-month period is the primary business goal of most small business vendors.

REVENUE FORECASTING USING THE EXPECTED VALUE OF CONTRACTS

An exceptionally effective way to forecast revenue, particularly if you are going to be in the business of bidding on Fortune 500 contracts, is to use a method that I call "the expected value of contracts." Here is how it works.

Assume the following scenario: You recently started your business, a small chemical plant, and you have identified three contracts that you believe you have a reasonable chance of winning. Contract A, for $150,000, is with Air Products and Chemicals (205); contract B, for $100,000, is with BASF (149); and contract C, for $80,000, is with Celanese (132).

If you were an extreme optimist, you would assume the winning of all three contracts and forecast a revenue of $330,000. Since this outcome is not likely, further analysis is needed in order to produce a revenue forecast that more closely reflects the dynamics of the marketplace.

Suppose that for contract A you know of only two other firms that are bidding on the same contract and you have substantial reason to believe your firm to be far superior to these competitors. On contract B, you are not sure how many other firms are bidding. However, you do know that there are at least four or five competitors and that you are only in the middle of the pack, having no particular competitive advantage. On contract C, you feel that you are as good as "wired." Though your company is in a start-up phase, you have already visited the Celanese people twice; they like you, and they have just about said, "The contract is yours." Now, how does this information on the three contracts affect the revenue forecast?

First, construct a table that, to the best of your knowledge, accurately portrays the current situation.

Corporation	Size of Contract	Number of Competitors	How You Stand
Air Products and Chemicals	$150,000	2	1st of 3?
BASF	100,000	5	3rd of 5?
Celanese	80,000	0	1st of 1?

The potential contract with Air Products and Chemicals totals $150,000, and clearly whoever wins the contract will realize that full amount. At the moment, however, the best information you have indicates that your company is the leading candidate among the three companies that are bidding for the job. On the basis of probability you might be inclined to say that you have a 40 or perhaps 50 percent chance of winning the job. As you can quickly see, assigning probabilities is a highly subjective art. I advocate that you regard your probability of winning to be no more than 30 percent, and an even lower figure might suffice just as well.

You can never count on having accurate knowledge of the situation— things may change, and it is best to be cautious and conservative when forecasting revenue. For the purposes of this example, a 30 percent probability is reasonable. Multiplying this percentage by $150,000, the face amount of the contract, yields an expected value for contract A of $45,000. More on this shortly.

On the contract with BASF, your firm could be one of 5 or even 10 firms bidding. And you have no apparent advantage. Arithmetically, you might say that you have a 10 or 15 percent chance of winning. However, assigning a 5 percent chance, or less, is more realistic. The expected value of this contract is $100,000 times 5 percent, or $5,000.

On the contract with Celanese, you might be inclined to say that you have a 70 or 80 percent chance of winning what appears to be a contract that is "sewn up." But it would be wiser to assign a probability of winning at 50 percent or less. You just never know, and only fools count their chickens before they are hatched. Thus the expected value of this contract is $40,000 ($80,000 × 50%).

Summing the expected value for the three contracts on which you have bid yields a total expected value of contracts of $90,000. Surprise. No single contract equals $90,000, yet to the best of your knowledge and ability this represents the most appropriate revenue forecast for your firm.

Corporation	Size of Contract	Probability of Winning	Expected Value of Contracts
Air Products and Chemicals	$150,000	30%	$45,000
BASF	100,000	5	5,000
Celanese	80,000	50	40,000
			$90,000

This example is simple since it assumes that your company is a new one with no backlog, that you are faced with only three new contract possibilities, that you know the approximate number of the competitors involved and where you stand among them, that the amounts of the contracts are fixed, and that the contracts will all be let within a 12-month period.

However, the method works the same no matter how many potential contracts, starting dates, and payoffs are involved. The one factor that remains extremely difficult to assess is the probability of winning. In many cases, you will have little or no information as to where you stand. There may be myriad competitors, and your probability of winning may not exceed 1 percent.

The expected value of contracts method for revenue forecasting points up the need to play the numbers game—bid on many, many contracts, and try to get as much information as possible on where you stand in relation to competitors.

The more contracts you bid on and the longer you have been in business, the better the expected value of contracts method for revenue forecasting will work for you. As time passes and contract awards are made, your forecasts change. For example, if you win the Celanese contract, the probability changes from 50 percent to 100 percent and the expected value of the contract becomes the full $80,000. Thus your overall expected value of contracts jumps up to $130,000.

Corporation	Size of Contract	Probability of Winning	Expected Value of Contracts
Air Products and Chemicals	$150,000	30%	$ 45,000
BASF	100,000	5	5,000
Celanese	80,000	100	80,000
			$130,000

Once the BASF contract goes to another firm, your probability of winning becomes 0 percent and the expected value of that contract becomes $0. Your revenue forecast then decreases $5,000. Similarly, as you bid on other contracts and obtain additional information regarding those contracts, your forecast can be updated further.

SIX ADDITIONAL COMPONENTS OF AN EFFECTIVE MARKETING PLAN

Having discussed the need to produce a one-sentence marketing definition, the power of goal setting, and methods of revenue forecasting, we will now review the remaining components of a simple but effective marketing plan.

Defining Your Trade Radius

Precisely define the trade radius in which you intend to do business. This can include planet earth, selected continents, North America, the United States, sections of a country, a state, a county, a town, whatever. Next prepare a precise description of the target market. Who will your customers be, and what are their needs? What industries can you most readily serve? How big are these industries? How many firms are in these industries? What are their operating characteristics? Much of the information that you will need to research targets is presented in detail in Chapter 7.

One small electronics firm targeted the electronics manufacturers between Fortune 300 and Fortune 500. In this way, it was able to profile more concisely the operating characteristics and needs of corporations in this size range.

One of the greatest pitfalls facing entrepreneurs is falling into the trap signified by the boast "We already know who our customers are."

Once this type of mind-set takes hold, the possibilities of constantly redefining and retracking the marketplace are greatly diminished.

The application and use of your product or service are apt to be such that your company can always benefit from increased exposure to new prospects. Also, the dynamics of the marketplace, including changing needs and personnel turnover, ensure that yesterday's marketing research and yesterday's marketing strategy will not do for today. It is necessary to establish long-term relationships that generate significant follow-on or repeat business. Companies that focus solely on familiar territory run the risk of quickly being surpassed by competitors.

Distribution Channels

An examination of channels of distribution will provide information on how to most effectively serve the customer profitably.

Any sequence of participants within the marketing chain that connects what you're offering to the end user, in this case Fortune 500 corporations, is a channel of distribution. The first chart on page 44 provides a brief look at typical channels of distribution.

Many other channel combinations are possible, depending on your goods or services and the industries to whom you sell. The second chart on page 44 depicts possible channels of distribution for an electronic components manufacturer.

Successfully marketing to Fortune 500 firms requires nothing less than a professional sales effort. The selling options include face-to-face selling, catalog sales, trade show sales, and responses to requests for bids, quotations or proposals. This book (see Chapters 4 and 5) stresses the face-to-face method of selling because in the end purchasing agents select vendors whom they know and like. And being known in the marketplace increases the effectiveness of the other selling methods.

Sales Force Training and Deployment

Who will be representing your company? You? A hired professional staff? Distributors or manufacturers' representatives? Fully describe the marketing sales background of the people who will be representing your company. Do they have the basic prerequisites to do the job? If not, can they be trained to do the job? What are the income, age, occupation, education, and sex of the purchasing agents to whom you or your representatives will be making presentations? These factors should not be ignored

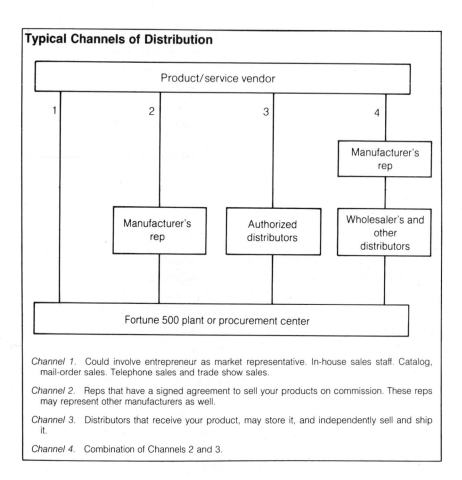

Typical Channels of Distribution

Product/service vendor

1   2   3   4

Manufacturer's rep

Manufacturer's rep

Authorized distributors

Wholesaler's and other distributors

Fortune 500 plant or procurement center

Channel 1. Could involve entrepreneur as market representative. In-house sales staff. Catalog, mail-order sales. Telephone sales and trade show sales.

Channel 2. Reps that have a signed agreement to sell your products on commission. These reps may represent other manufacturers as well.

Channel 3. Distributors that receive your product, may store it, and independently sell and ship it.

Channel 4. Combination of Channels 2 and 3.

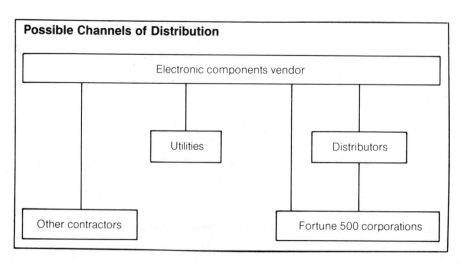

Possible Channels of Distribution

Electronic components vendor

Utilities

Distributors

Other contractors

Fortune 500 corporations

in the overall sales effort. Yet many small vendors focus their efforts on producing superior products or services while shortchanging the ability to sell those products and services professionally.

What types of training will be offered to your salespeople? What books will they read? What courses will they attend? What self-study programs will they complete? Noted sales trainer Jim Cathcart, CPAE, observes that "selling is now a profession"—there are simply "no more peddlers."

Your salespeople will need to be fully briefed on the benefits and features of using your product or service and must be able to present them in a professional manner. They will need to learn how to handle objections, which words to use, how to professionally close, and other selling fundamentals. (See Chapters 4, 9, and 14).

The 80/20 rule, also known as the Pareto principle, applies in the area of professional selling. It is likely that 20 percent of your sales force will produce 80 percent of your sales and that 80 percent of your sales force will produce only 20 percent of your sales. In addition, 20 percent of your products or services will account for 80 percent of your revenues, while 80 percent of your products and services will account for only 20 percent of your revenues. Oh, that we could all identify and drop the 80 percent that yield only 20 percent of our returns and concentrate solely on the fecund 20 percent that yield 80 percent.

Deployment of your sales force involves assigning territories, developing compensation structures, and establishing quotas (see Chapter 5).

Promotion

While a full-scale advertising campaign is not necessary to successfully sell to Fortune 500 firms, an effective promotional program is. At a minimum, you will need a brochure or flier, perhaps a capability statement, business cards, mailers, specifications or boilerplate sheets, product descriptions, and, depending on the nature of your product or service, a catalog.

Undoubtedly, you will want to be listed in the yellow pages and perhaps in directories of trade groups and associations and with state and local business development agencies and other support groups. You may consider joining professional societies and local civic groups such as the Chamber of Commerce, the Rotary Club, and the Kiwanis Club. To increase your firm's visibility, you may decide to exhibit at trade shows offering professional displays and demonstrations.

Each time a targeted corporate purchasing agent is favorably exposed to your firm, you have enhanced the efforts of the salespeople in the field and moved one step closer to making a sale. Your marketing plan should include a description of all the promotional techniques that you will use to favorably influence the target market (see Chapters 5, 6, and 11).

What types of public relations activities will you undertake? Maintaining contact with customers and prospects keeps your firm's name in front of them. You can do this by mailing greeting cards, newsletters, or press releases announcing new products or services. Attending key conventions and maintaining a high profile in civic and business organizations improve public relations. The contacts you make at civic and business functions enhance and enlarge your potential for new business.

Your employees also represent public relations opportunities for your firm. Your marketing plan should discuss how you plan to include all of your company's employees in the marketing process from answering the phones, to handling mail, to serving customers on-site.

Facilities and Equipment

The success of your marketing efforts is dependent on having the proper facilities and equipment to carry out your plan. Do you currently have the space you need for adequate production? Could you easily expand your operations if necessary? Do you have the money required to expand or increase production on short notice? What types of equipment would you like to have? Is the design of your facility consistent with your revenue goal—for example, can you ship enough products or provide enough services to reach the desired sales level?

An examination of your facilities and equipment and their respective capacities will enable you to determine whether your resources are consistent with your marketing goals. Many small vendors find that their facilities and equipment are underutilized and off the top of their heads they are quite confident that increases in business can be absorbed easily. Under fire, some of those vendors learn that the optimal capacity of their facilities or equipment is actually less than they had thought. Such vendors have in essence become the cause of their own bottlenecks.

How does your plant or office measure up to that of competitors? What is the probable first impression that a corporate representative will have when visiting you on-site? Are you willing to make the expenditures necessary to work with major corporations for the long term?

Organization and Staff Support

An often overlooked component of the marketing plan is your organization and supporting staff. What contribution do they make to your marketing efforts? Is your company able to respond to requests for information in a timely manner? If you promptly deliver poorly typed bids or proposals that are otherwise conceptually sound, you may still be penalized. Are the documents, packages, and other items submitted to customers and prospects of the same high quality as the products or services you offer?

Is your staff/customer relationship focused, and if not, what is your plan for instilling focus? Jim Cathcart says, "Marketing is not a department; it's a philosophy." Strategist Peter R. Johnson adds that, at the end of any plan should be added a written commitment, such as, "This is our plan, and we're going to follow it."

The following outline lists all the major components of the marketing plan discussed in this chapter.

COMPONENTS OF THE MARKETING PLAN

1. One-sentence definition of your business.
2. Choosing a market niche.
3. Revenue forecasting, goal setting.
4. Defining your trade radius.
5. Distribution channels.
6. Sales force training and deployment.
7. Promotion.
8. Facilities and equipment.
9. Organization and staff support.

THE ACID TEST

If I flew to your plant or office today and asked you to show me your marketing plan, could you? The only way to get a marketing plan prepared is to give it priority status. There are a host of obstacles to producing such a plan. These obstacles include the time it takes to put the plan together, difficulties in getting needed input from others, and uncertainty as to how to handle some of the elements. Also, for those responsible for producing marketing plans who are not company owners or presidents, there are additional obstacles such as gaining full acceptance, handling differences of opinion, and updating the plans as necessary.

The vendors who get the contracts have taken the time to produce a marketing plan and to follow it to the best of their ability.

HOW ONE COMPANY APPROACHES MARKET PLANNING

Here is a minicase on how one company approaches market planning.

One small but growing firm located in southern California, which we'll call MNO, defines itself as being in the business of providing hardware/software system integration and related services to the domestic aerospace and defense industry. MNO maintains a four-pronged approach in its market planning. Let's take a look at the actual language it uses in its plan.

MNO possesses key distinct competitive advantages that enable it to succeed in the marketplace:

1. Its underlying marketing philosophy.
2. The types of individuals it employs.
3. The long-term marketing effort it undertakes for key opportunities.
4. Its superior marketing research capabilities.

Marketing Philosophy

MNO believes in the full-service approach to serving the needs of industry in the areas of hardware/software integration, communications network analysis and design, systems engineering, systems maintenance, and automated office systems design. The company's existing commitment to maintain hardware and software support for computer systems, for example, spans the continent. MNO has established a strong technical base while maintaining a people-oriented operation.

In the past, 60 percent of MNO's business has been follow-on. Growth or expansion is undertaken only after careful planning, analysis of risk, and assembling of the requisite resources. MNO has maintained a reputation for quality and timeliness, and it charges a fair price for the value of its products, services, and performance.

This marketing philosophy has enabled MNO to become a $3.5 million–plus company, and it serves as the cornerstone for further growth. Having maintained a track record for outstanding performance, MNO enjoys a strong competitive advantage in acquiring new business with existing clients and in attracting potential new clients through third-party referral.

Types of Individuals Employed

MNO employs top computer service professionals with proven performance records. It matches employees with challenging tasks in familiar environments. These talented individuals are able to discuss client problems in the client's own terminology, and they understand contract requirements from both sides of the fence.

These employees afford MNO's top management a continuous supply of inside marketing information and marketing opportunities. MNO project managers provide the level of effort mandated by the contracts to which they adhere, and serve as a network of inside "salespeople" obtaining first-person primary market data for the company in its most lucrative market area.

MNO's strategy in obtaining the right type of contract managers is to identify marketing targets "sole source, noncompetitive in nature," of somewhat modest size, that could be used to bring the desired types of individuals on board. MNO is presently bidding on contracts for which such individuals can be hired, recognizing the value of their services in the marketing effort required for systems integration.

MNO's staff is supported by excellent working conditions, specialized training when necessary, and a vast array of sophisticated support materials.

Long-Term Marketing Effort

MNO's marketing philosophy and the types of individuals it employs firmly support the company's third and most important vehicle in achieving a competitive advantage: a long-term marketing effort. Solid marketing intelligence requiring long lead times for tracking is required before any solicitation is made by MNO. Intelligence gathering is a two-way street. The company maintains an active file of all potential projects. Then, once a promising new business target takes shape, MNO calls on its various data sources and prepares a marketing strategy.

Solicitations are generally *not* bid unless they have been tracked over a period of time and a significant amount of intelligence has already been gathered. MNO prefers to have key contacts within a corporation and to know how receptive that corporation would be to an MNO bid.

MNO's marketing intelligence gathering is supported through continuing contact with client representatives; review of industry directories and research reports; membership in trade and professional associations;

attendance at prebid conferences, marketing seminars, trade shows, and federal government expositions; and leads generated as a result of its five years in the marketplace.

MNO's working agreements with original equipment manufacturers, hardware and software firms, and other computer services firms enable it to provide competitive products and services.

Marketing Research Capabilities

MNO maintains superior marketing research capabilities that enable it to perform in-depth analysis of market opportunities, industry growth and trends, and intensity of competition. MNO also monitors the configuration of other installations at key client locations. All of the above enhance MNO's focus on a potential market opportunity.

GETTING STARTED ON YOUR PLAN

Your marketing plan need not be longer than 10 pages. The best time to start on it is now. "Later" is good for updating.

FURTHER READING ON MARKETING PLANS

Connor, Richard A., Jr., and Jeffrey P. Davidson. *Marketing Your Consulting and Professional Services.* New York: John Wiley & Sons, 1985. 219 pp.

Husack, Glen A., and Gordon P. Kraemer. *Do-It-Yourself Marketing Plan.* Buffalo: Institute for Small Business, 1982. 99 pp.

Kotler, Philip. *Marketing for Nonprofit Organizations.* Englewood Cliffs, N.J.: Prentice-Hall, 1982, "The Format of a Marketing Plan," pp. 177–82.

Luther, William. *The Marketing Plan.* New York: AMACOM, 1982, "The Marketing Plan," chap. 4.

Quagliaroli, John A. *How to Write a Marketing Plan.* Tarrytown, N.Y.: Center for Entrepreneurial Management, 1979. 44 pp.

Skacel, Robert K. *The Marketing Plan: How to Prepare It . . . What Should Be in It.* Towson, Md.: MPM Associates, 1976. 64 pp.

Stanford, Melvin J. *New Enterprise Management.* Englewood Cliffs, N.J.: Prentice-Hall, 1982, "Outline for Business Development Plan," pp. 345–51.

Any plan is better than no plan, and as Pete Johnson says, an "unsophisticated plan that is followed" is infinitely more valuable than a "sophisticated plan that sits in a desk drawer."

CHAPTER FOUR

There's No Substitute for Effective Selling

*The world is before you, and
you need not take it or
leave it as it was when
you came in.*

JAMES BALDWIN

You can be offering *the* greatest product or service in the world, but if you or your marketing staff haven't mastered the fundamentals of selling—on a one-on-one basis—your quest to successfully market to Fortune 500 firms will be continually thwarted. This chapter highlights the three common denominators of successful selling, focuses on word power and effective listening, offers proven closing techniques, provides instruction on handling objections, and examines the traits of supersellers.

There are numerous books worth reading that are devoted entirely to the topic of face-to-face selling, among them, *How to Master the Art of Selling,* by Tom Hopkins, and *Successful Cold Call Selling,* by Lee Boyan. In addition, several recent books incorporating the latest sales techniques are reviewed on pages 64–66.

THE THREE COMMON DENOMINATORS OF SUCCESSFUL SELLING

The three common denominators of successful selling are: total unshakable belief in yourself, belief in your product or service, and the ability to close successfully.

Belief in Yourself

You will never be successful in selling until you fully believe in yourself. You may have a superior product or service. You may have many skills in selling. You may have hot prospects and a sales territory that is a bonanza. However, you will never be consistently successful in sales until you firmly and steadfastly believe in yourself.

The intensity of your belief in yourself is transmitted to your prospects and clients regardless of what you say or what style of selling you use. According to sales star Betty R. Arbuckle, an insurance consultant, "What's inside your head is the most important element in the selling process. If the prospect buys 'you,' he or she buys your product or service." Entrepreneur and inventor Richard Levy confirms this view. Levy, who has sold dozens of product ideas and inventions to such Fortune 500 firms as Procter & Gamble (22), General Foods (38), and Mattel (300), says, "The first thing that must be sold is yourself. From there, the potential for product sales increases." Belief in yourself is so important in selling that without it the best-trained and most professional salesperson might as well seek another profession.

Belief in Your Product or Service

The second common denominator of successful selling is belief in your product or service. You must believe strongly that the product or service you are offering represents a sound investment for your prospects. Your product doesn't have to be the best one on the market. What is important is that you believe it to be the best *value* for the investment. If you drive a Chevy, you can't sell a Ford as effectively as the man or woman who owns a Ford, drives a Ford, and believes in a Ford. Veteran sales trainer Alan Cimberg believes that selling in the 80s and 90s should also be synonymous with helping—a highly useful and practical insight.

A salesperson's commitment to his product or service is magically transmitted to the prospect or client. About the most dramatic example of commitment to one's service that I can think of is that of Harvey W. Austin, a McLean, Virginia, cosmetic surgeon. Austin, who at age 50 looked several years younger, underwent a face-lift to demonstrate his commitment to and belief in the service he offered. The enthusiasm you possess for your product or service is contagious; moreover, it cannot be feigned on a sustained basis. If you are prone to oscillation and don't believe in what you are selling, you can't possibly expect your customers or prospects to do so—and they won't.

The best and easiest way for you to reap the benefits that can be derived from selling is to offer a product or service to which you are fully committed.

The Ability to Close Successfully

The third common denominator of successful selling is the ability to close. Without that ability, your sales presentations will meander hopelessly, and the sales you make will represent a fraction of those that you could make with proper closing techniques.

What is a closing sentence? It is any question whose answer confirms that the sale has been made. Some salespeople, such as William Leader of Springfield, Massachusetts, are natural closers; they were born with the ability to close. Leader has no qualms about repeatedly asking for the order. And his success over the years indicates that he has closed on an awful lot of orders. For most of us, however, closing techniques must be learned. Fortunately, closing ability can be acquired through proper instruction.

A good time to close is as soon as you perceive a positive response to your sales presentation. Another is any time the customer indicates verbally or nonverbally that he or she has interest in your product or service. Since studies have shown that it takes at least six "no's" in a sales presentation before that one sweet yes is obtained, it is strongly advised that a variety of closing questions be learned:

- Which do you prefer, cash or check?
- In view of the benefits, can you afford to put off this investment until later?
- Would you like to OK this order?
- Don't you agree that anything worth having is worth having now?
- Your pen or mine?
- Would you like it by August 1 or August 15?
- Would you like me to stop by for the check on Monday?
- How much of a deposit would you like to leave?
- What color do you prefer?
- Will one be enough?
- Would you like it gift wrapped?
- Will we ship it directly?
- Would you prefer early morning delivery?
- Will you be needing accessory items?
- Where would you like it to be installed?

There are dozens of effective closing techniques. However, my first boss, William Murray, of the Burroughs Corporation (72), advocated learning a few that are consistent with your style rather than trying to master a large number of them. Here are six closing techniques, one of which may be right for you:

Pluses and Minuses.   Ask the customer to make a list of pluses and minuses. By the time he or she is finished, the result will resemble your original proposal.

Similar Situation.   Mention competitors or successful people that have also made a purchase.

Sharp-Angled Close.   If the customer asks, "Will it do this?" respond with the close, "Do you want it if it does?"

Benefits versus Price Illustration.   On a sheet of paper show the benefits of your product or service in terms of dollar savings over several years. Under that, in a tiny figure, write the selling price of your product or service.

The False Exit.   If the customer wants to think it over, make a false exit, then ask, "What better time is there to think it over than right now?"

Assumptive Close.   Start filling in the details of the sale during the give-and-take subsequent to the presentation.

The only way to become a strong closer is to practice. Try closing too soon and too often rather than too late or too infrequently. Closing takes guts, and top salespeople expect to take at least six "no's" while making a presentation.

During a sales presentation, a customer may exhibit a buying signal, indicating that the sale is not far away. Customers who lean forward, ask many questions, and listen intently to your answers are givng you buying signals. As soon as you perceive a positive response, move in to close the sale.

However, any time you close is a good time, and the earlier you start closing during a presentation, the better off you'll be in the long run. After making a closing statement, stop talking. At this point silence is golden. Let the customer speak next—you'll have either a sale or an opportunity to continue. Speaking first weakens the impact of the question, or as California-based Howard Shenson, "the consultant's consultant," says, "The next person to speak loses."

All great salespeople are strong closers. With each close you are indicating to the customer that you have confidence, that you see a need for the product and service, and that you and your company are ready to fulfill that need. In that sense, closing is nothing less than assuring the customer that when he reposes his confidence in you and

---

SALES AND MARKETING ASSOCIATIONS

American Marketing Association, 250 South Wacker Drive, Chicago, IL
60606. Professional society of marketing and marketing research executives, sales and promotion managers, advertising specialists, teachers,
and others interested in marketing.

National Association of Professional Saleswomen, Box 255708, Sacramento,
CA 95865. Offers training and education to women in professional sales
and marketing careers. Publishes *"Successful Saleswomen."*

Sales & Marketing Executives International, 6151 Wilson Mills Rd., Cleveland, OH 44143. Sales and marketing management, research, training,
and distribution. Conducts marketing information center. Grants awards
to executives and educators.

Academy of Marketing Science, School of Business Administration, University of Miami, Coral Gables, FL 33124. Education in marketing science,
professional standards. Promotes research and widespread dissemina-
tion of findings; facilitates transfer of marketing knowledge to developing
countries; contributes to the solution of marketing problems encountered
by individual firms, industries, and society as a whole.

Public Relations Society of America, 845 3rd Avenue, New York, NY 10022.
Professional society of public relations practitioners. Has speakers bureau
and information center.

---

your company, he is making no mistake. And once you prove yourself
to a buyer through carrying out your word in terms of delivery, quality,
and other factors, you'll find that closing becomes easier the next time
you meet with this buyer. Corporate purchasing agents are people just
like the rest of us. The people at J. P. Stevens & Co. (201) or Cincinnati
Milacron (373) want to be sold. Once they have been sold, and satisfied,
the ease and likelihood of additional purchases increase.

TALK THEIR LANGUAGE

To be most effective during a sales presentation, one must literally use
the language of the prospect. This requires research and experience. If
you're not communicating in the prospect's terms, then you're not communicating at all. The boxed listing that follows briefly defines some of
the latest "purchasing parlance." But be forewarned that other terms
and methods are bound to replace some of those defined here.

PURCHASING PARLANCE—ACCENT ON ACRONYMS

CCM—centralized commodity management. A purchasing program whereby a commodity manager buys for all plants or divisions regardless of his or her home base. This eliminates responsibility for commodity purchases by buyers at individual plants and tends to increase contract longevity with the vendor.

CPM—certified purchasing manager. Professional designation awarded by the National Association of Purchasing Management to individuals demonstrating broad experience, competence, and integrity.

JIT—"just in time". A program for reducing cost or eliminating waste by assembling only the minimum resources necessary to add value to a product. Is often mistakenly regarded as an inventory program because low inventories are one of its essential elements. Is customer or sales focused rather than production focused.

MRO—maintenance, repairs, and overhaul. Purchasing department expenditures for the preservation or enhancement of existing capital assets or resources.

MRP—material requirements planning. A systematic approach to purchasing that includes forecasting needs, identifying sources, establishing delivery schedules, and monitoring progress.

PM—purchasing manager. One who coordinates, directs, and possibly trains buyers and assistant purchasing managers while also maintaining buying responsibilities.

SIC—Standard Industrial Code. A uniform classification system wherein goods and services are assigned a four-digit code. Used by the federal government, particularly the Department of Commerce's Bureau of the Census, as well as private industry.

SPC—statistical process control. A quantitative tool for enhancing quality control. Relies on probability theory and random sampling to assure that predetermined standards are maintained.

VA—value analysis. An approach to cost reduction in which components are analyzed to determine if they can be redesigned, standardized, or produced by less costly methods.

CLARIFY TO BE UNDERSTOOD

Tony J. Alessandra, chairman of Alessandra and Associates in La Jolla, California, and coauthor of *Non-Manipulative Selling* and *The Business of Selling,* offers a simple test that illustrates the need we all have to be more precise in communication. Alessandra suggests that you quickly jot down what you think would be meant if someone said the following to you:

> "I'll be there in a minute . . ."
> "It isn't very far . . ."
> "We'll provide you with a small number of these at no cost . . ."
> "Call me later and we'll discuss it . . ."

These statements are ambiguous. When they are used in normal conversation, there is a high probability that they will be misinterpreted unless they are clarified. For instance, observes Alessandra, when a person says, "Call me later and we'll discuss it," does he mean 15 minutes from now, one hour from now, tomorrow, or next week?

All of these statements have an unrestricted meaning, which can create misunderstanding in communication. We use such statements in everyday conversation and expect other people to clearly understand what we are saying. Alessandra believes that unless statements of this kind are clarified and their meaning confirmed, miscommunication is likely.

GIVE AND GET DEFINITIONS

Alessandra also points out that interpretations of words or phrases vary among people, groups, regions, and societies. When we assume that words have only one meaning, we may believe we understand others when we really don't. The words you use in your everyday conversations often have multiple meanings. Therefore, Alessandra advises that we give and get definitions while questioning and listening.

During interpersonal communications, it is dangerous to assume that the other person thinks or feels as you do. The other person may have a frame of reference totally different from your own. He or she reacts and perceives according to what he or she knows or believes to be true, and his or her reactions and perceptions may be very different from your own. Alessandra advises you not to assume that you and the other person are talking about the same thing, that your words and phrases are automatically being understood.

LISTEN EFFECTIVELY

Shh! Here's a top secret—the best salespeople are good listeners. But good listening must be learned.

Why don't we listen as well as we should? Dr. Chester L. Karrass, director of the Center for Effective Negotiating, based in Santa Monica, California, offers several reasons.

- We often have a lot on our minds, and it's not easy to switch gears quickly to fully absorb and participate in what is being said to us. (I find this to be so true that I started taping meetings. When I played back the tapes, I just couldn't believe what I had missed the first time.)
- We have adopted the habit of talking and interrupting too much and do not let the other party continue even when this may be to our benefit.
- We are anxious to rebut what the other person has said, and we are afraid that we may forget to make our point if we do not do so right away.
- We allow ourselves to be easily distracted by interruptions that occur while the meeting takes place. (Have you ever asked your secretary to hold all phone calls during meetings? More than 10 years ago, I had a full day of interviews at the Ford Motor Company (4), not one of which was disturbed by phone calls. The people I saw there were interested in listening to me, and they showed it.)
- We jump to conclusions before all the evidence has been presented or is available.
- We discount or "write off" some statements because we minimize the importance of the party who is making them.
- We tend to discard information that doesn't match what we want to hear or that we don't like.

Dr. Karrass, who has delivered hundreds of programs to Fortune 500 executives, points out that "poor listeners often drop out of a conversation in the hope that they will catch up later. This seldom happens."

Developing good listening habits is one way to become more effective in handling purchasing agents. Active listening improves your interpersonal skills, your human relations capabilities, and your ability to make sound buying judgments. In the long run, good listening can enhance your professional marketability and pay real dividends when you call on corporate purchasing agents.

HANDLE OBJECTIONS

Jim Cathcart, CPAE, based in La Jolla, California , has provided extensive training in the area of sales techniques and handling objections and has worked with such companies as ITT (25), General Electric (10), and Sperry (63). Cathcart says that "too many salespeople cringe at the thought of objections, often considering them a form of personal rejection. Experienced salespeople, while not encouraging objections, consider them a means of determining what to do to complete the sale."

From a salesperson's perspective, an objection is anything that presents an obstacle to the smooth completion of the sale. Salespeople are most concerned about objections in the early part of the sale, when they are trying to initiate a relationship, and toward the end, when the time has come to close the sale.

Cathcart observes that too many salespeople react to objections by tensing up. They tend to misinterpret and overreact to them. However, salespeople should view objections, not as roadblocks, but rather as "crossroads" to the sale.

Objections are opportunities. By objecting, the prospect is participating in the sale and telling you something. This presents you with an opportunity for increased understanding and more effective tailoring of your sales presentation to the prospect's needs. Objections are like a guidance system. The prospect is saying to you, "Don't go that way. Go this way."

How Do You Recognize Objections?

"You recognize objections by listening and observing," says Cathcart. "If you are preoccupied with what you are saying, you'll miss many of the cues the client gives you." Listen carefully and watch for indications that tell you something is wrong. Such indications can be likened to stoplights.

Behavior that says, "No, absolutely not," is like a red light that says, "Stop; do not proceed until you resolve my concern." Behavior that sends you a "mixed message" because the prospect is not comfortable with what you are saying or doing is like a yellow light that says, "Proceed with caution." Positive feedback is like a green light that says, "Go ahead; everything is fine."

Seven Techniques for Handling Objections

Here are seven basic techniques that Cathcart has found effective for handling objections.

1. *Feel/Felt/Found.*   "I understand how you *feel.*" (I'm empathizing with you.) "Many people have *felt* the same way." (You are not alone in feeling this way.) "However, they have *found* that . . ." (Now you present your solution.) Here is another way the idea might be used. "I understand your thinking. I thought the same thing when I first saw this product. However, I have found . . ."

2. *Convert to a Question.*   When the prospect makes a statement, it may be difficult to answer. However, you can convert the statement into a question that allows you to answer it more easily. Example: "I don't think I could use that product." Your response might be, "There is an important question in your statement, and that is, 'How can you gain maximum use for a product like this?' Is that the question?" Now you can proceed to answer the *question* rather than arguing with the statement.

3. *Echo Technique.*   Sometimes you are faced with a response that doesn't give you enough information. In this case, you can reflect or echo the response back to the prospect. The prospect might say that the price is too high. Here you can say "Too high?" The prospect will then generally give you more feedback and information. From there, you can address the concern about price from the prospect's perspective.

4. *Lowest Common Denominator.*   In this case, you take an objection that looms large in the prospect's mind and reduce it to a figure much easier to comprehend and handle. Example: "$300 is too much." Response: "$300 does seem like a large price tag until you consider that you will probably be using this 3,000 times a year. This means that your cost per use is only 10 cents, a small price to pay for the increased convenience and profitability that comes from this product."

5. *Boomerang Technique.*   Think of a boomerang and what it does. Once thrown, it makes a wide arc and then comes right back to the individual who threw it. You do the same thing with a prospect's concern. He or she says, "I'm too busy right now to implement this new procedure." You boomerang the objection right back: "The fact that you are too busy today means that you need the time savings that will come to you as a result of using this product."

6. *Change the Base.*   Change the basis upon which the prospect is founding the response so that he or she can see things in a different light. Example: The prospect says, "This won't perform the X-process." Your response: "You were interested in this because it does the Y-process so well. It would be nice if it did both, but your main concern is the Y-process, isn't it?"

7. *Compensation Technique.* Sometimes an objection is based on a very real shortcoming that must be acknowledged. Example: "This unit is too large for the space." Your reply could be, "I agree that the unit is larger than the present space, but the benefits are so great that it wouldn't be right to deny them to yourself simply to avoid moving to another space." Admit the shortcoming, but override it with added benefits.

As you encounter objections, your knowledge, skills, and intentions will allow you to choose the right path—the path to increased sales and increased personal satisfaction.

SELL SOFTLY

"Selling softly" sounds like a contradiction in terms. However, David H. Sandler, a sales seminar trainer from Stevenson, Maryland, believes that contrary to most popular conceptions, the supersalesperson is a softseller, not a hardseller. He or she says and does the unexpected and thus gets the customer to reveal important needs. Then he or she tailors the pitch to meet those needs and makes the sale.

These are marks of the supersalesperson, according to Sandler:

- Brings up objections before the customer thinks of them.
- Doesn't try to impress the customer about how much he knows about his product. Concentrates completely on what will make the sale.
- Spends the first part of the sales meeting asking questions about the customer's problems.
- Spends most of the rest of the time getting the customer to suggest how the problems might be lessened.
- Then makes the sales presentation, tailored to the customer's needs.
- If the customer is hostile, gently tries to neutralize him. If that doesn't work, doesn't try to sell but lays the foundation for a callback.

The purchasing agent who gave you a hard time on Monday may have repented by Thursday! I was once kicked out of a company because a sales representative from my firm had previously oversold the company and had not adequately installed the equipment. Dismayed, I made my way slowly out the door, only to be called back just before getting into my car. The prospect had had a change of heart and conceded that my integrity and his present need overruled his initial, emotional response. Betty Arbuckle points out that those toughest to sell to often become strong advocates "after you've lived up to your words through action." So stand your ground even on the toughest sales calls. Your missionary efforts may ultimately yield a songbird that sings the praises of your products and services to others.

PLAY THE NUMBERS!

Many salespeople, even those who have mastered selling skills, choose to be discouraged and abandon ship after a relatively short time. The winners, however, realize that successful marketing means paying homage to the numbers game, that if you don't call enough people, it is guaranteed that you will not be a successful marketer.

The key to a successful, personal sales effort, in addition to making a sufficient number of contacts, is to offer a personal touch. Obviously, this is done best in a face-to-face discussion with the prospect. In fact, as society becomes more technologically sophisticated ("high tech") the need for "high touch" increases. (John Naisbitt almost used the title *High Tech, High Touch* for his best selling book; however, Nansey Neiman, the publisher of Warner Books, came up with *Megatrends* instead!) Many erroneously believe that time can always be saved by following up requests for information through the mail or on the phone. If you've taken the time to define an appropriate target market and you can readily visit the corporate plant site, why take shortcuts by using the mail or phone instead of making a personal appearance?

You may be a truly talented person, but if you're not making a sufficient number of in-person sales visits, your marketing program will suffer. It is essential to properly "work" the prospect list that you have developed. This means calling all of the prospects, using spaced intervals between calls. It also means not letting the results of the first few calls dampen the enthusiasm you may have generated originally. AMAX (183), Allis-Chalmers (315), and Smith International (387) have sustained large losses over the last few years. So their purchasing people may be less receptive than those of Baxter Travenol Laboratories (160), or Texaco (6), which have been very profitable of late. But all of these corporations have needs, so who knows? The point is to hang in there.

It is not unusual for salespeople to place too much reliance on lists that haven't been kept up-to-date or have aged. On pages 159–72 is a list of nearly 200 purchasing departments that was updated just before this book went to press. But 20 percent of the items on this list will be outdated 12 months later. Canned lists age quickly. Though considerable effort may be necessary, use lists that you've generated and updated yourself. It is discouraging to make several calls and be told each time that your party "is not at this number."

Playing the numbers has an additional meaning. The average sale is made after the prospect has said no six times! If the world's best salesman requires six "no's" per prospect before getting a sale, who are we to assume that our selling efforts will require fewer "no's" to be successful?

All other things being equal, the marketer who takes the time to get organized and stay organized in working a prospect list will do far better than the poorly organized, easily discouraged marketer.

HOW SUPERSELLERS SELL

How do they do it? How do supersellers earn $100,000, $200,000, and $300,000 or more per year? The goal of supersellers involves *helping* the prospect.

Supersellers, according to Alan Cimberg, are superhelpers. More than ever, salespeople are acting as consultants to those to whom they sell and the process of selling has become a two-way street. Charles Porter, a partner with Coopers & Lybrand, holds that any time two people meet, one is selling something. To view this another way, at any given time one of these people has the potential to help the other. Supersellers are constantly on the lookout for ways to help purchasing customers in crucial areas such as cost control, quality improvement, and inventory control. Supersellers help with just-in-time (JIT) delivery systems, material requirements planning (MRP), and value analysis (VA).

Robert Ellis of Motion Industries, in Cincinnati, Ohio, helps his buyers by pointing out available product substitutes that can prevent massive downtime costs. Joe Macaluse of W. W. Grainger, in Houston, Texas, helps his customers to systematize and standardize their purchases so as to achieve volume discounts and lower inventory costs. He also makes available a wide variety of alternative solutions to customer problems.

Robert Shoults of Bay City Container Corporation, in Pico Rivera, California, continuously monitors his customers' needs for more functional and cost-effective made-to-order packaging. Another superseller arrives on the scene as early as 4 A.M. for one customer who checks in at that time.

There is no composite profile of supersellers. However, a *Purchasing* magazine study indicates that this core of traits and behaviors seems to characterize the superseller:

- Offers professional, thorough presentation and timely follow-up.
- Offers support to buyers within the supplier firm.
- Maintains familiarity with the buyer's product line.
- Maintains expert knowledge of his or her own product line or services.
- Stays abreast of the industry and shares information with buyers.
- Creatively applies his or her products or services to the buyer's needs.
- Makes regular sales calls.
- Has a technical education or background.
- *Prepares* sales calls.

"A winner," according to Denis Waitely, Ph.D., "is someone who never meets you just halfway." Winners go all the way in making sure that the customer understands how their products or services will satisfy the customer's needs. Supersellers look like and act like winners.

BONE UP ON YOUR SELLING CAPABILITY

Inspired? Here are some of the latest crop of books on selling.

Non-Manipulative Selling. By Dr. Tony Alessandra. Box 2767, La Jolla, CA 92038. 182 pp. This popular book explains how to increase sales by removing pressure and building trust. It offers proven insights on such topics as: how to "size up" prospects; the art of asking questions; listening your way to more sales; image: the silent persuader; selling without words: the language of nonverbal communications; and the information-gathering, presentation, commitment, and follow-through processes.

The Business of Selling. By Dr. Tony Alessandra. Box 2767, La Jolla, CA 92038, 200 pp. This book shows you how to gain more control over your career and increase client satisfaction. Its topics include strategies and tactics for account management, territory management, and self-management; professionalism; goal setting; time management; prospecting and promotional strategies; and preparing for the sales call. It will show you how to run your own selling career as a highly successful and profitable business.

Strategic Selling: The Unique Sales System Proven Successful by America's Best Companies. By Robert B. Miller and Stephen E. Heiman, with Tad Tuleja. William Morrow, 105 Madison Avenue, New York, NY 10016. 309 pp. A guide to sales based on customer-needs analysis and satisfaction and an ''I win–you win'' point of view.

The New Sales Manager's Survival Guide. By David A. Stumm. AMACOM, 135 West 50th Street, New York, NY 10020. 233 pp. This handbook for beginning sales managers covers many selling topics and discusses management by objectives (MBO), running a sales meeting, and developing a personal management style. It also explores the question of why salespeople fail and what can be done about it.

Power Selling: A Three-Step Program for Successful Selling. By James H. Brewer, J. Michael Ainsworth, and George E. Wynne. Prentice-Hall, Englewood Cliffs, NJ 07632. 126 pp. Focuses on power, not motivation, as the key to selling. Tells how to assess prospect's personality type and quickly create the perfect sales strategy.

Selling on the Phone: A Self-Teaching Guide. By James D. Porterfield. John Wiley & Sons, Somerset, NJ 08873. 143 pp. This handbook offers a five-step system to teach basic selling skills. It includes numerous self-assessment exercises and application activities along with sample call-flow plans and advice on script development.

Managing the Successful Sales Force. By James M. Comer and Alan J. Dubinsky. Lexington Books, 125 Spring Street, Lexington, MA 02173. 141 pp. Presents and draws conclusions from previous research on sales management issues, with a focus on first-line activities. Includes an extensive glossary and numerous charts and tables.

Gary Goodman's 60-Second Salesperson. By Gary S. Goodman. Prentice-Hall, Englewood Cliffs, NJ 07632. 96 pp. Tells how to open and close telephone sales calls within 60 seconds. Advises on psyching yourself up, then building rapport, positioning yourself believably, effectively describing your products or services, making the offer, creating commitment, and then closing the sale, each within 10 seconds.

Managing Sales and Marketing Training. Edited by Patrick Forsyth. Gower Publishing, Old Post Road, Brookfield, VT 05036. 352 pp. This guide for practitioners covers training tools and techniques and organization of the marketing-training function, along with international sales training and evaluation sales training.

In addition, the publishers of *Selling Direct,* a monthly magazine, offer these titles:

Top Secrets of Successful Selling: Thought Plus Action. By Jack Wardlaw. 235 pp. Methods of putting positive thoughts into action from the initial contact with the prospect to the closing of the deal are outlined in this concisely written book.

How to Turn Your Ideas into Big Money. By Vernon Brabham, Jr. 102 pp. Demonstrates how anyone can develop, produce, and successfully market an idea.

Making Money with the Telephone. By M. T. Brown. 200 pp. Telephone selling is the sales skill of the future, and it is in great demand today! This book teaches the techniques of successful telephone selling and shows how to sell smarter and get better results.

The 36 Biggest Mistakes Salesmen Make and How to Correct Them. By George N. Kahn. 205 pp. This book tells how to recognize and correct the 36 mistakes that keep thousands of salespeople from reaching their peak performance.

The Soft Sell. By Tim Conner. 169 pp. Looks at selling in a new way. A "how-to" book that promises personal growth and increased sales and income.

The Power of Positive Intimidation in Selling. By Dave Johnson. 249 pp. Written for the working salesperson, this guide demonstrates how to use the power of positive intimidation to greatly increase your sales.

Successful Personal Selling through TA. By Maurice F. Villere and Claude P. Duet. 261 pp. Techniques for dealing with an unreasonable customer through transactional analysis.

Making Successful Presentations: A Self-Teaching Guide. By Terry C. Smith. 193 pp. How to plan, organize, develop, and deliver presentations. Poise and skill-building resources are stressed.

How to Increase Sales and Put Yourself Across by Telephone. By Mona Ling. 262 pp. With 77 million telephones available to the salesperson, here is the telephone technique that can produce immediate results for the individual or company sales program.

For information, write to:

Communication Channels, Inc.
Attn: Book Department
6255 Barfield Road
Atlanta, GA 30328

CHAPTER FIVE

Managing the Marketing and Sales Effort: A Never-Ending Task

The secret of success is not in doing your own work but in recognizing the right person to do it for you.

ANDREW CARNEGIE

Mastery of sales technique assures effective performance in the field. Mastery of sales management techniques assures efficient performance of the overall selling effort and, because sales is the most important component of marketing, of the overall marketing effort. Even if your designated staff or sales representatives master all of the skills discussed in Chapter 4, all will be for naught if you cannot effectively manage your company's overall sales effort.

Firms that are successful when marketing to Fortune 500 corporations characteristically document their strength through the use of capability statements, company brochures, and sales literature. They have defined their target markets well in advance, collected research or background information on selected targets, and, of most importance, followed a weekly marketing plan. They are able to respond quickly to new opportunities as these become evident while still maintaining a methodical approach to penetrating the market.

My observation in working with over 225 companies since 1975 is that successful firms are not overreliant on a few large clients but instead strive to achieve a balanced client mix. Some, though not the majority, employ aggressive promotional techniques to bolster their marketing efforts. Finally, of great significance, small vendors that are effective marketers have a designated marketing coordinator to carry out the ongoing program of calling on corporate prospects.

HIRING MARKETING HELP

One of the turning points in the evolution of an emerging firm occurs when the entrepreneur recognizes that a marketing manager or sales staff must be added because he or she can't do it all alone.

Bill Sharer, executive vice president of Exxel Management and Marketing Corporation, Flemington, New Jersey, says that "done well, hiring salespeople is a risky, imperfect process. After all, you are examining someone's past but hiring his or her future. Done poorly, staff selection is a horror show."

Even years of training and experience do not guarantee uniformly good results. Small wonder that even seasoned entrepreneurs approach the task with trepidation. Despite the difficulties, Sharer believes that careful attention to, and avoidance of, the most common mistakes improves one's odds dramatically.

Here are common mistakes in seeking sales support that Sharer has observed, along with their antidotes.

1. Cloning. Many entrepreneurs tend to hire in their own image and likeness, believing that they can best relate to people who share their values, interests, and background. However, people who think differently than you do may be better for your organization. They may be harder to manage, but the best salespeople often are.

2. Piracy. If you make competitors your source of sales talent, you are playing a risky game. Piracy erodes overall market credibility. Retreads who move from one vendor to the next can arouse customer suspicion and reflect badly on your company's integrity. Moreover, a person who leaves a position for a better one sometimes continues to search for another that's better still.

3. Chicken or Egg Hangup. Should you hire good technicians and teach them to sell, or should you hire good salespeople and teach them the technical aspects of the job? Either strategy can succeed. Your training capability is the key. Which are you better able to teach? Except in highly technical fields, product knowledge is usually easier to teach. So it's often best to select a salesperson.

People who know how to sell and like to sell will learn what they need to know about products, markets, and applications because this knowledge is a means of reaching their goals.

4. Hiring the Nonsalesperson.   Previous sales experience is not an absolute must—everyone has to start somewhere—but a desire to sell is. Beware of anyone who doesn't really want to sell. Such people are usually easy to spot. Among them is the candidate who is looking at a half-dozen career options, the candidate with no understanding of the selling environment, and the candidate who has vague or shallow reasons for choosing sales, such as the desire to work independently, to meet people, to travel, or to earn big money.

Look for evidence of assertiveness, professional aggressiveness, and a clear desire to sell.

5. Stereotypes.   To hire good salespeople, you may have to change some deep-seated beliefs. Give every applicant a chance to present his or her case. Listen fairly and objectively. Question what troubles you, but don't just try to justify your emotional perceptions.

Studies show that interviewers usually make a decision in the first five minutes, then spend an hour searching for evidence to support it. That's not only discrimination; it's also self-defeating. Supersellers come in all shapes, sizes, and genders!

6. Overselling the Opportunity.   Interviewers often glamorize the opportunity they offer. This practice is especially dangerous with salespeople since salespeople tend to be goal-oriented. Many candidates who accept an ''inflated'' offer quickly become disgruntled and leave.

7. The ''Best Available'' Trap.   After a lengthy search and many rewarding interviews, managers sometimes choose the ''best available'' candidate, even when they know that he or she is unsatisfactory. Most often you'd be better off with a vacant territory than with one filled by an incompetent. Among the many strategies that are preferable to adding a known or probable loser to your staff are temporary assignment, phone coverage by inside staff, direct mail, territory realignment, and major account maintenance by you.

8. Gullibility.   People seeking work are often under stress. Job searches can be discouraging and humiliating. It's human nature to present oneself as favorably as possible. However, one study showed that Harvard had no record of 4 percent of the candidates whose ostensible graduation from that institution employers called to verify. Check the references of any candidate to whom you intend to make an offer. *Checklist Manage-*

ment: The Eight-Hour Manager (Bethesda, MD.: National Press, 1986) provides numerous suggestions for verifying credentials. Because sales is a high-interface profession, try for a cross section of references— boss, subordinates, peers, customers, and personal acquaintances.

9. Lack of System. If your overall personnel policies are haphazard, your hiring practices are likely to follow suit. Many companies have vague definitions of success, poor or no standards of performance, and loose or no appraisal procedures. If you can't say what on-the-job success is, it's doubtful whether you'll hire someone who can achieve it.

You should state objective performance expectations for 30-day, 60-day, 90-day, and six-month periods. As new employees meet each benchmark, recognize and reward them. As they don't, weed them out.

Ross Perot said, "Eagles don't flock. You have to find them one at a time." There are no shortcuts to good selection. "But the better the job you do," says Sharer, "the less frequently you'll have to do it and the easier your day-to-day management will be."

SALES TRAINING METHODS

Even if you are able to select the best possible person for your sales staff, some type of training must be supplied. This is particularly true if the person was hired from outside your company rather than shifted or promoted from within. Purchasing departments in such companies as Xerox (40), Boise Cascade (105), and Burroughs (72) commit substantial time and resources to developing first-rate purchasing systems and staff. And you must be no less committed to developing a professional sales staff.

At a minimum, you will want to acquaint sales staffers with your company's history, its organization, and its policies and procedures. Sales reps must also be thoroughly familiar with your products or services: the materials used in their production, their design features, and their performance capabilities. Once you have imparted information about your products or services, you must also provide whatever information you can on the products or services of competitors (see page 77).

Your training program must also focus on customers—who they are, where they are, and what their needs are. Your company's history of calling on customers as well as its successes and failures should be carefully detailed to the sales staff. They will need to know this in order to effectively represent you. Hopefully, the basics discussed in

Chapter 4 on sharpening selling skills have been or will be mastered by your sales staff. If not, your sales management training program must also provide instruction in the areas of prospecting, word usage, handling objections, listening, closing, and following up.

Depending on your product or service, the size of your staff, and your target market, your sales staff will be responsible for the following:

- Providing marketing information and feedback to you.
- Handling customer inquiries and following up on requests.
- Learning the nuances of corporate purchasing processes.
- Negotiating and closing on sales.
- Finding new applications for existing products and services.
- Relaying information to customers.
- Providing training to customers' personnel in effectively using your product or service.
- Representing you at meetings.
- Scouting the competition's goods and services.
- Handling customer complaints.
- Developing and maintaining good customer rapport.
- Seeking and obtaining new accounts.
- Collecting payments.
- Maintaining desired levels of service.
- Finding new ways to satisfy customer needs.
- Maintaining a professional image with prospects and customers.
- Effectively representing your company at all times.
- Maintaining visibility with selected targets.

Author and consultant Christopher W. Lovelock, Ph.D., based in Cambridge, Massachusetts, points out that these questions will be of continuing concern to you: Are your sales representatives allocating time effectively? Are they delivering the intended message, or are they modifying it? Is their behavior changing on the basis of the actions of the customers with whom they deal?

"Purchasing's responsibility is to get all the information it can, evaluate it, and make decisions as to whom it wants to do business with," says George H. Nusloch of Olin Corporation's (195) Chemical Group. According to Lovelock, your primary responsibility in managing the sales function will be to hire and train sales representatives, to motivate them to carry out their assigned selling task effectively, and to evaluate their performance. You will also be responsible for setting salaries and bonuses, establishing sales quotas, and evaluating sales performance.

If your business is large enough it might be useful or necessary for you to hire a sales manager who will relieve you of these responsibilities. For long-term, sustained success, a carefully planned, systematic approach to sales management is essential.

SALES QUOTAS AND TERRITORY MANAGEMENT

Ideally, the sales quotas that you establish for each sales representative and the territories that you assign will follow directly from your marketing plan. Realistically, in the day-to-day operations of your business, such coordination is difficult to achieve. Use your revenue forecast as the basis for establishing sales quotas and dividing up territories.

For companies with good track records, the forecast is often based on the trend of previous yearly revenues. The major problem with this method is that future sales are predicted largely on the basis of what has been done in the past. More often, a revenue target is simply based on the entrepreneur's experience and observation, and forces are then marshaled to achieve that sales figure.

An Uninformed Marketer's View of the United States

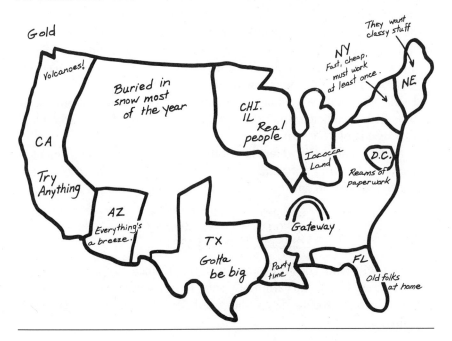

If you forecast sales of $2,400,000 for the coming 12 months, and your average sale is $50,000, then you will obviously need 48 sales to achieve your sales forecast, or 4 sales per month, although seasonal variations and other factors usually create havoc with such schedules. If a sales representative can effectively make 6 presentations a week, or 300 a year, and your sales history shows that roughly 5.3 percent of the presentations ultimately turn into sales, then you will need three full-time salespeople:

300 presentations/year $\times$ 5.3% closing rate = 16 sales

48 sales/year $\div$ 16 sales/sales rep = 3 sales reps

In this scenario, your average sales rep would bring in roughly $800,000 worth of business (16 sales $\times$ $50,000 average sale = $800,000). At a straight 8 percent commission, each rep would earn $64,000.

In making territorial assignments, your job would be to divide your target area—it could be the United States, your own state, or some multicounty area—into three territories such that each territory provides roughly the same potential as the others. This is not an easy task. Also, you may divide your territory, not by geographic area, but by customer characteristics, potential size of order, or any one of a number of other important criteria.

Major EDP manufacturers such as IBM (5), Digital Equipment (55), NCR (89), and Wang Laboratories (161) generally assign sales territories by type of customer within regional areas. So, for example, Digital Equipment sales reps in the Washington, D.C., area may cover the defense market, while others cover the federal government in general and still others cover commercial markets. Territory allocation should be modified periodically to reflect the dynamic nature of the marketplace and the needs of your firm.

For an excellent text devoted entirely to sales force management, I recommend *How to Plan and Manage Sales Territories Effectively,* published by Dartnell in an 8½ $\times$ 11-inch three-ring binder. Write to:

> Dartnell Corporation
> 4660 Ravenswood Avenue
> Chicago, IL 60640-9981

This text will help you to design territories to increase your sales and profits, the efficiency and earnings of sales reps, and sales to key accounts. It will also help you to determine whether a territory is increasing in potential.

TALK TO YOUR SALESPEOPLE

Surely one of the great tragedies of business marketing efforts occurs when the views of sales representatives go largely ignored. Yet, according to Don Waite, president of Sales Staff Surveys, few companies bother to ask their salespeople for their suggestions and then follow up on those suggestions.

Waite is a former manager of sales and marketing training for Continental Can, now Continental Group. His company aids sales executives in researching salespeople's opinions about policies and strategies. His clients include E. R. Squibb (180); Nabisco, now a part of R. J. Reynolds (23); Johnson & Johnson (59); and others.

"Surveys among 26 companies in a wide range of marketing activities—industrial, consumer, and service included—found that managers, on average, are not listening to their sales reps," says Waite. That's the firm conviction of the 8,000-plus sales reps and the more than 1,000 first-line managers who returned survey questionnaires. It's also proof that Lee Iacocca's best-selling autobiography hits the nail on the head in at least one area.

"Too many people," notes chairman of Chrysler, "fail to realize that real communication goes in both directions." Chrysler Corporation (13) has clearly demonstrated that under Iacocca it has been listening.

One of the prime questions that Waite asked respondents was how they rated their companies with regard to asking for their suggestions on how to improve overall sales effectiveness. "The results," Waite observes, "are startling." Of the 7,615 respondents, 46 percent rated their companies as below average. Also, the longer a sales rep stays with a company, the less he or she expects management to try to learn what sales reps have to say about increasing sales effectiveness. What a shame.

Another key question was, "How do you rate your company at listening to field concerns?" The answer? "Not very well." At least, that was the view of 45 percent of the 7,615 respondents. Among the most experienced reps, 58 percent rated their executives negatively in listening to field concerns, even though, Waite observes, "those worries often reflect customers' concerns." One respondent put it this way: "They only hear what they want to hear."

Giving recognition, it is argued, is a proven method for ensuring that the sales force is, and stays, motivated. As with Ivan Pavlov's dog, there's a stimulus-response effect. Also, we are often told, recognizing the accomplishments and efforts of veteran salespeople is an excellent way to keep them from "plateauing."

Jack Cohen, president of Sales Dynamics Institute, in Baltimore, Maryland, feels much the same as Waite. Cohen, whose 36-year career encompasses marketing, selling-skills training, sales communication, management consulting, and marketing support systems, says that "sales is the linchpin of the marketing strategy, yet sales reps are often abandoned or ignored. In the vibrant, ever-changing marketplace, entrepreneurs constantly seek new, more effective marketing strategies and more innovative and talented employees. I find it difficult to understand how these same entrepreneurs can overlook the importance of the sales rep."

"Marketing involves coordinating all activities from production of a product to its delivery to the customer." Observes Cohen, "Selling is but one of these activities, but it is the most important and exciting function in the entire marketing mix."

Enlightened management must operate the company with a customer focus, not a product focus. If priority is given to identifying customer needs and then satisfying them, the customer is king—again. "However," says Cohen, "to serve the customer requires teamwork." And establishing teamwork requires a strong commitment by you to ongoing training programs, open staff-management communication, and plenty of respect and recognition.

"The salesperson is the primary source of market information. He or she is the most current, most reliable, and least expensive research and planning tool available. Why, then," asks Cohen, "are salespeople so underused and poorly respected?"

ALL SALESPEOPLE ARE NOT CREATED EQUAL

In managing the selling function, it will quickly become apparent that different types of salespersons may be needed for different tasks. For example, account representatives generally call on a large number of preexisting customers to generate follow-on business, to ensure that your products are performing satisfactorily, and to handle any other needs of the customer.

A technical sales specialist, or sales engineer, differs from an account rep in that the sales engineer possesses technical know-how and can readily explain technical product or service features. The sales engineer often assists the customer in identifying and solving problems, and thus is looked upon as an adviser or consultant by the customer.

A service representative may interface with the same customers that are handled by account representatives or sales engineers. However, the service rep focuses more on following up provisions of contracts, maintaining customer relations, and highlighting benefits and other intangibles offered by your company to customers. Once you identify the different types of salespeople that your company may need, you are more likely to choose candidates with the appropriate backgrounds.

Dave Voracek, a marketing consultant based in Alexandria, Virginia, points out that in the next several years basic changes in America's sales forces will be occurring. Voracek cites Bureau of Labor Statistics figures indicating that more women will be hired in sales positions through at least 1995. He also notes that big gains in sales productivity will be achievable as older and more experienced sales professionals dominate sales staffs.

The cost of calling on new customers has risen dramatically. According to Cahners Publishing Company, the rise in the cost of selling continues unabated. A recent Cahners study of 2,400 manufacturers shows that the average cost of making a sale to a new customer is $1,490. Included in this cost are salaries, commissions, benefits, travel, sales materials, samples, advertising, follow-up, and additional mailings. Perhaps the greatest lesson to be learned from the high cost of selling is the importance of working hard to keep customers once your firm has landed them.

SCOUTING THE COMPETITION

Many of the marketing research sources and techniques that are discussed in Chapter 7 can be applied in the area of scouting your competition. Three particularly inexpensive methods that can easily be undertaken are the brochure scan, the phone book scan, and the literature scan.

Brochure Scan

An easy and convenient way to learn what your competitors are offering is to send for their brochures, their marketing literature, and their capability statements. In a free enterprise system, one of the chief sources of competitor information is very often the competitor. It is not unethical to request the brochure of an establishment that is open for business, and the odds are that your brochures, fliers, and other materials are already in the hands of your competitors.

On the major corporate level, you can bet the farm that electronics rivals such as Litton Industries (82) and North America Philips (86) try to learn as much about each other as possible, as do rubber products producers such as B. F. Goodrich (123), Goodyear Tire & Rubber (35), and Uniroyal (175). If you are leery of requesting such information on your corporate letterhead, have an employee make such requests from home using his or her personal stationery.

Continuously monitoring the new product and service offerings of your competitors is a good way to remain competitive. As you read the literature of rivals, note the specific benefits and features that they offer and you presently do not offer. Also, compare the brochures: Which ones appeal to you, and why? Are the photos helpful and eye-catching? What colors and textures of paper seem to work best? (See page 80.)

Phone Book Scan

To make a yellow pages scan, open your phone book to the yellow pages and find your industry. Then read all of the information in all of the advertisements placed by your competitors. You may wish to classify the items listed by "products and services" and "benefits and features."

If you list every product and service offering that the companies in your industry advertise, you will end up with a composite of what your industry has to offer. If available, obtain phone books of other major metropolitan areas. Obviously, no one vendor offers everything on the list you have generated.

The same technique may be applied to benefits and features. For example, one feature of working with ABC Company might be that it has been in the same location for 24 years, thus indicating stability. One benefit of working with ABC Company might be that it has an 800 number or that it is on call 24 hours a day. When this list has been completed, you will have a composite of all the benefits and features that your industry offers.

Both the products and services list and the benefits and features list may help to guide you in deciding what mix your company will offer.

Literature Scan

This is the third quick method for scanning the competition. Reviewing the *Business Periodicals Index,* monitoring regional and local business tabloids (see page 102), and maintaining a newspaper clipping file will enable you to generate information on your competitors at very little cost.

DYNAMICS OF THE MARKETPLACE

Seeking new customers is both time consuming and essential. The continual turnover of purchasing agents increases the difficulty and cost of calling on corporate agents. In this connection, Professor Philip Kotler, author and marketing guru, points to industrial magazine circulation records at McGraw-Hill (237). In a 12-month period, out of every 1,000 paid subscribers 304 are replaced, 56 change titles due to promotions and reorganization, 141 are transferred to different locations, and only 499, or about half, stay in the same job.

Many years ago, a classic McGraw-Hill advertisement highlighted the problems that sales reps face in trying to maintain information on customers and prospects and in keeping new purchasing agents familiar with the name of their company and with its products or services. The McGraw-Hill advertisement depicted a sales rep facing a corporate purchasing agent with the purchasing agent's thoughts running as follows:

> I don't know who you are.
> I don't know your company.
> I don't know your company's products.
> I don't know what your company stands for.
> I don't know your company's customers.
> I don't know your company's record.
> I don't know your company's reputation.
> Now—what was it you wanted to sell me?

Kotler notes that what the advertisement was suggesting was that sales reps should not be forced to use their time and skill to answer questions that could be better handled through mass selling—advertising.

While significant outlays for advertising are not essential to effectively market to Fortune 500 companies, and in most cases represent inordinate costs to small business entrepreneurs, it is essential to produce a brochure and other marketing support literature and to document your company's experience in a capabilities statement (see Chapter 6).

PREPARING A BROCHURE

The preparation of an effective brochure—even a simple one—is not an easy task. Your brochure serves as a central source of printed information to existing and potential customers. While there are no fixed rules about what a brochure must contain, an effective brochure contains, at the least, basic information on your company's history, philosophy, organizational structure, and service areas. Your brochure should help enhance your image, as it literally represents you on paper. It should also be designed to project uniqueness—to make you stand out from the competition.

Producing your firm's brochure is a complex undertaking and requires significant effort. You lay the groundwork for the development of the brochure, but outside assistance is needed for its completion. The first questions you may ask yourself in undertaking this project are: "What targets do I want to reach?" and "What message do I want to offer?"

Ted Eisenberg, president of Ted Eisenberg Associates, a New York graphic designer, says that your brochure "is, in effect, an expensive, illustrated calling card." Many vendors produce brochures that gratify their own egos but do not satisfy the information needs of the customer. Your brochure is not for you; it is for your prospects and customers, and it should focus on their needs.

In addition to the basic information mentioned above, a prospective customer will be interested in learning about:

- The qualifications of your skilled labor force.
- The quality of your product or service.
- The size and location of your plants or offices.
- The range of your services.
- Your company's reputation.
- Your company's experience in specific industries.
- Others who have used your products or services.
- How long you've been in business.

A quick way to determine what type of brochure will be right for you is to assemble and study the brochures of your competitors (if you've undertaken a brochure scan, this will have already been done). Writing to companies outside your trade area might yield better results than writing to potential competitors.

After you've assembled these brochures, carefully review the features that appeal to you. There are literally hundreds of factors to consider. The following represent a mere subset of all the options that are available in developing your brochure: dimensions, quality of paper, weight (affects mailing cost), use of pictures, staff biographies, client lists, number of pages, use of color, use of flaps, pockets, fold-overs, use of testimonials, use of bulleted sections, action photos, sketches, style of print, layout, spacing, headings, and titles.

You will eventually need to turn over the development of your brochure to a marketing or graphics specialist. The key to effective use of an outside resource is to supply a rough prototype of your desired end product. On several pieces of paper, sketch the layout and content of each brochure page to the best of your ability.

In your selection of outside assistance, try to seek marketing or advertising professionals who have had experience in working with firms similar to yours and ask to see samples of their work.

Hugo-Dunhill, a division of Mailing List, Inc., reports that brochures that get action are carefully targeted to the right people and are built around benefits that prospects will enjoy when they buy your products or services. Here are eight tips that it offers on brochure preparation:

1. Focus on the prospect's needs and desires—not on your company. It is not your brochure that sells your products or services: what sells is the benefits that your brochure gets across to your prospects.
2. Avoid clichés, fuzzy words, buzzwords, empty adjectives, and outlandish claims. Busy people respond to straight talk.
3. Use short sentences, active verbs, present tense, and a lot of "how to's." Draw the prospect into the brochure by making it personal, positive, upbeat, and exciting.
4. Use a compelling layout, including lots of white space, strong and closely related graphics, and many powerful headings. Guide the reader from the front page to the last word: think of the brochure as a road map. Break up the copy into easily readable bits.
5. Make the brochure believable by backing up every strong claim with data, endorsements, and proof statements from your previous customers.
6. Tell prospects precisely what they will receive and when, where, and how they will receive it. Emphasize "You will get . . ." rather than "We will give you . . ."
7. Make it easy for prospects to tell at a glance how they will benefit from what you can do for them.
8. Protect your investment by printing and mailing fewer brochures rather than by cutting corners on professionally produced copy and artwork, layout and design, and photography. Use good paper and a top-notch printer. The results are worth the cost.

The Vicissitudes of Business Life

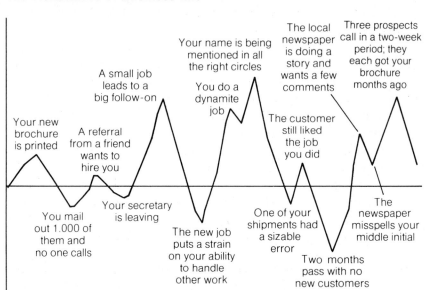

Harry A. Olson, Ph.D., president of Maximum Potential, Inc., Reisterstown, Maryland, believes that any printed material disseminated by your company "must be a class act." According to Olson, "The best brochures concentrate on what is being offered to the customer," that is, the payoff for the target audience.

Olson knows what he's talking about when it comes to designing effective brochures. As a small business entrepreneur successfully marketing his services to dozens of major corporations, he initially produced what he terms a completely disastrous brochure. His second, redesigned, streamlined, more customer-focused brochure won a national design award from the National Speakers Association in Phoenix, Arizona.

OTHER SUPPORTING LITERATURE

Other effective marketing vehicles that can be used in the marketplace include fact sheets, pamphlets, and announcements.

Fact sheets can be one-page, professionally printed sheets outlining distinct aspects of your company's operations—the types of problems your customers encounter and how you overcome them, your company's background and corporate history and how your reputation for quality benefits all customers, or detailed information about a product or service that you offer.

Pamphlets can be produced on a wide variety of topics such as your company's history, the expertise of your staff, specific product or service offerings, or how others have benefited by using your products or services.

Announcements may be in the form of bulletins or news or press releases. This type of message usually focuses on a single item, offering details on an event that will take place, news about your company, news about a specific product or service, and so forth. Announcements should be made with an air of urgency. A detailed discussion of marketing support literature is presented in my other books, *Marketing Your Consulting and Professional Services,* coauthored with Richard A. Connor, Jr., (New York: John Wiley & Sons, 1985) and *Blow Your Own Horn,* (New York: AMACOM, 1987).

All marketing support literature must be developed far in advance of actual sales calls and should be professionally prepared and designed so as to augment and increase your effectiveness or that of your sales representatives. Marketing is a numbers game, and you will have to make many, many contacts with corporations in order to be successful with a few. Therefore, your marketing support literature must be produced in quantities that are sufficient to reach all of your many targets.

Managing the marketing and sales effort is truly a never-ending task. There are always new improvements to be made in presentations and supporting materials, new marketing leads to explore, more follow-ups to be made, and so forth. If by now you have concluded that you need additional sales and marketing help, consider yourself ahead in the game.

CHAPTER SIX

Documenting Your Capabilities for Presentation

> *But words are things,*
> *And a small drop of ink,*
> *Falling like dew, upon a thought,*
> *Produces that which makes thousands,*
> *Perhaps millions,*
> *Think.*

LORD BYRON

Having the capabilities to successfully serve as a product or service vendor to Fortune 500 and other major corporations is certainly a prerequisite to calling on them. However, you must be able to *document* your company's ability to do the job. The purchasing agent with whom you deal will be keenly interested in your capabilities regarding the big three: price, quality, and delivery. According to expert Vic Morris, purchasing agents will also undoubtedly require considerable documentation relating to your firm's history, track record, and overall capabilities.

This chapter summarizes the minimum information requirements for a successful marketing presentation—the information that Morris says "you must have in your briefcase" and be able to supply upon request. That information is arranged in 13 topic areas:

Ownership	Labor relations
Market served	Plant and equipment
Products/services	Quality assurance
Projects/activities	Financial capabilities
Management expertise	Price
Research capabilities	Security
	Other documentation

OWNERSHIP

A description of ownership is generally the first item in your capability statement. How is your business organized? The purchasing agent or buyer will want to know whether your firm is a sole proprietorship, a partnership, or a corporation, and indeed vendor application forms required by many companies, for example, Grumman (131) and Dow Chemical (28), ask for form of ownership immediately.

In a nutshell:

- Sole proprietorships are owned by a single individual.
- Partnerships are owned by two or more individuals.
- Corporations are legal entities formed under the laws of the state.

If your business is a corporation, list the members of your board of directors and the stockholders, with their respective ownership percentages.

If your business is a sole proprietorship or a partnership, list the members of your advisory board. Incidentally, if you don't have an advisory board, consider creating one, using experienced businesspeople, retired bankers, and/or college professors with specialties in your field, and seek their advice. Have the temerity to solicit those individuals that can make a difference in your business.

If your business is a minority business, say so—and elaborate on the percentage of minority ownership. Be sure to mention whether your business is certified as a minority-owned firm by federal, state, or local agencies or by any other organizations (e.g., a public utility). Scores of Fortune 500 corporations, such as Zenith (225), Todd Shipyards (462), General Motors (1), Northrop (71), McDonnell Douglas (29), Harris (163), and Upjohn (176), are particularly receptive to minority-owned business.

MARKET SERVED

Specify what market you are attempting to serve and why your products or services meet the needs of this market. Many entrepreneurs make halfhearted attempts to penetrate first one market, then a second, and then a third. They never stop to decide which market they should penetrate first. This quixotic approach simply doesn't work.

An important step in effective prospecting is to set aside time to learn about the operating characteristics of the industry and businesses

Market Served—Sample Background Information

SENCORE

3200 Sencore Drive, Sioux Falls, South Dakota 57107

Sencore was started in 1951, in downtown Chicago, Illinois, by R.H. ("Herb") Bowden. Herb, originally from Hurley, South Dakota, founded Sencore after his technical education at the American Institute of Technology in Chicago. As the business grew, Mr. Bowden relocated the firm to Addison, a suburb of Chicago. In 1970, the decision was made to move the entire Sencore operation to Sioux Falls, South Dakota. Since that time, we have made a real home for the business in Sioux Falls and are proud to be a part of this community.

Sencore designs, manufactures, and markets electronic test equipment for such customers as service dealers, technical schools, communications businesses, technical industrial customers, and others. Sencore markets test equipment primarily across the United States, along with sales in Canada, Europe, and other export markets. Examples of our products are video analyzers, oscilloscopes, component testers, and digital volt meters, to name just a few.

When Sencore first started business, we sold our instruments with the aid of independent representatives. These "independent reps" called on distributors, who bought our products, stocked them, and then sold them to our end-users.

As technology advanced, we decided that we needed our own technical sales people calling on these distributors so that we could have more control over the quality of the representation of our distributors. Hence, Sencore changed from using independent reps and switched to our own technical representatives, or "tech reps", as we called them.

Several years later, approximately 1977, after looking at the new advancing technology in electronics, and realizing that this was going to have a major impact on Sencore's instruments and the marketing of those products, management decided to alter our sales vehicle one last time; this time deleting the last step between our final customer and Sencore. At that time, Sencore made the major move to go factory direct to our end-users across all 50 of the United States. We are now calling directly on our final customers and have found that we can offer the market better service through our direct sales program, while at the same time, being more efficient internally.

With our new direct marketing program in motion, we are anxiously looking forward to the future, where we anticipate even more growth and profitability. This is made possible through new innovative products as well as products on the drawing boards, sound financial controls, and most of all, through the efforts and productivity of fellow team members within our company.

to which you wish to sell. What in your past experience can be drawn upon and used as a competitive advantage in penetrating your chosen market? What do you presently offer that is consistent with the changing needs of that market?

A product or service that fulfills the needs of a specifically defined group is preferable to one that compromises to suit widely divergent needs. By targeting a particular segment, you can tailor your product to more closely serve your customers' needs. The closer the match, the greater is the potential for sales. Descriptive terminology in this section might encompass geographic area—climate, terrain, natural resources, population density, and cultural values; usage rate for product—heavy, moderate, or light; type of organization; customer size; and use of product.

For example, one company's market for sales of uniforms consists of corporations, hospitals, police departments, fire departments, laboratories, fast-food chains, grocery store chains, municipal workers (e.g., sanitation workers, road crews), and prisons within a 200-mile radius of its mill.

PRODUCTS/SERVICES

At Boeing Corporation (21), it's widely rumored that the hard copy documentation for a 747 aircraft outweighs the plane! Thank your stars that whatever you are offering can be described a bit more easily.

Your firm's products or services should be clearly and completely described, and the addresses and phone numbers of all of your firm's locations, including the one at which you can be most readily found, should be listed.

Leslie Rhatican asks, ''Are you innovative in your approach to product/ service offerings?'' Innovative means providing better and more economical goods and services. From General Motors (1) to Winnebago Industries (500), the ''word is out'' that vendors ''must be involved'' increasingly in almost a partnership type of relationship, in many cases starting from the design level. If you can, identify features of your product or service that distinguish it from those of competitors. Make your product stand out from the others.

Examples of innovation include:

- Lower prices.
- New and better product—even at a higher price.
- Finding new uses for existing products or services.
- New design.

A Customer Testimonial

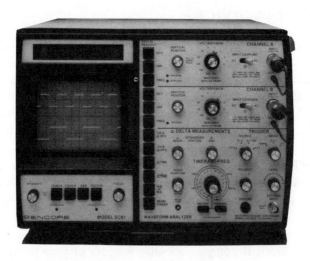

"

*Sencore, from all my experience,
means reliability, service (if ever required),
technical support, and engineering and
design with the user in mind.*

"

Robert Glazier
Communications Coordinator
Commonwealth Edison
Byron, IL

Reprinted with permission from Sencore, Inc.

- New distribution method.
- New production method.
- New or improved servicing.
- New marketing techniques.

Innovations for product offerings might also include:

- Greater durability.
- Portability.
- Ease of replacement.
- Add-on features.
- Guarantees beyond industry norms.
- Extended product life.
- Consultations.
- Training.
- After-hours service.

Innovation is as important for service companies as for manufacturing or engineering firms. Innovation in service offerings might include:

- Safety guarantees.
- Accelerated levering.
- On-site services.
- Reduced turnaround time.
- Dual functions.
- Special requests.

PROJECTS/ACTIVITIES

A concise description of recent projects on which your firm has performed well should be included in this section. If you have references or testimonial letters commending your firm and the job you have done, be sure to include these. Purchasing agents like to know up front who else you've done business with. Obtain permission from satisfied customers to use their names as references for potential new customers. Describe your firm, and state how long it has been in business.

PROJECT DESCRIPTIONS OF WORK PERFORMED BY A SYSTEMS INSTALLATION FIRM

TURNKEY AUTOMATED OFFICE SYSTEMS IN 12 LOCATIONS

CLIENT: Pacific Coast Aerospace Corporation

PROJECT DESCRIPTION:

Phase 1. Feasibility study and recommendations, which include:

Survey of existing systems.
Current and future application requirements.
Analysis of requirements.

Systems cost analysis of competing hardware.
Operational and communications requirements.
Development of functional specifications.
Development of procurement package.

Phase 2. Selection, procurement, and installation of equipment:

Equipment selection, procurement management.
Installation and component testing.
Communications and interfaces.
Development of all operational guides/procedures.
Orientation and training.
Data conversion, maintenance.
Establishment of a prototype automated office center.

ADVANCE PROGRAMMING ANALYSIS AND
DOCUMENTATION SERVICES

CLIENT: Chicago Area Research and Development Group

PROJECT DESCRIPTION:

ABC Systems Corporation has successfully performed advance-level work in the area of interpolating data. The ABC personnel performed work in (a) featuring data by statistical distribution curves using the method of least squares and (b) revising programs to make them shorter, easier to understand and maintain, and more efficient.

COMPUTERIZED SPACE MANAGEMENT PROGRAM

CLIENT: MidWest Manufacturer and Distributor

PROJECT DESCRIPTION:

ABC Systems developed a software package for a DEC system to inventory office and other space by type, create a file of company personnel by title and office, and collect data identifying the degree of interaction between offices. ABC also developed a model for the optimum location and allocation of space, the optimum being defined as the location and allocation that would result in a weighted minimum slack time related to interaction among offices. This effort involved:

Data analysis.
Creation of large data files and routines for file manipulation.
Mathematical analysis using the theory of graphs.
Software development.
System documentation.

AUTOMATED GUIDEWAY TRANSIT TECHNOLOGY SYSTEM

CLIENT: State Mass Transit Authority

PROJECT DESCRIPTION:

The two major objectives of this project were to assist in developing the optimum interface between the IBM 5100 computer terminal and the software developed by the AGTT program and to assist in monitoring AGTT project performance. ABC Systems thoroughly investigated the capabilities of the IBM 5100 in order to make recommendations as to the most effective software to be developed or purchased for it and to identify additional hardware requirements. Based on these investigations, ABC developed the software 'and generated a user's guide for agency personnel. ABC also determined whether and to what extent simulations and models could be executed in a local mode.

ABC designed and developed a project monitoring system that included a set of project monitoring tools. A data base was developed that contained project deliverables and their status.

MANAGEMENT EXPERTISE

This section should include résumés of the key members of your organization, outlining their training, education, and experience. How long has each of these key members been with your firm? Your public library has books that can guide you in preparing résumés and that illustrate various formats. A uniform style for the résumés will enhance the professional image of your firm.

RESEARCH CAPABILITIES

If your company does research, explain specifically what your capabilities include. This information is important and could enhance your chances as a prospective vendor.

LABOR RELATIONS

Describe the composition of your labor force. What is the average length of employment? If you have valued long-term employees, this demonstrates the stability of your work force, good working conditions, and most important, the probable continued availability of these people to your company.

Are your employees unionized? If so, a potential buyer may associate their higher skill levels with higher labor costs. To a potential buyer, the threat of a strike means that delivery of his orders may be threatened. If there have not been any strikes at your company, Vic Morris advises that you be sure to include this point.

Is your business located in a state with right-to-work laws? Right-to-work laws prohibit "union shops," which require new employees to join the union. Under such laws, wages *may* be lower with potentially lower labor costs. Are your employees paid the minimum wage? This may indicate easily replaceable employees and lower labor costs to a buyer.

Are both skilled and unskilled labor available for your business? Vic Morris points out that a potential buyer wants to know how easily you can enlarge your staff to handle an order. A large labor supply indicates that your current employees will remain with you due to greater competition for available jobs. Particularly if you are a manufacturer, you will need to describe the availability of workers in your area. Also, list the hourly rates of your current employees and the rates of any new additions to your work force that might be necessary on the new contract you are seeking.

PLANT AND EQUIPMENT

If appropriate for your firm, list the types of machinery that you use, including the capacity, age, and number of each type. Photos of plant or equipment, if available, are always helpful.

Also, accurately list the size of your plant or office in square feet and your daily output when operating at your maximum level. This information may be requested by purchasing agents.

QUALITY ASSURANCE

If the customer has specifications that you must meet, and nearly all customers will, explain how your product or service will be checked to determine adherence to specifications. One way to demonstrate the integrity of your product or service is to offer a guarantee or warranty. If you do guarantee your service, describe the scope of the guarantee and how you will uphold it. Federal Express became famous for guaranteeing delivery of your package "when it absolutely, positively has to be there overnight." Now that is some guarantee, and it reflects a magnificent obsession with commitment.

The wording of any guarantee or warranty should be checked with an attorney to ensure that you are not getting in over your head. When offered, guarantees and warranties are a strong marketing tool that can enhance your selling effort.

Fortune 500 corporations want to know about your quality control program (see Chapter 10). At Scott Paper Company (130), close relationships with a few quality control–conscious vendors has paid off in both improved quality and lower cost. If your firm has an established program to monitor the quality of production or the level of service provided, briefly describe it and the benefits to the recipient. In addition, describe any measurement or inspection capability. Itemize any equipment that you use for testing and inspection, and state the tolerance, range, or capacity of that equipment.

FINANCIAL CAPABILITIES

Though you would probably prefer not to supply information on your financial capabilities, the corporate representative with whom you deal will probably request a copy of your latest balance sheet, profit and loss statement, and line of credit information, if applicable. Some corporate representatives may require your financial statements for the past three years. Even if your financial statements do not appear as healthy as you would like them to be, you cannot avoid such requirements. Thus, it pays to have them readily available. (See Chapter 15 for help in strengthening your financial position.)

PRICE

The price of your product or service depends on many variables. A successful marketing presentation will identify and itemize factors affecting price, including:

- Initial charge.
- Development charges.
- Engineering charges.
- Tooling charges.
- Special equipment charges.
- Testing charges.
- Material charges.
- Machine rates.

A one-paragraph description of why the customer will be obtaining a good value for the price you are charging will bolster your presentation. To meet the challenge of competition, offer your best price, along with your best quality and your best delivery date. While remaining competitive, you must strive to attain a minimum of deviation from the customer's requirements and your plans to meet them.

SECURITY

Vic Morris has observed that since the late 1960s industrial and corporate security have assumed great importance. Increasingly, such corporations as U.S. Steel (15), Boise Cascade (105), and Raytheon (60) have been sharing information with key vendors so that both sides can become more efficient in these areas. You must be prepared to explain how you will guarantee that trade secrets, confidential information, or new product and service plans will not be divulged. Also, describe in detail the security measures that are in place for your plant, office, storage yard, or other facilities. How does your firm safeguard important documents, and who has responsibility for the maintenance of security? Your firm's ability to provide a high level of security to private-sector corporations will enhance your marketing position. This is particularly true if you deal with federal defense or aerospace contractors such as Rockwell International (415), United Technologies (16) and Sundstrand (258).

OTHER DOCUMENTATION

Make sure that your firm's organization chart and the proposed organization for the specific project are available (see examples below). How does your firm handle regulation and legal compliance? Cite any regulations—federal, state or local—that you are required to meet and how you plan to meet them. This information helps convey that you are "on top of the situation."

THE RUTHLESS RULES OF REALITY

You cannot avoid the reality: effective marketing to private-sector corporations requires a great deal of documentation. I expect that the typical reaction of most of the entrepreneurs who read this chapter will be, "Well, that's all fine, but we don't have the time to round up all this

A Typical Company Organization Chart

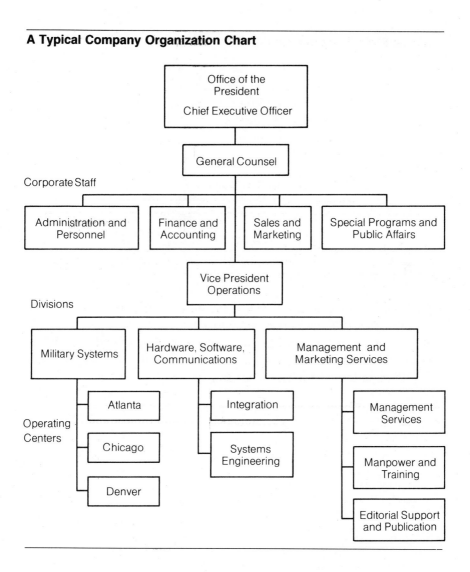

data.'' In case you decide to slip back among those who have ''cut themselves from the team,'' consider that it is usually costly and time consuming for major corporations to prequalify small suppliers, not because of poor quality in the products or services they provide, but because of their inadequate documentation, control, and accounting.

Successful vendors can demonstrate competence in providing quality products and services, and solid capability in the area of management *documentation* and controls. Lack of documentation is a basis on which

A Typical Project Organization Chart

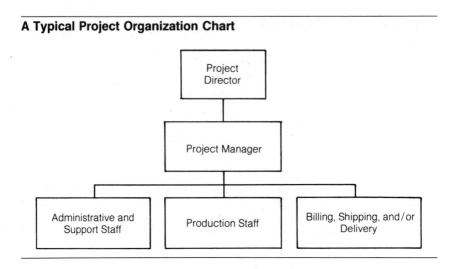

purchasing agents can easily weed out those firms that appear to be incapable of meeting corporate requirements.

Smart entrepreneurs will prepare as much of the required material as possible in advance, thus minimizing the burden that has to be borne when it's time to make a new marketing call.

CHAPTER SEVEN

Researching Your Targets

So little done,
So much to do.

CECIL JOHN RHODES

As Ernest Carruthers read his morning paper, he noticed an item of particular interest. A Fortune 500 firm located in the next county had announced an expansion of its product line to include hydraulic brakes. Ernie owned and managed a firm that produced components that could be used in these brakes.

FINDING YOUR WAY THROUGH THE CORPORATE MAZE

Recognizing a potentially large new market for his components, Ernie called corporate headquarters to speak with the purchasing people. The receptionist informed him that no purchasing personnel were located at the headquarters of the firm. Ernie then asked for the correct location to call and was placed on hold while the receptionist checked. Since this was a long-distance call, Ernie counted the dollars as the minutes passed. The receptionist finally returned with the name of the East Coast plant where purchasing activities took place and gave Ernie the phone number—another long-distance call.

Ernie was tenacious. Knowing that this was a solid marketing lead for his firm, he called the East Coast plant. More time and money were spent as Ernie and the receptionist attempted to identify the correct purchasing manager for this new product line.

Success at last! Ernie was connected with the proper office only to be told that this purchasing manager circulated through the region and would be at the Tennessee plant for three weeks. Ernie got the telephone number for the Tennessee plant and placed his third long-distance call. He located the purchasing manager and began his "sales pitch" for the components he produced. Unfortunately, this purchasing manager was not the right person after all. He told Ernie that another purchasing manager would have to be reached.

This probably sounds painfully familiar to you. You spend time and money running through the corporate maze, and you get nowhere. It is tough to navigate through corporate channels. A purchasing manager for Exxon (2), the nation's largest oil refiner, admitted that he had trouble finding the right people within his own corporation. At times it seems that only Drucker's "monomaniac on mission" can break through.

There are steps you can take to make this process easier. "Fishing" attempts by telephone, such as Ernie's, almost always lead to frustration. Ernie had the right idea in following up a marketing lead, but he chose the wrong way to do it. If you have the corporate headquarters address, here are three simple ways to navigate the corporate maze.

Seek Vendor Guides

Write to the purchasing department (see list on pages 159–72) if its address is available, and ask to receive copies of any vendor guides (see Chapter 12), vendor application forms, and lists of products purchased. If the address of the purchasing department is not available, send the letter in care of corporate headquarters.

Ask for Corporate News

Write to the public relations office and ask for copies of the company's newsletter, in-house publications, and any recent press releases on what the company is doing. These services may contain useful information that can help you tailor your marketing pitch. The editor of an in-house monthly magazine for a U.S. corporation that employs over 200,000 says, "You can always write to the public relations office and request one sample copy of in-house publications. It's not likely that you'll be put on the mailing list. However, the samples you do receive will certainly give you a sense of how the company operates and some of the things it values."

Contact Small Business Liaison Office

Write a letter to the small business coordinator explaining your product or service and your interest in becoming a vendor to the corporation.

Dow Corning (336), Owens-Illinois (108), Varian (311), and Minnesota Mining and Manufacturing (47), as well as hundreds of other firms, provide names and phone numbers of plants and purchasing agents. Even if the firm does not have a small business coordinator, you will receive a response indicating the name, title, and location of a person who can handle your request.

Only a few handwritten letters are needed to obtain materials that contain a wealth of information. Determine the appropriate division, plant, and persons to call. The more you can narrow your search and the more you know about the company you're calling on and the trends in the industry, the better.

For more in-depth research sources and techniques, read on. This chapter will provide specific references to aid your marketing efforts and offer some effective ways for gathering research information quickly and inexpensively.

USING THE PUBLIC LIBRARY

Your public library maintains a copy of the *Business Periodicals Index,* the *Readers' Guide to Periodical Literature,* and the *Readers' Guide to Scientific Literature.* Through these indexes, you may scan for the latest articles in selected topic areas. For example, if you want to see whether any articles have been written recently on a particular corporation, you could use the *Business Periodicals Index* to obtain a listing of all the articles on the corporation that appeared in the last month, quarter, or year (or several decades!) in such nationally known business journals as *Business Week, Fortune, Forbes,* and *Harvard Business Review,* as well as numerous other business periodicals.

Your public library also maintains a generous supply of phone books for both your geographic area and major cities across the United States. These may serve as reference points for identifying customers and suppliers.

USING ANNUAL REPORTS AND 10K REPORTS

First, obtain the address of corporate headquarters. This can be done by telephone if you know the city in which the company is located. Or you can go to your local library and look up the corporate address in the business reference section in *Moody's, Dun & Bradstreet,* or *Standard & Poor's Index.* Better yet, simply obtain the address over the phone from the reference desk of your local library. Then write a letter to the company's shareholder information department and ask for a copy of the annual report. This may contain addresses and phone numbers of various plant sites or divisions.

ANNUAL REPORTS: WHAT THEY TELL YOU

Chief executive officer's report

Expansion plans.
Warning of "streamlining" operations (may indicate closing of some facilities).
New social responsibility or awareness programs.
New product lines.
Diversification.

Consolidated income statements

Net revenue over time.
Percentage changes over time.
Observed increases or decreases.

Auditor's letter

Exceptions or notes to financial statements.
"Onetime" accounting entries.
Changes in accounting methods.

The Securities and Exchange Commission (SEC), in Washington, D.C., requires annual filing of a 10K report. This document expands on information contained in the annual report and includes additional documentation and "hard numbers." The 10K report may be requested from the SEC for a fee, or from the corporation at no cost, although corporations do not send out 10Ks as willingly as they do annual reports.

Purchasing one share of stock is a relatively inexpensive and effective method of obtaining annual reports, 10Ks, quarterly reports, and entrée to shareholders' meetings. At age 12, I acquired a single share of Sperry's (63) common stock. For the duration of my investment, I was constantly updated on the company's earnings and activities and Sperry faithfully paid me my $0.10 quarterly dividend!

ASSOCIATIONS AS RESOURCE TOOLS

There now exists, for virtually every industry and type of business, a professional or trade association. A sampling of such associations is provided in Chapter 13. Most of these associations maintain a membership directory that, depending on your needs, may serve several purposes. Association membership directories are often free or available at a minimum charge.

Many associations maintain a list of publications and serve as a reference center for the type of industry they serve. The National Association of Manufacturers, headquartered in Washington, D.C., for example, maintains an extensive array of books, films, pamphlets, and training materials designed to assist member companies.

Associations also provide trend information, surveys, publications, trade fairs, lobbying support and monthly newsletters and magazines.

Many associations sponsor seminars and conferences that provide intensive training and specialized industry information. These meetings also enable members to exchange ideas with one another.

Association directories offering the names, addresses, and phone numbers of your industry's trade and professional associations can be found in any library. These two association directories collectively offer over 10,000 listings:

>*Gale's Encyclopedia of Associations*
>*National Trade and Professional Associations* (NTPA)

The American Marketing Association is a professional society of marketing research executives, sales and promotion managers, advertising specialists, teachers, and others interested in marketing. It conducts research, sponsors seminars and conferences on marketing, and publishes several periodicals: *Marketing News,* bimonthly; *Journal of Marketing,* quarterly; and *Journal of Marketing Research,* quarterly. It also publishes a variety of pamphlets and books on marketing. It is a good source of marketing data and other promotional or technical information.

>American Marketing Association
>250 South Wacker Drive
>Chicago, IL 60606
>(312) 648-0536

PERIODICAL INDEXES

If you need to find an article or information on a corporation that appeared in your local newspaper, often your public library will contain a newspaper index that abstracts newspaper articles by topic and cross-references this listing by date. Your metropolitan area may also be served by one or more area business publications (see list on pages 102–13). You can write to the Association of Area Business Publications, 202 Legion Drive, Annapolis, MD 21401, for a complete list of such publications. Also, *The Wall Street Journal Index* is available in many public libraries in major cities.

To identify a specific industry or trade journal, consult *Working Press of the Nation, Writer's Market,* or the *Standard Periodicals Directory,* all of which can be found in a library. These annually updated directories collectively contain listings of over 10,000 technical and trade publications. Here are two other valuable directories:

> *All-in-One Directory*
> Gebbie Press, Inc.
> P.O. Box 1000
> New Paltz, NY 12561
> (914) 255-7560

The *All-in-One-Directory* lists daily newspapers, weekly newspapers, radio stations, television stations, general consumer magazines, trade magazines, professional business publications, and news syndicates.

> *Bacon's Publicity Checker* (2 vols.)
> Bacon's Publishing Company
> 332 South Michigan Avenue
> Chicago, IL 60604
> (312) 922-2400

Bacon's lists consumer and trade magazines and daily and weekly newspapers in the United States and Canada.

LOCAL, STATE, AND REGIONAL BUSINESS PUBLICATIONS

Advantage, Nashville's Business Monthly   (*Monthly*)
Advantage Companies, Inc.
1719 West End Avenue
Nashville, TN 37203–5120

Arizona Business Gazette   (*Weekly*)
Phoenix Newspapers, Inc.
305 North 1st Street
P.O. Box 1950
Phoenix, AZ 85001

Arkansas Business   *(Biweekly)*
Journal Publishing, Inc.
201 East Markham, Suite 200
Little Rock, AR 72201

Atlanta Business Chronicle   *(Weekly)*
Scripps Howard Business Publications
1800 Water Place, N.W., Suite 100
Atlanta, GA 30339

Austin Business Journal   *(Weekly)*
W.S. Publications, Inc.
1301 Capital of Texas Highway, Suite C200
Austin, TX 78746

Baton Rouge Business Report   *(Monthly)*
Louisiana Business, Inc.
P.O. Box 1949
Baton Rouge, LA 70821

Business Atlanta   *(Monthly)*
Communication Channels, Inc.
6255 Barfield Road
Atlanta, GA 30328

Business First of Buffalo, Inc.   *(Weekly)*
American City Business Journals, Inc.
361 Delaware Avenue, Suite 200
Buffalo, NY 14202

Business First of Columbus   *(Weekly)*
American City Business Journals, Inc.
274 Marconi Boulevard
Columbus, OH 43215

Business First of Louisville   *(Weekly)*
American City Business Journals, Inc.
607 West Main Street, Suite 300
Louisville, KY 40202

Business Journal—Milwaukee   (*Weekly*)
American City Business Journals, Inc.
2025 North Summit Avenue
Milwaukee, WI 53202

Business Journal of New Jersey   (*Monthly*)
Business Journal of New Jersey, Inc.
CN-2
Jamesburg, NJ 08831

Business Journal of Portland   (*Weekly*)
American City Business Journals, Inc.
P.O. Box 14490
Portland, OR 97214

Business Journal—Sacramento   (*Weekly*)
American City Business Journals, Inc.
2030 J Street
Sacramento, CA 95814

Business—North Carolina   (*Monthly*)
Shaw Communications, Inc.
212 South Tryon Street, Suite 1450
Charlotte, NC 28281

Business Record (Des Moines)   (*Weekly*)
516 3rd Street
Des Moines, IA 50309

Business Worcester   (*Biweekly*)
Central Mass Media, Inc.
P.O. Box 1000
Worcester, MA 01614

California Business   (*Monthly*)
California Business News, Inc.
4221 Wilshire Boulevard, Suite 400
Los Angeles, CA 90010

Capital District Business Review　(*Weekly*)
American City Business Journals, Inc.
76 Exchange Street
Albany, NY 12205

Caribbean Business　(*Weekly*)
Manuel A. Casiano, Inc.
1700 Fernadez Juncos Avenue
San Juan, PR 00909

Citybusiness/Twin Cities　(*Biweekly*)
MCP, Inc.
600 1st Avenue North, Suite 600
Minneapolis, MN 55403

Connecticut Business Journal　(*Weekly*)
Axon Business Publications, Inc.
201 Ann Street
Hartford, CT 06103

Corporate Report/Kansas City　(*Monthly*)
Dorn Communications
4149 Pennsylvania Avenue
Kansas City, MO 64111

Corporate Report Minnesota　(*Monthly*)
Dorn Communications
7831 East Bush Lake Road
Minneapolis, MN 55435

Crain's Chicago Business　(*Weekly*)
Crain Communications, Inc.
740 North Rush Street
Chicago, IL 60611

Crain's Cleveland Business   *(Weekly)*
Crain Communications, Inc.
140 Public Square
Cleveland, OH 44114

Crain's Detroit Business   *(Weekly)*
Crain Communications, Inc.
1400 Woodbridge
Detroit, MI 48207

Crain's Illinois Business   *(Quarterly)*
Crain Communications, Inc.
740 North Rush Street
Chicago, IL 60611

Crain's New York Business   *(Weekly)*
Crain Communications, Inc.
220 East 42nd Street
New York, NY 10017

Dallas/Ft. Worth Business Journal   *(Weekly)*
Scripps Howard Business Publications
11551 Forest Central Drive, Suite 130
Dallas, TX 75243

Delaware Business Review   *(Weekly)*
Independent Newspapers, Inc.
709 Market Street Mall
Wilmington, DE 19801

Denver Business Magazine   *(Monthly)*
General Communications, Inc.
100 Garfield Street
Denver, CO 80206

The Executive   *(Monthly)*
Executive Publications, Inc.
245 Fischer Avenue, Suite C-1
Costa Mesa, CA 92626

Executive Report   (*Monthly*)
Riverview Publications, Inc.
Bigelow Square
Pittsburgh, PA 15219

Florida Business/Tampa Bay   (*Monthly*)
Business Journal Publishing Company
5005 West Laurel, Suite 111
Tampa, FL 33607

Florida Trend   (*Monthly*)
Florida Trend, Inc.
P.O. Box 611
St. Petersburg, FL 33731

Focus/Philadelphia's Business News Weekly   (*Weekly*)
Business News, Inc.
1015 Chestnut Street
Philadelphia, PA 19107

Georgia Trend   (*Monthly*)
Florida Trend, Inc.
Georgia Pacific Center
133 Peachtree Street, Suite 4740
Atlanta, GA 30303

Hawaii Business   (*Monthly*)
Hawaii Business Publishing Corporation
P.O. Box 913
Honolulu, HI 96808

Houston Business Journal   (*Weekly*)
Scripps Howard Business Publications
5314 Bingle Road
Houston, TX 77092

Indiana Business   *(Monthly)*
BLM, Inc.
1200 Waterway Boulevard
Indianapolis, IN 46202

Jacksonville Business Journal   *(Weekly)*
American City Business Journals, Inc.
1851 Executive Center Drive, Suite 227
Jacksonville, FL 32207

Journal Record   *(Daily)*
Journal Record Publishing Company
621 North Robinson
Oklahoma City, OK 73102

Kansas Business News   *(Monthly)*
P.O. Box 511
Lindsborg, KS 67456

Kansas City Business Journal   *(Weekly)*
American City Business Journals, Inc.
3527 Broadway
Kansas City, MO 64111

Long Island/Business Newsweekly   *(Weekly)*
Long Island Commercial Review, Inc.
2150 Smithtown Avenue
Ronkonkoma, NY 11779

Los Angeles Business Journal   *(Weekly)*
Scripps Howard Business Publications
3345 Wilshire Boulevard, Suite 207
Los Angeles, CA 90010

Louisiana Business Journal   (*Monthly*)
455 2nd Street
Natchitoches, LA 71457

Memphis Business Journal   (*Weekly*)
Mid-South Communications, Inc.
4515 Poplar, Suite 322
Memphis, TN 38117

Miami Review and Daily Record   (*Daily*)
Miami Review, Inc.
100 North East 7th Street
Miami, FL 33132

Michigan Business   (*Monthly*)
Business Journal Publishing Company
Cranbrook Center, Suite 302
30161 Southfield Road
Southfield, MI 48076

Minnesota Business Journal   (*Monthly*)
Dorn Communications
7831 East Bush Lake Road
Minneapolis, MN 55435

Nashville Business Journal   (*Weekly*)
Mid-South Communications, Inc.
172 2nd Avenue North
Nashville, TN 37201

New England Business   (*Biweekly*)
Yankee Publishing, Inc.
Main Street
Dublin, NH 03444

New Hampshire Business Review   (*Biweekly*)
Business Publications, Inc.
795 Elm Street
Manchester, NH 03101

New Jersey Success　　(*Monthly*)
Success Publishing Company, Inc.
1138 North Broad Street
Hillside, NJ 07205

New Orleans Business　　(*Weekly*)
Guide Newspapers (Cox
　Newspapers Group)
401 Whitney Avenue
P.O. Box 354
Gretna, LA 70054

New Orleans Citybusiness　　(*Biweekly*)
MCP Incorporated
111 Veterans Boulevard,
　Suite 750
Metairie, LA 70005

Northern Ontario Business　　(*Monthly*)
Laurentian Publishing Group
158 Elgin Street
Sudbury, Ontario P3E 3N5

Oakland Business Monthly　　(*Monthly*)
Oakland Community Newspapers, Inc.
7196 Cooley Lake Road
Union Lake, MI 48085

Ocean State Business Magazine　　(*Biweekly*)
Central Mass Media, Inc.
4 Davol Square
Providence, RI 02903

Ohio Business　　(*Monthly*)
Business Journal Publishing Company
1720 Euclid Avenue
Cleveland, OH 44115

Oregon Business *(Monthly)*
MEDIAmerica Incorporated
208 South West Stark Street,
  Suite 404
Portland, OR 97204

Pacific Business News *(Weekly)*
American City Business Journals, Inc.
P.O. Box 833
Honolulu, HI 96808

Phoenix Business Journal *(Weekly)*
Scripps Howard Business Publications
1817 North Third Street, Suite 100
Phoenix, AZ 85004

Puget Sound Business Journal *(Weekly)*
Scripps Howard Business Publications
1008 Western Avenue, Suite 515
Seattle, WA 98104

Regardie's *(Monthly)*
1010 Wisconsin Avenue, N.W.,
  Suite 600
Washington, D.C. 20007

Rocky Mountain Business Journal *(Weekly)*
Scripps Howard Business Publications
2300 15th Street, Suite 110
Denver, CO 80202

St. Louis Business Journal *(Weekly)*
712 North 2nd Street
P.O. Box 647
St. Louis, MO 63188

San Antonio Executive   *(Weekly)*
Lammert Publications
1603 Babcock, Suite 159
San Antonio, TX 78229

San Diego Business Journal   *(Weekly)*
Scripps Howard Business Publications
3444 Camino Del Rio North
San Diego, CA 92108

San Francisco Business Journal   *(Weekly)*
Scripps Howard Business Publications
635 Sacramento Street, Suite 310
San Francisco, CA 94111

San Jose Business Journal   *(Weekly)*
American City Business Journals, Inc.
80 South Market Street
San Jose, CA 95113

South Florida Business Journal   *(Weekly)*
Scripps Howard Business Publications
3785 North West 82nd Avenue, Suite 204
Miami, FL 33178

Tampa Bay Business Journal   *(Weekly)*
Tampa Bay Business Publishing Company
405 Reo Street, Suite 210
Tampa, FL 33609

Texas Business Magazine   *(Monthly)*
Commerce Publishing Company
5757 Alpha Road, #400
Dallas, TX 75240

Vermont Business   (*Monthly*)
Manning Publications, Inc.
P.O. Box 6120
Brattleboro, VT 05301

Washington Business Journal   (*Weekly*)
Scripps Howard Business Publications
8321 Old Courthouse Road, Suite 200
Tysons Corner
Vienna, VA 22180

Washington Business Review   (*Weekly*)
Business Review, Inc.
138 Church Street, N.E.
P.O. Box 859
Vienna, VA 22180

Westchester Business Journal   (*Weekly*)
Axon Business Publications, Inc.
222 Grace Church Street
P.O. Box 31
Port Chester, NY 10573

Western Business   (*Monthly*)
Unicorn Communications/Lee
   Enterprises
401 North Broadway
P.O. Box 31678
Billings, MT 59107

Wisconsin Business Magazine   (*Monthly*)
Dean Communications, Inc.
7535 Office Ridge Circle
Eden Prairie, MN 55344

DIRECTORIES OF CORPORATIONS

As a general rule, the more intelligently you can discuss a corporation's current activities, financial standing and outlook, the easier it will be for you to gain the ear of purchasing agents. Fortunately, there are scores of publications available that aid further research on target corporations. Standard & Poor's *Register of Directors and Executives* offers the names, business, and home addresses of 75,000 topflight executives with biographies-in-brief that list their directorships, showing interlocking business affiliations, and their alma maters.

The *Register*'s corporate listings give you the type of business, ZIP-coded addresses, telephone numbers, and, in most cases, approximate annual sales and number of employees. A substantial number of listings also identify companies' accountants, primary banks, and primary law firms.

A special section breaks down the 37,000 companies into over 900 product categories coded by current Standard Industrial Classifications.

Thomas Register of American Manufacturers, Thomas Publishing Company, is a multivolume reference source that lists manufacturers' sources alphabetically by state and by city within state. Trade and brand names are also given alphabetically, along with company name, address, and a variety of other information about the companies listed. *Thomas Register* is good for locating the source of brand names, for providing sources for your goods, and for obtaining details on companies that you may want to contact (see accompanying ads).

Trade Name Dictionary, published by the Gale Research Company, indicates which companies manufacture which trade name products. The information it contains includes the trade name and a description of the product and the name of the company that manufactures it.

Dun & Bradstreet's *Middle Market Directory* lists over 31,000 companies with net worths ranging from $500,000 to $999,999, represented alphabetically by business name and geographically by business address. It states the size, chief executives, and products of these companies and provides financial information on them.

The Corporate 1000 provides facts on the top 1,000 manufacturing and service corporations in the United States and enables readers to locate quickly and easily every key executive and every prime purchasing and decision-making individual in these corporations.

Facts for Sellers about
THOMAS REGISTER

Only THOMAS REGISTER gives you a $400-million a day sales opportunity.

Why do more companies advertise in Thomas Register than in any other publication? For one reason only: sales results. Only Thomas Register brings them millions of dollars of directly traceable sales every day.

Just consider Thomas Register's major role in the industrial buying process...

- 97% of all new sales are initiated by the buyer...not the seller. The seller rarely knows of the opportunity until contacted by the buyer.
- 54% of all buyers say that they find their new suppliers through buying guides and directories.
- Thomas Register is their overwhelming first choice... used more than all other buying guides combined by both engineering and purchasing.
- As a result, they use Thomas Register in buying products and services at the rate of more than $400-million a day. No other industrial advertising medium has documented more than a fraction of this sales volume.

Thomas Register is used...

- 300,000 times a day...75 million times a year.
- by 1.5 million specifiers and buyers at 150,000 buying locations.
- in purchasing products and services at the rate of more than $400-million a day.

Your advertising and catalog in Thomas Register gives you...

- 91% coverage of the Fortune 500 companies.
- 85% coverage of all manufacturing companies listed on the New York Stock Exchange.

- Coverage of tens of thousands of other companies in both the manufacturing and service industries.
- Extensive coverage of Federal, State and Local Government procurement offices.
- Effective coverage in tens of thousands of buying locations and government reference centers overseas.

Your advertising is seen and used by prospects in...

- Purchasing & Procurement
- Production Management & Manufacturing Engineering
- Administrative Management & Administration
- Design & Product Engineering
- Research & Development
- Maintenance & Quality Control
- Warehousing & Shipping
- Marketing & Sales

Your advertising keeps working for you year after year after year...

- Subscribers pass on their old sets to other departments and locations each year when their new editions arrive.
- This "pass on" boosts Thomas Register's effective circulation to more than 150,000 sets in use at any given time.

No other buying guide comes close to the loyal usage that Thomas Register assures you...

- 98-out-of-100 Chief Purchasing Executives in Fortune 500 companies prefer Thomas Register over their next most popular buying guide.
- 80-out-of-100 Chief Engineers in Fortune 1000 companies prefer Thomas Register over their next most popular buying guide.

And only Thomas Register offers you a $400-million a day sales opportunity.

For full details on advertising contact...
Thomas Register of American Manufacturers
One Penn Plaza, New York, New York 10001. Or call...(212) 290-7225

Reprinted with permission from *Thomas Register of American Manufacturers.*

Facts for Buyers about THOMAS REGISTER

Only THOMAS REGISTER gives you a comprehensive 3-part Specifying and Buying System.

More than 1½ million specifiers and buyers around the world use Thomas Register on a regular basis to find the products, services, companies, and information they need. Because Thomas Register is by far the most complete specifying and buying guide to American industry available anywhere...it saves them vital time...

giving them fast, thorough, fingertip access to all of American industry.

While most other publishers give their buying guides away free, industry pays more than $10,000,000 to buy Thomas Register. That's just one indication of how important specifiers and buyers consider Thomas Register to be to their businesses.

Here's what the 21 volume Thomas Register gives you...

1. Products & Services

Volumes 1 thru 12 tell you who makes virtually any product you need... who's a prime source for virtually any service you require.

- More than 50,000 product and service headings are included.

- Under each heading, a comprehensive list of sources is reported... with addresses and asset ratings.

- To help you spot the closest qualified source...suppliers are listed geographically under each heading.

- Tens of thousands of illustrated product ads supplement these listings...providing detailed information on product availability, specs, etc.

- Each product and service section is fully cross-indexed to the Company Profiles Section...where you'll find important information on each company's locations and capabilities.

- Each section is also cross-indexed to the THOMCAT Catalog File Section ...where hundreds of manufacturers include detailed product specs.

2. Company Profiles

Volumes 13 and 14 give you comprehensive information to help you evaluate and contact more than 133,000 U.S. companies.

- Companies are listed alphabetically...with headquarter locations, phone numbers, nearest plants, nearest service locations, corporate affiliations, nearest distributors and asset ratings.

- Many companies also include a summary of their complete product line, facilities and special capabilities.

- Additionally, many of the country's largest corporations also supply multi-page profiles to help you locate the correct division or department for your needs.

- Volume 14 also contains a Brand Names Section...listing in alphabetical order nearly 105,000 trademarks and brand names...and the companies who own them.

- Volume 14 also gives you a comprehensive index to headings contained in the Products & Services Section.

3. Catalog File

Volumes 15 thru 21 put more than 8,800 pages of catalog data from more than 1,250 manufacturers at your fingertips. You'll have "instant access" to engineering and product performance data you need. No need to request, then wait for supplier literature. THOMCAT pre-files it all for you... alphabetically by company name.

- The reference line... "See our Catalog in THOMCAT"...in the ads and listings in the Products & Services Section (Vol. 1—12) will tell you when a supplier has catalog data in THOMCAT.

- The same reference line appears in that supplier's profile in the Company Profiles Section (Vol. 13—14).

- Alerted by these reference lines, you can turn directly to the appropriate Catalog (Vol. 15—21) for detailed specifying and buying information.

- By having "instant access" to this catalog data, you'll zero in more quickly on the supplier best able to meet your requirements.

For full details on subscription costs contact...

Thomas Register of American Manufacturers

Circulation Manager, One Penn Plaza, New York, N.Y. 10001. Or call...(212) 290-7277

Reprinted with permission from *Thomas Register of American Manufacturers.*

The Corporate 1000
Washington Monitor, Inc.
1301 Pennsylvania Avenue, N.W.,
   Suite 1000
Washington, DC 20004

The *Small Business Sourcebook* is a directory produced specifically for the small business entrepreneur. It is a guide to small business information services and sources available from associations, consultants, educational programs, franchisers, government agencies, reference works, statisticians, suppliers, trade shows, and venture capital firms. Write to: Gale Research Company, Book Tower, Detroit, MI 48226.

Also, suppliers' guides, often called blue books or red books, can be found in the business reference section of many public libraries. These books, which might bear such titles as the ''Blue Book of Metro Area Home Builders,'' and the ''Red Book of Plumbing Supply Contractors,'' are often distributed by the local associations serving these industries.

Other corporate guides are provided as special issues of business periodicals and are also available through major public libraries and other university libraries:

Financial World—''Financial World's 500: America's Biggest Money Makers.'' Annual, July 15 issue. Ranks companies by profits; also includes profit ranking by industry, the top 10 in net profits, return on common equity, return on total capital, top and bottom 20 on total return to investors.

Forbes—''Annual Directory Issue.'' May 15 issue. Lists ''the 500 largest corporations'' ranked by revenues, assets, market value, and net profit. The first issue each year, ''Annual Report on American Industry,'' ranks companies by profitability, growth, and stock price gain.

Fortune—''Directory of Largest Corporations.'' Annual, four parts, in May–August issues. The May issue lists the 500 largest U.S. industrial corporations; the June issue lists the 500 corporations that follow the 500 largest corporations; the July issue lists the 50 largest banks, life insurance, diversified-financial, retail, transportation, and utility companies; the August issue lists the 300 largest foreign industrial corporations and the 50 largest foreign banks.

Specific Industry Directories

Advertising Age—"100 Leading National Advertisers." Annual, last August issue. This issue also includes a table of the 100 leaders in advertising as a percentage of sales, by industry, and a comparison of the 100 leaders' media expenditures.

Chemical & Engineering News—"C&EN's Top 50 Chemical Producers." Annual, first May issue. This ranking is also in the "Facts & Figures" issue (annual, first June issue).

Chemical Week—"Chemical Week 300." Annual, last April issue. The listing of the "100 Top Foreign Chemical Processing Companies" is in the first August issue.

Electronic Business—"The Electronic Business 100." Annual, February issue.

Electronic News—"The Leaders." This is usually section 2 of an early July issue.

Engineering News-Record—"Top 500 Design Firms." Annual, around the end of May.

Iron Age—"Steel Industry Financial Analysis," a ranking of over 30 companies, and "Nonferrous Industry Financial Analysis," an alphabetical list of over 25 companies. Annual, last April issue.

National Petroleum News—"Oil Company Annual Financial Reports." Mid-May issue each year.

Oil & Gas Journal—"How . . . Large U.S. Companies Fared Financially . . ." Annual, first May issue. Ranks over 25 companies.

International Corporations

Canadian Business—"2 + 2: The Top 200 plus the Next 200 of Canada's Largest Companies." Annual, July issue.

Financial Post (Canadian)—"Financial Post 300." Published separately in summer each year. Ranks top industrial, financial, merchandising, property, and resources companies.

Europe's 5000 Largest Companies (New York: Bowker).—Annual. Financial data on the 5,000 largest industrials and 1,000 trading companies. Includes rankings of the 500 largest industrials by profit, the 250 most profitable industrials, 50 money losers, and the largest companies by industry and by country.

German International—"The World's Largest Steel Producers' League." Annual, July issue.

Le Nouvel Economiste 5000—Annual, extra November issue. Includes ranking of the 1,000 largest European companies, arranged by industry.

Additional Industry Data

Robert Morris Associates produces an annual composite of balance sheets and income data with selected ratios for over 340 lines of business—manufacturers, wholesalers, retailers, services, and contractors. Figures are given in percentages but are translatable into "average" firm dollar figures. To obtain more information, write to:

> Annual Statement Studies
> Robert Morris Associates
> Philadelphia National Bank Building
> Philadelphia, PA 19107
> (215) 665-2874

Annual Statement Studies also provides references to hundreds of other industry data and statistical guides. Here is a sampling:

Statistics of Paper and Paperboard—American Paper Institute, 260 Madison Avenue, New York, NY 10016. (212) 340-0631. Annual. Financial data based on Department of Commerce reports. Covers sales, taxes, and profits going back to 1950. Also includes cash flow information, operating ratios, production capacity, consumption data, and import/export data.

Cost of Doing Business—Corporations—Dun & Bradstreet, Inc., 99 Church Street, New York, NY 10007. (212) 285-7669. Irregular, single copies free. Cost of goods sold, gross margins, and selected operating ratios for lines of business, based on a sample of federal income tax returns.

Cost of Doing Business—Proprietorships & Partnerships—Dun & Bradstreet, Inc., 99 Church Street, New York, NY 10007. (212) 285-7669. Irregular, single copies free. Selected profit and operating expense ratios for lines of business, based on federal income tax returns.

Annual Financial Survey of the Rigid Paper Box Industry—National Paperbox and Packaging Association, 231 Kings Highway East, Haddonfield, NJ 08033. (609) 429-7377. Annual. Includes operating ratios and expense percentages broken down by geographic divisions and sales volume.

The Lilly Digest—Eli Lilly & Co., 307 East McCarty Street, Indianapolis, IN 46285. (317) 261-6009. Annual. Comprehensive study of pharmacies showing a detailed breakdown of expenses with firms grouped according to sales volume and prescription activity. Also gives balance sheet data and selected financial ratios.

Special Statistical Report on Profit, Sales, and Production Trends of the Men's and Boys' Clothing Industry—Clothing Manufacturers Association of the U.S.A., 1290 Avenue of the Americas, Suite 1351, New York, NY 10104. (212) 757-6664. Annual. Report includes net profits on sales and on net worth for past 20 years, plus statistics on production and sales, industry size, employment, and earnings and population projections.

Aerospace Facts and Figures—compiled by Aerospace Industries. Published and orders processed by *Aviation Week & Space Technology,* 1221 Avenue of the Americas, New York, NY 10020. (212) 997-3289. Annual. Percentage values for current assets, income taxes, and net profits along with balance sheet and income comparisons covering the last few years.

Cost of Doing Business—Farm and Power Equipment Dealers—National Farm and Power Equipment Dealers Association, 10877 Watson Road, St. Louis, MO 63127. (314) 821-7220. Annual. Sales, expense, and balance sheet data on agricultural and industrial dealers. Studies include four volume size groups and three regions.

NHFA Operating Experiences—National Home Furnishings Association, 405 Merchandise Mart, Chicago, IL 60654. (312) 836-0777. Annual. Generally available to members only; on occasion available to financial and educational institutions at NHFA's discretion. Operating percentages for retail furniture stores classed according to sales volume. Additional statistics on various merchandise lines, credit experience, payroll, etc.

Lilly Hospital Pharmacy Survey—Eli Lilly & Co., 307 East McCarty Street, Indianapolis, IN 46285. (317) 261-6009. Annual. Presents the most recent and detailed information available on the operational statistics of hospitals in the United States.

Gas Facts—American Gas Association, 1515 Wilson Boulevard, Arlington, VA 22209. (703) 841-8497. Annual. Extensive collection of basic gas industry statistics, including balance sheet and income and expense figures shown in historical sequence. Includes selected analytic ratios for gas utilities. Published in third quarter of current year.

Statistical Year Book of the Electric Utility Industry—Edison Electric Institute, 1111 19th Street, N.W., Washington, DC 20036. (202) 828-7643. Annual. Data compiled from company reports, and other sources, on operational and financial aspects of the total electric utility industry. Categories include national and state statistics on installed capacity; electric generation and supply; and sales, revenue, and customers by class of service. Published in the fall.

Air Transport—Air Transport Association of America, 1709 New York Avenue, N.W., Washington, DC 20006. (202) 626-4000. Annual. Operating revenues and expenses in dollar amounts compared over a period of years. Also includes balance sheet data for various types of airlines.

INFORMATION FROM UNCLE SAM

The federal government is one of the largest publishers in the world. Through the Bureau of the Census of the Department of Commerce, you may obtain sales and revenue data on virtually any industry, by state, county, and standard metropolitan statistical area. Although the Bureau of the Census is known primarily for its population reports, it takes a census of business in the second and seventh year of each decade. The results of this census are generally available 18 to 24 months after it is taken.

Census information will be provided on more than 800 of the approximately 1,000 industries, businesses, and products classified according to the SIC system. In the 1982 census expense and production information was collected for about 1,000 material categories and quantity and value data for 16,000 product classifications. Separate censuses were conducted for manufacturers, mineral industries, construction industries, retail trade, wholesale trade, and service industries.

Printed documents of the 1982 census are available from the Superintendent of Documents, U.S. Government Printing Office, Washington, DC 20402.

Computer file tapes can be obtained directly from the Bureau of the Census. The Bureau of the Census also produces many special industry reports and offers several ways to access its files. To obtain a list of the bureau's publications, write to:

Public Information Office
Bureau of the Census
Department of Commerce
Washington, DC 20233
(301) 763-4040

The Department of Commerce annually publishes the *U.S. Industrial Outlook,* which traces the growth of 200 industries and provides five-year forecasts for each industry. The *U.S. Statistical Abstract* is a compilation of data and reports from the Department of Commerce, the Department of Labor, the Department of Transportation, the Small Business Administration, and other federal agencies.

If you need to access information within a specific federal government agency, it is best to call the public information office rather than the agency switchboard. When trying to identify a specific individual, ask for the locator's office, and when trying to identify a specific nonclassified document, use the Freedom of Information Office.

Many of the major publications produced by the federal government are on sale at the U.S. Government Printing Office. For a free catalog, write to:

Superintendent of Documents
U.S. Government Printing Office
Washington, DC 20401
(202) 783-3238

The federally sponsored National Technical Information Service, a division of the Department of Commerce, maintains abstracts and data bases in 28 technical areas, such as engineering, energy, and physics, and is the central source for the sale of government-sponsored research, development, engineering, reports, or other analyses by federal agencies. You may also obtain copies of the thousands of research reports that it has on file. Descriptive brochures may be obtained by writing:

National Technical Information Service
Department of Commerce
5285 Port Royal Road
Springfield, VA 22161
(703) 487-4600

The information provided by this service can help you in everything from marketing to product development.

STATE INFORMATION SOURCES

Nearly all of the 50 states have their own Department of Commerce and special offices established to assist small or small disadvantaged businesses. The state capitol, the state capitol library, and the governor's office, as well as the offices of your elected representatives, often maintain special reports, studies, and analyses that may prove useful in your marketing research efforts. Here is a listing of various state offices of commerce, international trade, and economic development.

STATE SMALL BUSINESS SUPPORT OFFICES

Alabama
Alabama Department of Economic
and Community Affairs
P.O. Box 2939
Montgomery, AL 36105–0939

Alaska
Office of International Trade
Pouch D
Juneau, AK 99811

Arizona
Office of Economic Planning and
Development
Business and Trade Section
Executive Tower, 4th Floor
1700 West Washington
Phoenix, AZ 85007

Arkansas
Arkansas Industrial Development
Commission

1 State Capitol Mall
Little Rock, AR 72201

California
Office of Small Business
Development
1121 L Street, Suite 600
Sacramento, CA 95814

Colorado
Colorado Business Information
Center
1525 Sherman, Room 110
Denver, CO 80203

Connecticut
Department of Economic
Development
210 Washington Street
Hartford, CT 06106

Delaware
Delaware Development Office
99 Kings Highway
P.O. Box 1401
Dover, DE 19903

District of Columbia
Office of Business and Economic
  Development
1350 Pennsylvania Avenue,
  N.W., Room 208
Washington, DC 20004

Florida
Bureau of International Trade and
  Development
Collins Building
107 West Gaines Street
Tallahassee, FL 32301

Georgia
Georgia Department of Industry
  and Trade
P.O. Box 1776
Atlanta, GA 30301

Hawaii
Small Business Information
  Service
250 South King Street, Room 724
Honolulu, HI 96813

Idaho
Department of Commerce
Statehouse, Room 108
Boise, ID 83720

Illinois
Illinois Department of Commerce
  and Community Affairs
310 South Michigan Avenue,
  10th Floor
Chicago, IL 60604

Indiana
Indiana Department of Commerce
1 North Capital, Suite 700
Indianapolis, IN 46204

Iowa
Iowa Development Commission
600 East Court Avenue
Des Moines, IA 50309

Kansas
Kansas Department of Economic
  Development
503 Kansas Avenue, 6th Floor
Topeka, KS 66603

Kentucky
Kentucky Commerce Cabinet
Capitol Plaza Tower, 22nd Floor
Frankfort, KY 40601

Louisiana
Office of Commerce and Industry
P.O. Box 94185
Baton Rouge, LA 70804–9185

Maine
State Development Office
State House Station 59
Augusta, ME 04333

Maryland
Department of Economic and
  Community Development
45 Calvert Street
Annapolis, MD 21401

Massachusetts
Department of Commerce
100 Cambridge Street, 13th Floor
Boston, MA 02202

Michigan
Department of Commerce
P.O. Box 30225
Lansing, MI 48909

Minnesota
Small Business Assistance Office
150 East Kellogg Boulevard,
　#900
St. Paul, MN 55107

Mississippi
Department of Economic
　Development
Marketing Division
P.O. Box 849
Jackson, MS 39205

Missouri
Department of Economic
　Development
Harry S. Truman Building
P.O. Box 118
Jefferson City, MO 65102

Montana
Department of Commerce
1424 9th Avenue
Helena, MT 59620

Nebraska
Nebraska Department of
　Economic Development
301 Centennial Mall South
P.O. Box 94666
Lincoln, NE 68509

Nevada
Small Business Development
　Center
University of Nevada, College of
　Business Administration
Business Building, Room 411
Reno, NV 89557–0016

New Hampshire
Office of Industrial Development
P.O. Box 856
Concord, NH 03301

New Jersey
Department of Commerce
1 West State Street
Trenton, NJ 08625

New Mexico
New Mexico Economic
　Development and Tourism
　Department
Bataan Memorial Building, #201
Santa Fe, NM 87503

New York
Department of Commerce
230 Park Avenue, Room 834
New York, NY 10169

North Carolina
Department of Commerce
430 North Salisbury Street,
　Room 282
Raleigh, NC 27611

North Dakota
Economic Development
　Commission
Liberty Memorial Building
Bismarck, ND 58505

Ohio
Department of Development
P.O. Box 1001
Columbus, OH 43216–0101

Oklahoma
Department of Economic
　Development
4024 North Lincoln Boulevard
P.O. Box 53424
Oklahoma City, OK 73152

Oregon
Oregon Economic Development
　Department
595 Cottage Street
Salem, OR 97310

Pennsylvania
Department of Commerce
Forum Building, Room 483
Harrisburg, PA 17120

Rhode Island
Department of Economic
   Development
7 Jackson Walkway
Providence, RI 02903

South Carolina
State Development Board
P.O. Box 927
Columbia, SC 29202

South Dakota
Department of State Development
Box 6000
Capitol Lake Plaza
Pierre, SD 57501

Tennessee
Department of Economic and
   Community Development
Rachel Jackson Building,
   7th Floor
320 6th Avenue, North
Nashville, TN 37219

Texas
Economic Development
   Commission
P.O. Box 12728, Capitol Station
Austin, TX 78711

Utah
Economic and Industrial
   Development Division
6150 State Office Building
Salt Lake City, UT 84114

Vermont
Agency of Development and
   Community Affairs
109 State Street
Montpelier, VT 05602

Virginia
Department of Economic
   Development
1000 Washington Building
Richmond, VA 23219

Washington
Department of Commerce and
   Economic Development
312 1st Avenue North
Seattle, WA 98109

West Virginia
Governor's Office of Economic
   and Community Development
State Capitol, Room B-517
Charleston, WV 25305

Wisconsin
Department of Development
P.O. Box 7970
Madison, WI 53707

Wyoming
Department of Economic Planning
   and Development
Herschler Building, 3rd Floor
Cheyenne, WY 82002

Puerto Rico
International Division
Puerto Rico Department of
   Commerce
P.O. Box 4275
San Juan, PR 00905

NEWSLETTERS

Newsletters have become a valuable source of marketing research information. Newsletters are now published by government agencies, industry groups, associations, political groups, and virtually every corporation. The *Oxbridge Newsletter Directory* lists several thousand newsletters, arranged by functional area. The *National Trade and Professional Association Directory* (NTPA) indicates which of the thousands of associations listed maintain a newsletter. The *Newsletter Yearbook* is also a valuable guide. By accessing these directories and others that your local librarian may suggest, you can obtain late-breaking news and information of concern to your business and your industry.

If you have a computer and modem, you can subscribe to hundreds of business-oriented newsletters—even if you are not a subscriber to any of them through NewsNet. This is an information delivery and retrieval service that produces electronic editions.

Current newsletter issues, and back issues for the past year, are stored in NewsNet's main computer. By dialing a local telephone number, NewsNet users access that data base. They pay a modest rate to read the newsletters. A small minority of newsletter publishers impose a surcharge for those who are not subscribers to the printed version of their newsletter.

More information is available from:

> NewsNet
> 945 Haverford Road
> Bryn Mawr, PA 19010
> (800) 345-1301

LOCAL RESOURCES

On a regional or local basis, various planning communities, the research department of newspapers, highway commissions, local libraries, and the county courthouse are just a few of the information sources that you may wish to tap, depending on your research need. Many entrepreneurs have found that a wealth of information can be gained right over the phone or by simply visiting nearby organizations or agencies.

Local publications offer such business nuggets as:

- Plant openings or closings.
- Office buildings being erected and announcements of tenants.

NEWSLETTER DIRECTORIES

If you're interested in reviewing a wide range of industry newsletters, in particular those that your marketing targets read, the following directories are helpful:

Standard Periodical Directory
Oxbridge Communications, Inc.
150 5th Avenue
New York, NY 10011
(212) 741-0231
Lists over 72,000 magazines, journals, newsletters, directories, house organs, and association publications throughout the United States and Canada.

Oxbridge Directory of Newsletters
Oxbridge Communications, Inc.
150 5th Avenue
New York, NY 10011
(212) 741-0231
Lists approximately 5,500 newsletters in the United States and Canada.

National Directory of Newsletters and Reporting Services
Gale Research Company
Book Tower
Detroit, MI 48226
(313) 961-2242
Lists thousands of newsletters issued by commercial and noncommercial publishers.

Hudson Newsletter Directory
Newsletter Clearinghouse
44 West Market Street
Rhinebeck, NY 12572
(914) 876-2081
Lists 2,600 newsletters offered through subscription.

- New products or services offered by a large company, potentially creating a need for your services.
- Industry trends.
- New programs for small businesses sponsored by corporations and by federal, state, or local governments.

Also consider these valuable information sources:

- Chamber of Commerce studies.
- University research publications.

- Purchasing trade journals (see Chapter 8).
- Data obtained from your dealers, suppliers, and customers.

The local Chamber of Commerce has figures for the types of businesses in your area and their estimated profits, the number of new people moving into the area, listings of local media, and so forth. On both the local and national level, it is a valuable source of information. Local colleges and universities can also be a useful source of information on the size and accessibility of your market. These institutions can sometimes offer assistance or advice through graduate research programs.

RESEARCH THROUGH NETWORKING

Other information may be generated through membership in business and professional associations. These groups often maintain local chapters in large metropolitan areas:

> Administrative Management Society
> American Society for Training and Development
> Board of Realtors
> Business and Professional Women's Club
> International Management Council
> Purchasing Management Association
> Sales and Marketing Executives International
> Other professional societies (bankers, accountants, engineers)

USING DATA BASES TO REDUCE YOUR RESEARCH EFFORTS

Ken Wexler, managing director of Infotech Research Corporation, Trumbull, Connecticut, believes that computerized data bases are a powerful tool that small business can use effectively when researching markets.

Of particular interest, computerized data bases permit the gathering of hard-to-find information on small industrial niche markets. Such information is usually difficult to gather using conventional market research tools.

Some examples, offered by Wexler, of industrial niche markets are hot-melt adhesives, disposable industrial protective garments, residential doorknobs, industrial microwave drying equipment, and extra strong shipping containers.

Research regarding industrial markets usually involves information on market size, the major players in the market, market growth rate, technological trends, distribution channels, and product pricing.

Wexler notes that data bases can be searched by specific product names, company names, or index terms or by free-text searching, using pertinent key words in appropriate combinations, such as "residential and door and knob."

"A researcher has access to several hundred data bases through a single-source data base vendor who markets a broad mixture of data bases from data base producers, allowing researchers to access several hundred data bases with one password and one search language," says Wexler.

Vendors offering a wide selection of data bases include Lockheed and Mead Data Central. Together, Lockheed's Dialog system and Mead's Nexis system yield the most appropriate combination of several hundred data bases with which to gather information on industrial markets.

Dialog, Nexis, Dow Jones News, and virtually every other data base can be located by using one or more of the following directories:

Computer-Readable Databases
American Library Association
50 East Huron Street
Chicago, IL 60611
(312) 944-6780

Directory of Online Databases
Cuadra Associates, Inc.
2001 Wilshire Boulevard, #30
Santa Monica, CA 90403
(213) 829-9972

Federal Database Finder
Information USA, Inc.
12400 Beall Mountain Road
Potomac, MD 20854
(301) 983-8220

Data Base Directory
Knowledge Industry Publications
701 Westchester Avenue
White Plains, NY 10604
(914) 328-9157

The North American Online Directory 1987
R. R. Bowker
204 East 42nd Street
New York, NY 10017
(800) 521-8110

The *Source Directory* is an annual listing of over 5,000 sources of business information. This directory includes many publishers of data bases.

> Source Directory
> Predicasts, Inc.
> 11001 Cedar Avenue
> Cleveland, OH 44106
> (216) 795-3000

Author and consultant Jeffrey Lant, Ph.D., of Cambridge, Massachusetts, in his self-published book *Tricks of the Trade* reviewed 10 data bases of interest to those wishing to gather information on specific Fortune 500 firms:

ABI Inform.   A general business data base with lengthy abstracts of articles from over 650 business press publications. Dates back to 1971. Available on many systems, including BRS, SDC, Dialog, and VU/TEXT.

The Computer Database.   Provides indexing and abstracting of articles from about 500 computer publications. Superb source for information on hardware, software, telecommunications, and networking. Available on Dialog and BRS, among others.

Disclosure II.   Contains business and financial information extracted from documents filed with the Securities and Exchange Commission (SEC) by over 10,000 publicly held companies. Available on many systems, including Dialog, CompuServe, and Dow Jones News/Retrieval.

Dow Jones News.   Contains news stories dating back to 1979 from *The Wall Street Journal, Barron's,* and the Dow Jones News Service. Over 10,000 U.S. and Canadian companies in 50 industries are covered. Available on Dow Jones News/Retrieval.

Dun's Market Identifiers 10+.   Provides marketing information and company history for U.S. businesses, both public and private, that have more than 10 employees. Coverage includes parent companies, subsidiaries, headquarters information, products, and services. Available on Dialog.

Investext. Contains the full text of industry and company research reports produced by financial analysts of leading investment firms in the United States, Canada, Europe, and Japan. Available on several systems, including the Source and Dialog.

Magazine Index. Provides indexing for articles from over 400 popular magazines. In many cases, the full texts of the articles are provided. This includes information on many subjects, including consumers, restaurants, and travel. Available on Dialog, Mead's Nexis System, and BRS.

Management Contents. This general business data base contains information from over 500 business publications. Available on Dialog, Mead, BRS, SDC, and others.

National Newspaper Index. Contains indexing for articles from such national newspapers as the *New York Times, The Wall Street Journal,* and the *Christian Science Monitor* as well as the *Washington Post* and the *Los Angeles Times.* Available on Mead, BRS, and Dialog.

PTS Prompt. This is a must for industry information. It includes data on both private and public companies and is international in scope. Abstracts with citations to the full text cover thousands of publications that have appeared since 1972. Available on several systems, including Dialog, BRS, and VU/TEXT.

Lant's book also contains comprehensive information on how to use data processing technology to your best advantage. Write to: JLA Publications, 50 Follen Street, Cambridge, MA 02138.

Even the most difficult market can be researched using computerized data bases. An example offered by Wexler is research on industrial protective garments. Here the researcher would use search terminology such as protective garments, industrial garments, or SIC 3842–351. He or she would then view on a terminal the data base records that referred to these types of products, by name or seven-digit Standard Industrial Classification code, and would print them for later reference.

Here are some other examples of data base use offered by Wexler:

- A business-oriented data base containing abstracts of articles from more than 80 business-oriented publications that cover the chemical and processing industries.

- A listing of industry directories and special issues of trade journals for 65 major industries.
- An engineering-oriented data base covering about 3,500 engineering journals and selected government reports.
- A summary of published market forecasts by SIC code.
- A listing of published market research reports.

The computerized data bases can also be used for pricing strategy, distribution channel selection, advertising and promotional budgeting, and requests for venture capital.

IN SUMMARY

The basic ability to effectively gather information to support your market planning is directly related to how organized you are. Maintenance of a Rolodex or other type of phone system is essential. It is also necessary to befriend information sources such as librarians, publishers, and federal agency representatives, because you may need to call on these people a number of times. Once you or your staff have become familiar with the techniques and the reference sources cited in this chapter, the task of generating timely, effective marketing research information will become less difficult.

CHAPTER EIGHT

The Corporate Purchasing Manager and Purchasing Departments

*You must look into people,
as well as at them.*

LORD CHESTERFIELD

Today's corporate purchasing manager is the "bull's-eye" for small vendors and suppliers who want to target new commercial business opportunities with major corporations. William J. Holleran, director of media relations with Earle Palmer Brown Public Relations, says that the more you know about purchasing management at major corporations, the better your chances will be for marketing success. Holleran has actively studied the role and responsibilities of corporate purchasing agents and has been instrumental in generating small business vendor opportunities at several plants of Fortune 500 firms.

WHO THEY ARE

Corporate purchasing departments today are staffed with well-educated, well-trained, and broadly experienced professionals. Holleran's research disclosed that in the 40 years since World War II purchasing moved from the status of little more than a clerical function to a position as a full-fledged member of the corporate management team. It has emerged as an important strategic managerial function.

A study by *Purchasing World* magazine shows who is managing the business of buying in American industry today. This study is based on responses from more than 1,300 *Purchasing World* readers selected at random. It shows that the typical *Purchasing World* reader is an educated, experienced decision maker with wide-ranging responsibilities and authority. According to the findings, the typical *Purchasing World* reader:

- Attended college (69 percent). Nearly 10 percent of the respondents hold advanced degrees. The major field of study mentioned most often is business administration (60 percent); 14 percent of the respondents majored in engineering; 12 percent in liberal arts.

- Has about a dozen years of experience in the purchasing function. About half of the respondents have been in purchasing for more than 10 years.
- Has not generally spent all of his or her business career in purchasing. Other work cited by the respondents included production (38 percent), inventory control (37 percent), management (31 percent), and sales and marketing (24 percent).
- Is a member of company-wide committees, most often those concerned with cost reduction (75 percent), standardization (45 percent), and product design (28 percent).
- Earns, on the average, between $34,000 and $39,000, although the respondents encompassed a wide range of readers with varying levels of experience.

WHAT THEY DO

Fortune 500 corporations are pushing to upgrade the purchasing function even further. *Purchasing* magazine, a competitor of *Purchasing World,* recently examined how purchasing is changing and found that purchasing involvement in corporate affairs is expanding and that "professional purchasing now includes innovation in contracting and management methods, and the ability to sell new ideas." U.S. Steel (15), Corning Glass Works (217), and General Electric (10) now have a vice president of purchasing.

According to *Purchasing World,* "Purchasing is getting more involved in such areas as corporate strategy and long-range planning; long-term agreements with major suppliers in different parts of the world; research and negotiation on critical materials to assure continuity of supply; major studies on make or buy; and close coordination with vendors and user departments on significant quality problems."

By the early 1990s the majority of corporate purchasing departments will have additional responsibilities in the areas of packaging study and design review. A significant number will also be involved in new plant location.

Today's purchasing professionals, says *Purchasing World,* have "to distinguish between the strategic and tactical responsibilities of their departments and allocate time and effort to each according to its importance." The tactical responsibilities—placing orders, expediting, working with material control, checking vendor performance—are only half of the job. The other half is the strategic responsibilities—long-range planning, forecasting, maintaining engineering interface, negotiating major contracts, and setting goals and objectives. At Boise Cascade (105), for example, an all-out effort is being undertaken to involve purchasing in all of the management functions at their origin.

The *Purchasing World* survey of its readers sheds new light on the duties and responsibilities of today's purchasing manager. The findings show that the *Purchasing World* reader:

- Has over a dozen decision-making responsibilities, including the selection and evaluation of suppliers, the control of inventories, and the specification of the mode or carrier for outbound shipments. More than four out of five of the respondents specify the mode or carrier for inbound shipments.
- Spends more than $65 million a year for equipment, supplies, and services. One quarter of the respondents spend an average of close to $200 million annually.
- Works closely with other key functions, primarily production (82 percent) and top management (60 percent). Over half also work with finance.

In addition, the number of *Purchasing World* readers reporting directly to top management has increased by more than 10 percent.

THE CHANGING PICTURE OF PURCHASING

According to *Purchasing* magazine, "What purchasing is becoming more intensely with each passing year is a high-risk, high-visibility, high-gain field. It's an exciting, but increasingly perilous, place to be. One clear reason: the answers to virtually each and every one of business' biggest long-term problems depends on how well and smartly . . . professional buyers work with [their] most reliable vendors."

Purchasing is moving out of the corner of Fortune 500 corporations and into the mainstream. Appointments to top-level purchasing jobs in the industry are going to people with broad experience. There is an evolution toward more entrepreneurial leadership—more decision making—closer to the everyday operating level. Chief executive officers who were interviewed said that they were looking for purchasing types with a broad understanding of their own companies' long-range strategies, an acute awareness of how purchasing could contribute to those strategies, and the professional ability to make that contribution. Such is the case at Xerox (40), Eaton (107), and Pillsbury (80), among many other corporations.

Holleran observes that intense, expert, and comprehensive evaluation of suppliers continues to be a prime responsibility of purchasing. In the environment of the late 1980s and 1990s, says the purchasing vice-president of a top chemical producer, purchasing's charter means "more analysis, more study, more detail. You have to probe more deeply into all suppliers' qualifications. Purchasing agents need all the information they can get to evaluate vendors and make decisions as to whom they want to do business with." At Anheuser-Busch (51), purchasing personnel are expected to know the economics of supplying industries and to be aware of supplier capabilities and production problems. At other corporations, purchasing officials are playing a bigger role in new product development.

At a major aerospace corporation, the purchasing staff was restructured. The goal, says the new vice president for materials management, who spearheaded this initiative, was to "make our people professional managers of external manufacturing."

WHAT THEY LOOK FOR

The purchasing manager or executive can make or break any effort made by a Fortune 500 corporation to find and use qualified small business vendors. Small business purchasing coordinators are important contact points because they can put the purchasing department in touch with qualified small firms. "But it is the corporate purchaser," says Holleran, "who is responsible for hiring new vendors and suppliers, and small firms have to know what today's purchasing professionals seek."

Major corporations choose their vendors and suppliers with care, to obtain a good "fit" of products and processes. Life of the program contracts used by such companies as Amdahl (348) and corporate-sponsored vendor training signal an era in which supplier dependability is an element upon which purchasing departments rely. Unfortunately, a growing number of Fortune 500 purchasing departments, such as those of Xerox (40) and Air Products and Chemicals (205), are involved in major pushes to do business with fewer, higher-quality, more reliable suppliers. Approximately one third of corporate purchasing departments want to pare down their vendor list. Nevertheless, vast opportunities exist for resourceful vendors. Corporate top brass at such companies as Digital Equipment (55), Honeywell (56), and Corning Glass Works (217) wants suppliers with innovative ideas and the financial strength to implement them.

Vendor performance, in all its aspects, is purchasing's major concern today. Key performance factors include:

- Quality of purchased items.
- Lead times.
- Communication between supplier and buyer.
- Vendor representatives' level of knowledge and technical expertise.

Of these factors, *demonstrated* quality and reliability are by far the most important. In the past, cost reduction may have been the overriding concern for many corporate purchasing managers, but no longer. At an annual conference of the National Association of Purchasing Management, this message came through loud and clear. One speaker, vice president for a leading international telecommunications corporation, said, "If you don't demand the best from your suppliers, your company won't end up with the best product. That vendor is part of your company when it is supplying parts or services. You are the link with this critical area of supply, and you are responsible for the quality."

Philip Kotler observes that the purchasing office or buying center often draws up a list of desired supplier attributes and their relative importance. In selecting a chemical supplier, a buying center listed the following attributes in order of importance:

1. Technical support services.
2. Prompt delivery.
3. Quick response to customer needs.
4. Product quality.
5. Supplier reputation.
6. Product price.
7. Complete product line.
8. Sales representatives' caliber.
9. Extension of credit.
10. Personal relationships.
11. Literature and manuals.

Kotler says that the members of the buying center will rate the suppliers against these attributes and will identify the most attractive suppliers.

Buyers may attempt to negotiate with the preferred suppliers for better prices and terms, according to Kotler, before making the final selection. In the end, they may select a single supplier or a few suppliers. Many buyers prefer multiple sources of supply so that they will not be totally dependent on one supplier if something goes wrong and so that they will be able to compare the prices and performance of the various suppliers.

Quality-conscious buyers will want to see references on the general business ability of the small business vendor. Some buyers will want to visit the plant or facility of any new supplier.

Surprisingly, over 75 percent of purchasing agents are still not using computers in the vendor rating systems for either plant visits or contract performance. This situation will change rapidly in the next few years.

Understanding how the world of the purchasing professional works is an important step on the road to marketing prosperity in dealing with Fortune 500 firms. If you can put yourself in the purchasing manager's shoes, the trip can be a lot easier than you might expect!

THE PURCHASING HIERARCHY

Here is the typical hierarchy of positions within a corporate purchasing department, according to the National Association of Purchasing Management.

Vice President or Director of Purchasing

The vice president or director of purchasing is often on a par with other corporate VPs in marketing, administration, plant and operations, and finance. This is the top-ranked purchasing position, and it is primarily an administrator's position.

The head of a purchasing department (regardless of the title) is a member of the management team in the company. He or she has a multitude of major responsibilities and policies to supervise and administer.

Manager of Purchasing

The number and kinds of duties assigned to a manager of purchasing will depend to a considerable extent on the level of management to which he or she is assigned. In most companies, the manager of purchasing functions at two levels. He or she does some buying and, at the same time, supervises the buying activities of subordinates. In the capacity of supervisor over buyers and assistant purchasing managers, the manager is responsible for their training and development.

Procurement Engineer

The duties of a procurement engineer are to analyze technical data, design preliminary specifications, and appraise manufacturing limitations, suppliers' facilities, and the availability of materials and equipment. The procurement engineer consults with engineering personnel to establish performance criteria and construction and test specifications.

The procurement engineer investigates equipment makers and interviews supplier representatives regarding specifications, costs, inspection, and similar matters. The procurement engineer arranges and participates in conferences between suppliers and engineers, purchasers, inspectors, and other personnel to facilitate material inspection, substitution, standardization, rework, salvage, and utilization and the economical procurement of equipment.

Purchasing Analyst

The duties of a purchasing analyst are to compile and analyze statistical data to determine the feasibility of buying products, to establish price objectives for contract transactions, and to keep informed on price trends and manufacturing processes. The purchasing analyst obtains data for cost analysis studies, confers with suppliers, and analyzes suppliers' operations to determine the factors that affect prices.

Expediter

The duties of an expediter, in companies where such a position has been established, depend largely on the method of expediting and on the degree of expediting employed. The expediter's job is either to speed up delivery from suppliers or to see that suppliers adhere to the delivery commitments they have made. In many companies, the job of the expediter is basically clerical, involving the maintenance of an adequate set of tickler files and the follow-up of purchase orders to secure acceptances of the order and delivery date promises.

Traffic Manager

The traffic function is occasionally assigned as a subdivision of the purchasing department. Traffic management deals primarily with the problems inherent in securing delivery of purchased materials.

Buyer

A buyer may perform one or more of the following duties in connection with the purchase of raw materials, components, or finished parts (chemicals, paper and board, office equipment and supplies, printing, electrical and electronics equipment and supplies, building supplies, metals, pipe and fittings, various services, etc.):

1. Edits requisitions and confers with departments regarding specifications, quantity and quality of merchandise, and delivery requirements. Recommends substitutes where a savings in cost and improved delivery will result.
2. Solicits and analyzes quotations for new or nonstandard items. Negotiates with suppliers to obtain the most favorable terms of purchase. Recommends or approves awarding of contracts or purchase orders, ensuring that all purchases comply with government regulations and accepted trade practices.
3. Interviews suppliers and their representatives personally and maintains close contact by correspondence, telephone, and plant visits.
4. Arranges with appropriate subcontractors to fabricate special equipment to company blueprints. Checks blueprints to ensure freedom from accidental errors and completeness of information so that the subcontractors can comply with special requirements.
5. Carries out necessary follow-up and expediting activities to ensure delivery as required by production schedules.
6. Serves in an advisory capacity to assist other departments in obtaining proper specifications, quotations, delivery terms, and cost.
7. May examine and approve all invoices covering purchase orders placed.
8. Handles adjustments with suppliers involving replacement of materials not conforming to purchase specifications, return of material declared surplus as a result of engineering changes, cancellation of orders, and so on; prepares shipping orders and ensures that appropriate credit is received.
9. Maintains an appropriate file of catalogs, price lists, and so on to assist departments in obtaining the latest information on new products.

In many Fortune 500 corporations, the duties of buyers call for highly trained specialists who buy a narrow range of commodities. According to the National Association of Purchasing Management, there may be several categories of buying, including general products buying, construction buying, production materials and components buying, raw materials and commodities buying, and governmental and institutional buying.

Buyer Categories

1. General Products Buyer.   The buying of general products is characterized by the handling of a wide range of materials, generally of low unit value, which may include maintenance materials, tools, spare parts, and operating supplies. This is likely to be the first buying assignment given to the novice buyer in the larger company.

2. Construction Buyer.   Construction buying is at the opposite extreme from general products buying in terms of the responsibilities involved. A construction buyer handles the negotiations for buildings and facilities and the procurement of major items of equipment. This type of buying position is likely to be found only in the larger companies.

In general, personnel assigned to construction buying are far removed from other categories of buyers. This is not the beginner's assignment. Almost universally, companies require a college education for this type of assignment. In many cases, such assignments go to engineering graduates.

3. Production Materials and Components Buyer.   Production materials and components include items purchased to the user's specifications and design for incorporation into the final product. The buyer of such items must have a wide knowledge of processing and manufacturing techniques. In many instances, companies assign subcontracting negotiations to such buyers.

4. Raw Materials and Commodities Buyer.   Buyers in this category are generally specialists. In many cases, such buyers may even be members of the executive group of the company. This might be the case where the basic raw material constitutes a substantial portion of the company's total purchases, as with grain buying by flour millers and the buying of hides by tanneries. In many companies, the volume of purchases of the basic raw material is so great that no other buying is assigned to the person who buys it. An example would be the coal buyer for a large electric utility.

Successful buyers in this category must be able to study and forecast market trends and general business conditions. The position of raw materials and commodities buyer calls for a college graduate in either the technical or business field and possibly an MBA.

5. Governmental and Institutional Buyer.   The individual seeking a career in governmental and institutional purchasing will find that the type of work, the qualifications, and the opportunities are much the same as those for purchasing positions with industrial firms.

GETTING "INSIDE" PURCHASING: INFORMATION SOURCES ABOUND

"Once an entrepreneur gets comfortable with a strong set of business contacts," observes Holleran, "it is possible for him or her to begin lagging in a very important aspect of small business growth—new business prospecting. New business prospecting should remain a top priority on any entrepreneur's task list, no matter how reliable existing contacts are."

New business prospecting (see Chapter 4) is the most difficult and arduous part of selling. However, it can also be the most rewarding part. You can begin by canvassing buyers and customers with whom you are currently doing business, or with whom you have previously done business, and ask for names of buyers representing large firms that you wish to solicit. The referral approach is a more personal approach than prospecting and it eliminates some of the rigors involved in prospecting. Purchasing agents, for example, can put you in touch with key engineering and technical personnel (see Chapter 9) who generate the work requirements.

Having "inside" information on purchasing opportunities is the key to staying ahead of the competition. Surprisingly, the inside information you want is not hidden away in corporate files. It is readily available, says Holleran, at nominal cost, in the form of purchasing magazines, journals, and handbooks.

Purchasing Periodicals

Here are the leading trade periodicals read by purchasing managers. You should be reading them too. As a purchaser yourself, you qualify as a subscriber to those offered at no charge.

Purchasing Subscription Form

Purchasing

Free Subscription/Change of Address Form

Please answer all questions, **sign and date the card.**
Incomplete forms cannot be processed or acknowledged.
The publisher reserves the right to serve only those individuals who meet the publication qualifications.

PUR-460

A Please send/continue to send free copies of
Purchasing magazine   Yes ☐ No ☐

X _____
YOUR SIGNATURE (REQUIRED)   date

Your name (please print) _____

Title (please print) _____ (   ) _____
                                business phone

B For change of address—Please make changes on label
and affix below.

┌─── **Please Affix Label Within This Box** ───┐

company name

division   department

mailing address

city   state   zip code
└──┘

C Is the above your home address?   Yes ☐ No ☐

D If your title is not a purchasing title, is purchasing
your function?   1 ☐ Yes   2 ☐ No

E Number of purchasing professionals with buying authority
at this location. (Check 1 box)
3 ☐ 1-2   4 ☐ 3-5   5 ☐ 6-9   6 ☐ 10-19
7 ☐ 20-49   8 ☐ 50-99   9 ☐ 100+

F What is your level of authority? (Check 1 box)
10 ☐ I am primarily a manager
11 ☐ I have some management authority
12 ☐ I have a staff position

G Name and title of the individual to whom the Purchasing
department reports:

13/ _____ 14/ _____
   name   title

H Approximate number of employees at this location.
(Check 1 box)
15 ☐ 1000+   17 ☐ 500-999 19 ☐ 250-499
16 ☐ 100-249 18 ☐ 50-99   20 ☐ 20-49   21 ☐ 1-19

I What is the primary end product manufactured
(or service performed) at this location? (Be specific)

If this is a manufacturing company and there is no
manufacturing at this location, check if:
25 ☐ Central or District Administrative Office
26 ☐ Research Laboratory   28 ☐ Warehouse
27 ☐ Sales Office   29 ☐ Other

Please do not write above this line.

J 1. In the performance of my job, I buy or supervise the buying
of the following products or services: (check all that apply)
2. Please also check if you buy some or all the products
through a distributor:

Buy or supervise the buying of:	Buy some or all through distributors	(Check one or both)
30 ☐	53 ☐	Assembly Components
31 ☐	54 ☐	Chemicals
32 ☐	55 ☐	Electronic components, Equipment and supplies
33 ☐	56 ☐	Electrical equipment and supplies (motors, switches, batteries)
34 ☐	57 ☐	Hydraulic, pneumatic & fluidic equipment & supplies (hose pumps compressors)
35 ☐	58 ☐	Instruments (measuring, metering and recording)
36 ☐	59 ☐	Lubricants & other petroleum products
37 ☐	60 ☐	Materials handling equipment and supplies (trucks, conveyors, hoists)
38 ☐	61 ☐	Mechanical parts (stampings, springs, forgings)
39 ☐	62 ☐	Non-ferrous metals (aluminum, brass)
40 ☐	63 ☐	Non-metallic materials except chemicals, petroleum and plastic products (rubber, glass)
41 ☐	64 ☐	Computers, peripherals, software
42 ☐	65 ☐	Office/business machines and equipment
43 ☐	66 ☐	Furniture, filing systems office
44 ☐	67 ☐	Office and business supplies
45 ☐	68 ☐	Packaging (cartons, labeling, strapping)
46 ☐	69 ☐	Plant & personnel health or safety equipment & supplies (clothing, towels, eyewear)
47 ☐	70 ☐	Plant services & facilities (lighting, manual valves, energy)
48 ☐	71 ☐	Plastics (materials, parts, resins)
49 ☐	72 ☐	Power transmission products (V-belts, gears, bearings)
50 ☐	73 ☐	Production equipment (power tools, cutting tools, welding)
51 ☐	74 ☐	Steel and other ferrous metals
52 ☐	75 ☐	Other (please describe) 76 _____

I have no responsibility to buy or
supervise the buying of any of the
products or services listed above. 77 ☐

Do not buy through distributors 78 ☐

K In the performance of my job, I specify, recommend,
approve or purchase the following transportation
services: (Check all that apply)
80 ☐ Motor freight   83 ☐ Package express service
81 ☐ Rail carriers   84 ☐ International transportation
82 ☐ Air freight   85 ☐ Other transportation services
                    86 ☐ None of the above

L Check the publications below that you personally receive.
90 ☐ Business Week   93 ☐ Electronic Buyers News
91 ☐ Industry Week   94 ☐ Iron Age
92 ☐ Purchasing World
              95 ☐ None of the above

M 99 ☐ Check here if you do not wish to receive
promotional mail from Purchasing.

Reprinted with permission from *Purchasing* magazine.

Purchasing (every two weeks), Cahners Publications, 270 St. Paul Street, Denver, CO 80206.

Purchasing World (monthly), 6521 Davis Industrial Parkway, Solon, OH 44139.

Industry Week (weekly), Penton Publishing, 1111 Chester Avenue, Cleveland, OH 44114.

Industrial Distribution (monthly), Technical Publishing, 875 3rd Avenue, New York, NY 10022.

Purchasing Digest (monthly), Gordon Publications, 13 Emery Avenue, Randolph, NJ 07869.

Business Marketing, Crain Communications, 740 Rush Street, Chicago, IL 60611.

Distribution (monthly), Chilton Company, Chilton Way, Radnor, PA 19089.

Industrial Management (monthly), Institute of Industrial Engineers, 25 Technology Park, Norcross, GA 30092.

Industrial Purchasing Agent (monthly), Publications for Industry, 21 Russell Woods, Great Neck, NY 11021.

Handling and Shipping Management (monthly and twice in September), Penton Publishing, 1111 Chester Avenue, Cleveland, OH 44114.

Journal of Purchasing and Materials Management (quarterly), National Association of Purchasing Management, 496 Kinderkamack Road, Oradell, NJ 07649.

Industrial Development (bimonthly), 40 Technology Park, Norcross, GA 30092.

These publications contain articles with inside information directed toward purchasing professionals. You will find material on how vendors are found, vendor evaluations, negotiation tactics, purchasing law, and other purchasing management tips. The November 6, 1986 issue of *Purchasing,* in particular, is worth its weight in gold. The issue provides detailed information on the volume of purchases made by "the 100 largest buying shops in industrial America."

In addition, many issues spotlight purchasing programs and people at major corporations. Over the past few years, for example, *Purchasing* or *Purchasing World* ran in-depth features on Chrysler (13), Alcoa (69), Olin (195), U.S. Steel (15), Eaton (107), Xerox (40), Westinghouse Electric (32), General Motors (1), Tektronix (245), and many other large corporations. These articles, a veritable "Who's Who" of corporate purchasing executives, can be a gold mine of marketing contacts.

There are regional purchasing periodicals published by affiliates of the National Association of Purchasing Management that can help you keep current on issues and opportunities "closer to home." Titles and addresses of regional publications are presented in the accompanying box.

Purchasing Handbooks

Small business entrepreneurs who really want to immerse themselves in what makes the purchasing professional tick can obtain one or more of the many purchasing management handbooks. Here is a sampling of what is available:

Purchasing Negotiations. By C. Wayne Barlow and Glen P. Eisen. 1983. Van Nostrand Reinhold, 115 5th Avenue, New York, NY 10003.

The Buyer and the Law. By C. Wayne Barlow. 1982. Van Nostrand Reinhold, 115 5th Avenue, New York, NY 10003.

Purchasing and Materials Management: Integrated Strategies. By Joseph L. Cavinato. 1984. West Publishing, 50 West Kellogg Boulevard, St. Paul, MN 55166.

Purchasing and Materials Management: Texts and Cases. By Dean D. Dobler and Lemar Lee. 1984. McGraw-Hill, 1221 Avenue of the Americas, New York, NY 10020.

Basic for Buyers: A Practical Guide to Better Purchasing. By Somerby R. Dowst. 1971. Van Nostrand Reinhold, 115 5th Avenue, New York, NY 10003.

Purchasing: Principles and Applications. By Stuart F. Heinritz and Paul V. Ferroow. 1981. Prentice-Hall, Englewood Cliffs, NJ 07632.

Purchasing Management. By John Howard Westing. 4th ed., 1976. John Wiley & Sons, Somerset, NJ 08873.

Guide to Purchasing. Volume IV, 1986, National Association of Purchasing Management, 496 Kinderkamack Road, Oradell, NJ 07469.

Purchasing and Materials Management. By Lawrence D. Miles. 2nd ed., 1972. McGraw-Hill, 1221 Avenue of the Americas, New York, NY 10020.

Purchasing Principles and Techniques. By P. J. H. Bailey and D. Farmer. 1971. Pitman Publishing, 6 East 43rd Street, New York, NY 10017.

Purchasing Handbook. By George W. Aljian. 1973. McGraw-Hill, 1221 Avenue of the Americas, New York, NY 10020.

Purchasing Management—Materials in Motion. By J. H. Westing, I. V. Fine, and G. J. Zenz. 4th ed., 1976. John Wiley & Sons, Somerset, NJ 08873.

Profitable Purchasing Management: A Guide for Small Business Owners—Managers. By William Messner, 1982. AMACOM, 135 West 50th Street, New York, NY 10020.

REGIONAL PURCHASING PERIODICALS

Alabama Purchasor
P. O. Box 11506
Birmingham, AL 35202

Arizona Purchaser
1132 East Laurel Drive
Casa Grande, AZ 85222

Chicago Purchasor
201 North Wells Street, #824
Chicago, IL 60606

Cincinnati Purchasor
1001 East Linden, #19
Miamisburg, OH 45342

Columbus Area P.M.A.
% Bonded Scale and Machine Company
P.O. Box 27069
Columbus, OH 43227

Empire Niagara Purchaser
Purchaser N.Y. State
Purchasing Professional
1552 Hertel Avenue
Buffalo, NY 14216

Florida Purchaser
P.O. Box 1858
Jacksonville, FL 32201

Heart of America Purchaser
912 Baltimore Avenue, #900
Kansas City, MO 64105

Hoosier Purchasor
6100 North Keystone Avenue, #527
Indianapolis, IN 46220

Kentuckiana Purchasor
P.O. Box 35428
Louisville, KY 40232

Maryland Purchasing and Materials Management
6600 York Road, #109
Baltimore, MD 21212

Metropolitan Purchasor
% White Eagle, Inc.
2550 Kuser Road
P.O. Box 8307
Trenton, NJ 08650

Mid-Atlantic Purchasing
1342 Easton Road
Roslyn, PA 19001

Mid-South Purchasor
% Sperry-Vickers
P.O. Box 10177
Jackson, MI 39206

Milwaukee Buylines
% Red Carpet Leisure Industries
4747 South Howell Avenue
Milwaukee, WI 53207

Midwest Purchasing
1127 Euclid Avenue, #970
Cleveland, OH 44115

New England Purchaser
Connecticut Purchaser
185 Devonshire Street
Boston, MA 01220

New Golden West Purchasor
% Illustrated Features Corporation
P.O. Box 4000
Palos Verdes Peninsula, CA 90274

Northwest Purchaser
P.O. Box 1293
Spokane, WA 99210

Orange Empire Purchasing Manager
1695 Crescent Street, #663
Anaheim, CA 92801

Oregon Purchasor
5331 Southwest Macadam, #224
Portland, OR 97201

Pacific Purchasor
% Polar Publications
6090 West Pico Blvd.
Los Angeles, CA 90035

Pittsburgh Purchaser
% Community College of Allegheny County
610 Smithfield Street
Pittsburgh, PA 15222

Purchasing Management
% Bolger Publications, Inc.
3301 Como Avenue, S.E.
Minneapolis, MN 55414

Rock River Valley Newsletter
% W. A. Whitney Corporation
650 Race Street
Rockford, IL 61105

Southern Purchasor
P.O. Box Drawer V2
Greensboro, NC 27402

Southwest Purchasing
13531 North Central Expwy, #2020
Dallas, TX 75243

St. Louis Purchasor
% Admore Publishing Company
9701 Gravois Avenue
St. Louis, MO 63123

Washington Purchaser
% Murray Publishing Company
2313 3rd Avenue
Seattle, WA 98121

Yankee Purchaser
P.O. Box 924
Springfield, MA 01101

A useful guidebook for purchasing managers, *Practical Purchasing Management,* was published in 1984 by the editors of *Purchasing World* magazine. *Practical Purchasing Management* is a collection of article reprints, updated as needed, on a wide variety of purchasing management topics. This book covers the world of purchasing from the vantage point of those who know it best—the people who do it. Here are some of the topics of interest to small vendors:

- How to make suppliers justify cost increases.
- Checking the legal angle before buying.
- Improving buyer-seller relationships.
- Checking vendor financial reports.
- A look at purchasing from the outside in.
- How vendors rate purchasers.
- Why does it cost what it costs?
- Straight talk about purchasing ethics.
- Negotiation of sole-source items.
- Are you getting a fair value—or just low price?
- Expect more, get more, from suppliers.

Practical Purchasing Management can be obtained from *Purchasing World* magazine, 801 South Northwest Highway, Barrington, IL 60010. Another handy guide is *How Industry Buys,* which discusses how 15 progressive corporations do their buying. To order, write to *Purchasing* magazine, 221 Columbus Avenue, Boston, MA 02116.

Vendors with erudition and experience with corporate purchasing systems stand the best chance of accelerating their marketing efforts.

Local "Inside" Information

On a local basis, remember to consider business clubs such as the Chamber of Commerce, Rotary, and Kiwanis. These clubs generally have directories of members and their business affiliations. Join one of them, or at least get invited to one or several of the meetings. The weekly or monthly meetings of such clubs provide excellent opportunities to meet prospects and arrange for new business presentations on an informal basis. Such functions, if they are open to outside professionals, offer good opportunities to meet with local buyers. Also be on the lookout for directories of corporate purchasers in your region.

Look to those professionals who look to you for new prospects. Check with your insurance salesman for the names of executives of large firms in your area. Lawyers, stockbrokers, and consultants can all be useful in gaining inside information.

In summary, you and your company can get *very close* to the people who manage the busines of buying goods and services for the Fortune 500.

CHAPTER NINE

Calling on Corporations

*Our main business is not
to see what lies dimly at
a distance, but to do what
lies clearly at hand.*

THOMAS CARLYLE

Every vendor takes a series of steps to procure contacts with large corporations. The most critical of these steps is the meeting with the purchasing manager or other corporate representatives. At this one-on-one meeting, observes Vic Morris, you can "bring it all together" or watch a marketing opportunity fall apart. It is important to send experienced, mature sales representatives, particularly when dealing with purchasing agents who are responsible for buying millions of dollars of goods and services each year.

An unprofessional, poorly planned sales presentation can impair your company's image and restrict the size and frequency of contracts and purchase orders, even though you may be able to provide precisely the goods and services that are being sought.

CALLING ON PURCHASING AGENTS

Let's focus on the elements—the five *P*'s—for successfully calling on purchasing agents: preparation, professionalism, presentation, proof, and performance.

Preparation

Establishing productive business relationships with new customers is indeed a challenging task. Time is a valuable commodity for purchasing managers at most large corporations, and their first impressions of potential vendors are important.

The key to most triumphant presentations is advance preparation.

First, review all of the pertinent information about the prospect that you can get your hands on, including annual and quarterly corporate reports, product and service pamphlets, vendor guides, other company brochures, and industry information (see Chapter 7). Later, when making your presentation, you can refer to some of these items.

Next, identify and define the prospect's needs—to the extent possible—before shaping your presentation. Is the prospect coming off a profitable quarter and planning to expand? Is the prospect seeking to reduce inventories and costs? Is just-in-time (JIT) delivery preferable? What is the prospect's highest priority at this time—quality upgrades? low price?

Many Fortune 500 corporations designate the days of the week on which buyers are available for appointments. It is important to state in your letter or phone call to the buyer that you intend to make a new business presentation and would welcome the presence of any other company personnel. Suggest a time and date for a meeting.

If writing, include with your letter a brochure, pamphlet, or other printed materials that favorably reflect your firm's capabilities. If telephoning, offer to mail one of your promotional materials. Many buyers will immediately ask for these.

When you call, be prepared to appropriately direct the receptionist. Spread out in front of you the company information and keep track of the people with whom you speak. Should the receptionist suggest that you speak with Mr. Q, with whom you have already spoken, you will be able to point this out and eliminate wasting any more time with the wrong party. It is also useful to keep a record of the names of your contacts, because you may be talking with these people again. The annual report or vendors guide is a good place to note these names.

Marketing consultant Arnold Sanow, with the Business Source, suggests that you may want to have a staff person handle the preliminary steps and the exploratory telephone calls. This will save you time in identifying and locating the "right" person. After "the groundwork has been completed," says Sanow, you can then place the important marketing call to the appropriate purchasing agent.

Specify the amount of time that you would like the buyer to allocate for your presentation. Some buyers place strict time limits on appointments and new business presentations. Choosing an odd amount of time may prove extremely effective—after all, how many purchasing agents are told, "My presentation will require 17 minutes"? In any case, it is important to clarify beforehand the amount of time that will be available to you.

As the meeting time approaches, even more effort must be made on preparation. You can offer the best product or service in the world, but you must be able to convince the purchasing manager. Elise M. Giebel, advertising and public relations manager for the Centennial Development Corporation, advises meeting Fortune 500 purchasing agents on their own level. Centennial, a commercial real estate development firm that works with Sperry (63), Planning Research Corporation, and other major corporations, regards itself as the IBM of commercial real estate and stresses this in its presentation. Giebel says, "We want every contact we make to convey a high degree of professionalism, quality, and service. Our presentations are carefully tailored to the prospect."

Practice—with your staff, or on a tape recorder—so that ultimately you can make each presentation an "award-winning effort."

This type of preparation naturally leads you to consider the second *P*—professionalism.

Professionalism

The first meeting with a purchasing agent is usually accompanied by some anxiety. Confirm your appointment one day in advance by telephone. On meeting day, plan an early arrival at the plant or corporate headquarters. Use any extra time to collect your thoughts and to review your presentation while you sit in your car. Make critical checks. Is your briefcase organized so that you can easily obtain any documents you need?

Enter the meeting with confidence, enthusiasm, and drive, but never overpower a prospect. Jay Jaffe, chair of the Greater Washington Board of Trade Communication Division and president of Jay Jaffe Associates, marketing and public relations, typifies an effective "rainmaker." Jaffe arrives at meetings with energy and humor, nonstressed, *and* ready for business.

Dress for success, be well rested, and keep your mind clear of distractions. *Arrive at least five minutes early.* Richard Levy, who regularly sells to Fortune 500 companies, says, "The first several minutes, indeed seconds, of your encounter are crucial. We humans often form lasting impressions of someone based on our first impressions."

Presentation

Feeling and looking like a professional will produce results only if you have planned a professional presentation. The presentation should be

A Self-Analysis of Your Professional Image

A. How you believe others see you.
B. How you would like to be seen.

Prospects	*Present Customers/Clients*
Corporate Purchasing Agents	*Corporate Purchasing Agents*
A.	A.
B.	B.
Engineering, Technical Staff	*Engineering, Technical Staff*
A.	A.
B.	B.
Small Vendor Coordinator	*Small Vendor Coordinator*
A.	A.
B.	B.

brief but thorough. Mentally rehearse what you will say. A good guide on presentations is *An Executive's Guide to Meetings, Conferences, and Audiovisual Presentations,* by James R. Jeffries and Jefferson O. Bates (New York: McGraw-Hill, 1983).

Establish a common ground with your prospect. Some very brief small talk is a good icebreaker. Mention the name of one of your customers with whom you think the buyer might be familiar.

Consider using samples, audiovisual aids such as pictures, or a simple slide presentation. If the purchasing manager has never seen your location or met your personnel, he or she may appreciate such an approach. But the purchasing manager's major interest will be in how you can fulfill his or her buying needs. Since, increasingly, the buyer-vendor relationship is being looked upon as a long-term partnership, demonstrate that you are a vendor of caliber. Your chief task is to leave no doubt in the purchasing manager's mind that you can deliver.

Successful speaker and author Nido Qubien, who has done hundreds of thousands of dollars in business with Fortune 500 companies, believes that the ability to ask "good" questions is helpful in presentations, in sales situations, and in dealing with people in general. Intuitively, we know that it's important to ask the "right" questions. In many cases, it's better to ask "who, what, when, where, why, and how" questions rather than "yes–no" questions. Qubien advocates asking provocative, answerable questions that will provide information, clarification, or agreement. It's helpful to include the word *you* in questions (e.g., "What do *you* think about this?" "How did that work for *you?*" "What has been *your* experience in this area?" "How do *you* feel about . . .?").

"Good questions arise from our curiosity" says Qubien, "but be careful about the challenging" questions. It's tempting to point out to others where their logic is faulty, yet we know that it's better to enable them to shift their position, and save face, by skillfully asking self-enlightening questions.

Here's a checklist developed by Vic Morris to ensure that you turn in a superior performance during your presentation:

- *Be clear about your objectives.* Are you trying to close a sale on a specific item on this initial call, or are you seeking to make a contact and crystallize the buyer's needs?
- *Articulate the potential matches* between the buyer's needs and your goods and services. Be precise and clear about these matches.
- *Emphasize quality.* Generally speaking, quality goods and services are the highest priorities for purchasing managers. Give specific examples of your quality control procedures.
- *Focus on dependability.* Emphasize your commitment to timely and reliable delivery. Describe your warranty and liability protection benefits, if any. Mention how your dependability has helped customers.
- *Highlight your cost competitiveness.* Be prepared to justify your costs and the prices you charge with specific data. A simple cost-value

analysis on previous jobs should reveal cost-cutting factors and demonstrate your ability to minimize waste and rework.

- *Be specific about your contracting procedures.* Include a sample of your standard sales agreement, if appropriate.
- *Use visuals and other materials* to support your oral presentation. Graphs are an effective way to illustrate growth in sales revenues or increased production performance. If well done, brochures that describe your corporate capabilities lend an aura of professionalism to your business. However, there is no need to go overboard on audiovisuals.
- *Be positive, enthusiastic, and responsive* to the customer's wishes during the presentation. Be sensitive to the buyer's needs at all times; don't waste his or her time on topics about which no interest is indicated. Be prepared to answer questions during your presentation. Solicit additional questions at the end of your prepared remarks.

If possible, bring along one or two of your key employees who would be working on the prospective customer's account. They can answer specific questions and help establish the rapport necessary for good customer relations.

Conclude your presentation by establishing the steps for future action. Will you get a price quotation to the buyer by a specific date? Will you invite the buyer to tour your facility? Or will you call within a week to follow up the presentation? The mark of supersellers is follow-up; the mark of the majority of would-be suppliers is lack of follow-up.

Gauge whether the buyer is merely seeking bid quotes for a pricing decision or is exploring other purchasing issues as well. This will help you focus your remarks on his or her needs.

Two final steps should be taken within a day or two of your actual presentation:

- *Assess your presentation.* Create a "lessons learned" list—itemize what went well in the presentation and what needs to be changed in future presentations.
- *Write a follow-up letter* thanking the buyer for meeting with you and identifying what you plan to do next for him or her (see section on "Performance" below).

The first impression that you create is indeed critical. Unless the buyer is impressed with *you* personally and with the company you represent, he or she may never follow up the presentation with further qualification activities. As a result, he or she may never find out how good a product or service your company can deliver.

Proof

Although only a few words are needed in regard to proof, they are important ones. During your meeting with the purchasing manager, you must be prepared to *document* your company's ability to produce (see Chapter 6). A brochure, folder, or capability statement that describes what you can do is helpful. It can be bolstered by:

- Letters of recommendation and testimonials.
- References.
- Notices of certification.
- Certified capability statements.
- Copies of recent awards.

Performance

The fifth *P,* performance, relates not only to how you fulfill your contract but also to how you perform before the contract has been drawn up. The notes you took during your meeting form the base of the outline for your follow-up letter. That letter should:

- Review important points covered during the meeting.
- Provide answers to any questions that required research.
- Confirm actions that were agreed upon.

When the purchasing agent receives your letter, he or she will remember the meeting and will recognize that you are someone who follows through on details. Never promise more than you can deliver. If a purchasing agent begins to expect more than your company is capable of doing, let the truth be known; maintain your integrity. It is better to promise and deliver on a small or medium order than to overpromise on a large one and ruin your firm's reputation.

Some—not many—purchasing managers consciously use intimidation tactics. They may do this because they want to see how you handle yourself under pressure, or they may simply have very little time available. Your preparation and professional follow-through will give you a decided

---

CHECKLIST FOR CALLING ON A PURCHASING AGENT

Preparation

- ☐ Review the corporation's annual report, newsletters, vendor guides, etc.
- ☐ Identify and define the prospective buyer's needs.
- ☐ Phone or write for appointment.

Professionalism

- ☐ Confirm the appointment.
- ☐ Arrive at the plant early and become comfortable.
- ☐ Organize briefcase, documents, and notebook or pad.
- ☐ Check appearance.
- ☐ Arrive at the appropriate office five minutes early.

Presentation

- ☐ Plan a brief, but thorough, presentation.
- ☐ Rehearse.
- ☐ Use samples or simple audiovisual aids.
- ☐ Ask good questions.
- ☐ Listen attentively.
- ☐ Be positive.
- ☐ Assess your presentation.
- ☐ Use your meeting notes for a follow-up letter.

Proof

- ☐ Provide documentation on your firm's capability.

Performance

- ☐ Write a follow-up letter immediately.
- ☐ Prepare to repeat this cycle.

---

edge in handling such tougher situations. And that may give you an edge on getting the contract!

Here are the addresses of some 200 purchasing departments from Fortune 500 firms as well as other major corporations and nonmanufacturing organizations.

200 CORPORATE PURCHASING ADDRESSES

Purchasing
Vulcan Materials Company (309)
P.O. Box 7497
Birmingham, AL 35253
(205) 877-3000

Corporate Small Business Director
Northrop Corporation (71)
One Northrop Avenue
Dept. 6002/32
Hawthorne, CA 90250
(213) 970-6745

Purchasing Manager
Todd Shipyards Corporation (462)
710 North Front Street
P.O. Box 231
San Pedro, CA 90731
(213) 832-3361

Purchasing Department
Kaiser Aluminum Corp. (143)
300 Lakeside Drive
Oakland, CA 94643
(415) 271-3057

Purchasing Manager
Levi Strauss & Co. (148)
1155 Battery Street
San Francisco, CA 94106
(415) 544-6637

Purchasing Department
Litton Industries, Inc. (82)
360 North Crescent Drive
Beverly Hills, CA 90210
(213) 273-7860

Director, Employee Relations
Carnation Company
5045 Wilshire Boulevard
Los Angeles, CA 90036
(213) 932-6000

Small Business Coordinator
Hewlett-Packard Company (58)
3000 Hanover Street
Palo Alto, CA 94304
(414) 857-2796

Director of Purchasing
National Semiconductor (209)
2900 Semiconductor Drive
Santa Clara, CA 95051
(408) 721-6371

Central Purchasing Manager
Varian Associates, Inc. (311)
611 Hansen Way
Building 4A, MS, E-066
Palo Alto, CA 94303
(414) 493-4000, ext. 2442

Purchasing Department
Intel Corporation (251)
3065 Bowers Avenue
Santa Clara, CA 95051
(408) 987-8080

Purchasing Department
Hughes Aircraft Company
Building C2/B156
P.O. Box 1042
El Segundo, CA 90245
(213) 414-6059

Director of Purchasing
Teledyne, Inc. (122)
1901 Avenue of the Stars
Los Angeles, CA 90067
(213) 277-3311

Small Business and Economic
  Utilization
Rockwell International (30)
Dept. 067, Mail Code (ZE02)
P.O. Box 92098
Los Angeles, CA 90009
(213) 414-3954

Manager of Purchasing
Crown Zellerbach Corp. (128)
1 Bush Street
San Francisco, CA 94104
(415) 951-5575

Purchasing Manager
Transamerica Insurance Corporation
  of California
1150 South Olive
Los Angeles, CA 90015
(213) 742-2715

Purchasing Department
Lockheed Aircraft Corp. (36)
P.O. Box 551
Burbank, CA 91520
(818) 847-3448

Manager, Purchasing
Liquid Air Corporation of America
  (441)
1 Embarcadero Center
San Francisco, CA 94111
(415) 765-4500

Monfort, Inc. (241)
P.O. Box 6
Greeley, CO 80632
(303) 353-2311

Regional Purchasing
Stauffer Chemical Company
Nyala Farms Road
Westport, CT 06881
(203) 222-4132

Director of Purchasing
Lone Star Industries, Inc. (346)
P.O. Box 2550
Greenwich, CT 06836
(203) 661-3100

Director, Champion International
  Corporation (62)
1 Champion Plaza
Stamford, CT 06921
(203) 358-7000

Purchasing Manager
Amax, Inc. (183)
P.O. Box 1700
Greenwich, CT 06830
(203) 629-7041

Director, Procurement and
  Transportation
American Can Company (140)
American Lane
Greenwich, CT 06830
(203) 552-2000

Purchasing Manager
Dexter (404)
2 Elm Street
Windsor Locks, CT 06096
(203) 623-9801

Director, North American Operations
  Procurement
Otis Elevator Company
Corporate Headquarters
1 Farm Springs
Farmington, CT 06032
(203) 678-2000

Corporate Material Management
Combustion Engineering (127)
1000 Prospect Hill
  Road (6112-1916)
Windsor, CT 06095
(203) 329-8771

Purchasing Manager
Stanley Works (275)
195 Lake Street
New Britain, CT 06050
(203) 225-5111

Purchasing Agent
Olin Corporation (195)
120 Long Ridge Road
Stamford, CT 06904
(203) 356-2112

Great Northern Nekoosa Paper
   Corporation (188)
75 Prospect Street
Stamford, CT 06904
(203) 359-4000

Purchasing Department
Union Carbide Corporation (39)
Old Ridgebury Road (C1197)
Danbury, CT 06817
(203) 794-6851

Purchasing Department
GTE Service Corporation
1 Stamford Forum
Stamford, CT 06903
(203) 965-2000

Purchasing Director
Pitney Bowes, Inc. (204)
Walter H. Wheeler, Jr. Drive
Stamford, CT 06926
(203) 356-5000

Purchasing Department
Perkin-Elmer (256)
64 Danbury Road
Wilton, CT 06897
(203) 762-4349

Bangor Punta Corporation
   (Subsidiary of Lear Siegler)
1 Greenwich Plaza
Greenwich, CT 06830
(213) 452-6000

Purchasing Department
General Electric Company (10)
Corporate Headquarters
3135 Easton Turnpike
Fairfield, CT 06431
(203) 373-2211

Manager, Corporate Purchasing
Singer Company (156)
8 Stamford Forum
Stamford, CT 06904
(203) 356-4200

Corporate Procurement
Travelers Insurance Company
1 Tower Square
Hartford, CT 06183
(203) 227-2581

Purchasing Department
Uniroyal, Inc. (175)
Middlebury, CT 06749
(203) 573-2000

Vice President, Regional
   Procurement
Marriott Corporation
One Marriott Drive
Washington, DC 20058
(301) 897-9000

Purchasing Department
Coca-Cola Company (44)
P.O. Box 1734
Atlanta, GA 30301
(404) 676-2210

Vice President, Purchasing
Delta Airlines, Inc.
3550 Greenbrier Parkway
Atlanta, GA 30331
(404) 765-2810

Director of Purchasing
West Point-Pepperell, Inc. (276)
P.O. Box 71
West Point, GA 31833
(404) 645-4000

Director of Purchasing
Boise Cascade Corporation (105)
P.O. Box 50
Boise, ID 83728
(208) 384-7127, ext. 6413

Purchasing Department
Kraft, Inc.
Kraft Court
Glenview, IL 60025
(312) 998-2448

Director, Corporate Purchasing
Quaker Oats Company (111)
345 Merchandise Mart Plaza
Chicago, IL 60654
(312) 222-6957

Purchasing Department
Zenith Radio Corporation (225)
1900 North Austin Avenue
Chicago, IL 60639
(312) 745-3272

Director of Purchasing
Sunbeam Corporation
2001 South York Road
Oakbrook, IL 60521
(312) 850-5000

Mgr., National Contracts—
 Packaging and Purchasing
 Administration
Beatrice Foods Company (26)
2 North La Salle Street
Chicago, IL 60602
(312) 431-3600

Director of Small Business
Motorola, Inc. (66)
1301 East Algonquin
Schaumburg, IL 60196
(312) 576-6675

General Manager of Purchasing
Swift & Co.
115 West Jackson Boulevard, 6th
 Floor
Chicago, IL 60604
(312) 431-2000

Mgr., Contracts Purchasing
FMC Corporation (120)
200 Randolph Drive
Chicago, IL 60601
(312) 861-5770

Coordinator
Gould, Inc. (233)
10 Gould Center
Rolling Meadows, IL 60008
(312) 640-4000

Purchasing Manager
Hartmarx (291)
101 North Wacker Drive
Chicago, IL 60606
(312) 372-6300

Merchandise Support Group
Sears Roebuck & Co.
Sears Tower
Dept. 733 BSC, 43–08
Chicago, IL 60684
(312) 875-8839

Director of Corporate Purchasing
Borg-Warner Corporation (101)
200 S. Michigan Avenue
Chicago, IL 60604
(312) 322-8638

Manager of Purchasing
Audio-Visual Division
Bell & Howell Company (371)
7100 McCormick Road
Chicago, IL 60645
(312) 673-3300, ext. 4707

Purchasing Department
Abbott Laboratories (116)
Abbott Park
North Chicago, IL 60064
(312) 937-5052

Director, Administrative Services
Central Soya Company, Inc. (222)
1300 Fort Wayne National Bank
 Building
Fort Wayne, IN 46802
(219) 425-5364

Commodity Manager
Cummins Engine Company (174)
Box 3005—MC 10825
Columbia, IN 47202
(812) 377-6036

Purchasing Coordinator
Inland Steel Company (126)
3210 Watling Street
East Chicago, IN 46312
(219) 392-1200

Maytag Company (390)
403 West 4th Street North
Newton, IA 50208
(515) 792-7000

Purchasing Manager
Cessna Aircraft Company
Wallace Division Aircraft Facility
K-42 Highway at Hoover Road
P. O. Box 7704
Wichita, KS 67277
(316) 946-6582

Director of Purchasing and Materials
Santa Fe Industries
1906 Arrowhead
Topeka, KS 66604
(913) 357-2000, ext. 4305

Small Business Coordinator
Beech Aircraft Corporation
9709 East Central
P.O. Box 2903
Wichita, KS 67201
(316) 681-8312

Corporate Director, Facilities and
 Planning
Fairchild Industries (329)
20301 Century Boulevard
Germantown, MD 20767
(301) 428-6088

Purchasing Department
Martin Marietta Corporation (85)
6801 Rockledge Drive
Bethesda, MD 20817
(301) 897-6216

Director of Purchasing
Black & Decker Manufacturing
 Company (212)
186 Hanover Pike
Hampstead, MD 21074
(301) 239-5796

Manager, Corporate Purchasing
Norton Company (277)
1 New Bond Street
Worcester, MA 01606
(617) 853-1000

Purchasing Department
Wang Laboratories, Inc. (161)
1 Industrial Avenue
Lowell, MA 01851
(617) 459-5000

Purchasing Department
Raytheon Company (60)
141 Spring Street
Lexington, MA 02173
(617) 862-6600, ext. 2361

Purchasing Manager
Gillette Company (158)
Prudential Tower
Boston, MA 02199
(617) 421-7650

Purchasing Department
Polaroid Corporation (257)
400 5th Avenue
Waltham, MA 02254
(617) 684-3434

Supervisor, Purchasing
  Administration
Federal-Mogul (338)
P.O. Box 1966
Detroit, MI 48235
(313) 354-7700

Purchasing Department
Burroughs Corporation (72)
Burroughs Place
Detroit, MI 48232
(313) 972-9090

Manager of Supply Administration
American Motors Corp. (98)
14250 Plymouth Road
Detroit, MI 48232
(313) 493-2000

Purchasing Department
Ex-Cell-O Corporation (287)
Corporate Headquarters
2855 Coolidge
Troy, MI 48084
(313) 637-1212

Purchasing Department
Dow Corning Corporation (303)
3901 South Saginaw Road
Mail #142
Midland, MI 48640
(517) 496-4392

Vice President, Purchasing
Whirlpool Corporation (112)
2000 U.S. 33 North
Benton Harbor, MI 49022
(616) 926-3225

Purchasing Department
Dow Chemical (28)
Corporate Headquarters
2020 Willard H. Dow Center
Midland, MI 48640
(517) 636-0095

Vice President, Purchasing
Kellogg Company (138)
235 Porter Street
P.O. Box 3423
Battle Creek, MI 49016
(616) 966-2000

Manager, Corporate Purchasing
Upjohn Company
7000 Portage Road
Kalamazoo, MI 49001
(616) 323-4000

Director of Purchasing
Gulf & Western Manufacturing
  Company
P.O. Box 999
Southfield, MI 48037
(313) 355-8423

Manager, Special Supplier Program
Chrysler Corporation (13)
P.O. Box 2866
Detroit, MI 48288
(313) 956-6116

Purchasing Department
General Motors Corporation (1)
General Motors Building, Room
  4–168
Detroit, MI 48202
(313) 556-3439

Purchasing Department
Ford Motor Company (4)
American Road, Room 329 WHQ
Dearborn, MI 48121
(313) 594-7338

Manager, Purchasing
Economics Laboratory, Inc. (376)
370 Wabasha, Osborn Building
St. Paul, MN 55102
(612) 293-2428

Manager, Corporate Procurement
  Programs
Control Data Corporation (106)
901 East 78th Street
Bloomington, MN 55420
(612) 853-3010

Purchasing Director
George A. Hormel & Co. (235)
501 16th Avenue, N.E.
P.O. Box 800
Austin, MN 55912
(507) 437-5297

Corporate Material Services
Honeywell, Inc. (56)
Honeywell Plaza
Minneapolis, MN 55408
(612) 870-6664

Industrial Relations
Bemis Company (362)
800 Northstar Center
Minneapolis, MN 55402
(612) 340-6146

Corporate Purchasing Manager
International Multifoods Corporation
  (274)
Multifoods Tower
P.O. Box 2942
Minneapolis, MN 55402
(612) 340-3426

Purchasing Department
General Mills, Inc. (64)
9200 Wayzatta Blvd.
P.O. Box 1113
Minneapolis, MN 55426
(612) 540-3774

Director of Consumer Procurement
Pillsbury Center (80)
Mail Station 3818
Minneapolis, MN 55402
(612) 330-4506

Purchasing Department
3M Company (47)
P.O. Box 33327
St. Paul, MN 55133
(612) 733-1303

Purchasing Department
Monsanto Corporation (53)
800 North Lindburgh Blvd.
St. Louis, MO 63166
(314) 694-2656

Small Bus. Mgr.
McDonnell Douglas Corp. (29)
Dept. 710, Building NQ, #399
St. Louis, MO 63166
(314) 232-7775

Manager, Corporate Purchasing
May Department Stores
611 Olive Street, Suite 1350
St. Louis, MO 63101
(314) 342-6300

Director, Corporate Affairs
Anheuser-Busch Companies (51)
1 Busch Place
St. Louis, MO 63118
(314) 577-2230

Manager, Materials Services,
  Performance, and Planning
Trans World Airlines, Inc.
Kansas City International Airport
P.O. Box 20367
Kansas City, MO 64195
(816) 891-4125

Purchasing Department
Southwestern Bell Telephone
  Company
1010 Pine Street, Room 2119
St. Louis, MO 63101
(314) 247-1895

Corporate Director of Material
General Dynamics Corp. (42)
Pierre Laclede Center
St. Louis, MO 63105
(314) 889-8796

Operations Manager
Conagra (65)
Conagra Center
1 Central Plaza
Omaha, NE 68102
(402) 978-4135

Director of Purchasing
800 Group, Inc.
Corporate Headquarters
85 Chestnut Ridge Road
Montvale, NJ 07645
(201) 573-0800

Purchasing Department
American Cyanamid Company (109)
1 Cyanamid Plaza
Wayne, NJ 07470
(201) 831-3187

Director, Corporate Purchasing
Warner-Lambert Company (125)
201 Tabor Road
Morris Plains, NJ 07950
(201) 540-3548

Purchasing Department
Bendix
Columbia Road and Park Avenue
Morristown, NJ 07960
(201) 455-3677

Manager, Purchasing
GAF Corporation (374)
1361 Elps Road
Wayne, NJ 07470
(201) 628-3000

Purchasing Manager
Campbell Soup Company (100)
Campbell Place
Camden, NJ 08101
(609) 342-4800

Contract Purchasing
Ingersoll-Rand Company (145)
200 Chestnut Ridge Road
Woodcliff Lake, NJ 07675
(201) 573-3175

Purchasing Manager
Johnson & Johnson (59)
501 George Street
New Brunswick, NJ 08903
(201) 524-9034

Director of Purchasing
E. R. Squibb & Sons, Inc. (180)
P.O. Box 191
New Brunswick, NJ 08903
(201) 545-1300

Purchasing Department
Bristol-Myers Company (84)
345 Park Avenue, Room 436
New York, NY 10154
(212) 546-2841

Director of Purchasing
St. Regis Paper Company
237 Park Avenue
New York, NY 10017
(212) 808-6000

Purchasing Manager
Marine Midland Bank, N.A.
1 Marine Midland Center
Buffalo, NY 14240
(716) 843-4788

Purchasing Department
Eastman Kodak Company (33)
343 State Street
Rochester, NY 14650
(716) 724-3940

Purchasing Department
Bausch & Lomb (418)
1400 North Goodman Street
Rochester, NY 14692
(716) 338-6000

Purchasing Department Head
Manufacturers Hanover Trust
   Company
Bank Window
Church Street Station
New York, NY 10015
(212) 623-4310

Vice President, Purchasing
Lever Brothers Company (177)
390 Park Avenue
New York, NY 10022
(212) 688-6000

Purchasing Department
Xerox Corporation (40)
800 Phillips Road
Building 716
Webster, NY 14580

Merchandise
F. W. Woolworth Company
233 Broadway
New York, NY 10279
(212) 553-2000

Vice President, Purchasing
Crouse-Hinds
P.O. Box 4999
Syracuse, NY 13221
(315) 477-7000

Material Management
United Brands Company (124)
1271 Avenue of the Americas
New York, NY 10020
(212) 307-2000

Corporate Purchasing
ITT Corporation (25)
320 Park Avenue   .
New York, NY 10022
(212) 940-1026

IBM Corporation (5)
200 Purchase Street
Purchase, NY 10577
(914) 697-6469

Purchasing Agent
Time, Inc. (114)
Rockefeller Center
1271 6th Avenue
New York, NY 10020
(212) 586-1212

Purchasing Manager
J. P. Stevens & Co. (201)
1185 Avenue of the Americas
New York, NY 10036
(212) 930-2080

Director of Purchasing
Sperry & Hutchinson Company
330 Madison Avenue, 7th Floor
New York, NY 10017
(212) 983-2000

Purchasing Department
Grumman Corporation (131)
1111 Stewart Avenue
Bethpage, NY 11714
(516) 575-0574

Manager of Purchasing
W. R. Grace & Co. (49)
1114 Avenue of the Americas
New York, NY 10036
(212) 819-5500

Purchasing Department
Joseph Seagram & Sons (218)
800 3rd Avenue
New York, NY 10022
(212) 572-7166

Corning Glass Works (217)
Main Plant, 21-1
Corning, NY 14831
(607) 974-6725

Director of Purchasing
Amstar Corporation (255)
1251 Avenue of the Americas
New York, NY 10020
(212) 489-9000

Corporate Purchasing
Revlon, Inc. (154)
767 5th Avenue
New York, NY 10153
(212) 572-5000

Corporate Purchasing Services
Philip Morris, Inc. (27)
120 Park Avenue
New York, NY 10017   ·
(212) 880-4093

Purchasing Department
Pfizer, Inc. (99)
235 East 42nd Street
New York, NY 10017
(212) 573-2448

Purchasing Department
Carrier Corporation
Building TR-4, Door 25, Carrier
  Parkway
Syracuse, NY 13221
(315) 432-7496

Purchasing Department
Westvaco Corporation (215)
299 Park Avenue
New York, NY 10171
(212) 688-5000

Ogden Corporation (197)
277 Park Avenue
New York, NY 10172
(212) 754-4000

Purchasing Department
Colgate-Palmolive Company (73)
300 Park Avenue
New York, NY 10022
(212) 310-2000

Purchasing Department
Burlington Industries, Inc. (141)
P.O. Box 21207
Greensboro, NC 27420
(919) 379-2700, ext. 2146

Director of Purchasing
Blue Bell, Inc.
P.O. Box 21488
Greensboro, NC 27420
(919) 373-3400

Supply and Distribution
Celanese, Inc. (132)
P.O. Box 32414
Charlotte, NC 28232
(704) 554-2926

Section Chief
AT&T Technologies, Inc. (8)
P.O. Box 25000
Guilford Center
Greensboro, NC 27420
(919) 279-7001

Administrative Manager
Nationwide Insurance
1 Nationwide Plaza
Columbus, OH 43216
(614) 227-7111

Director of Purchasing
Technical Systems Division
NCR Corporation (89)
1700 S. Patterson Blvd.
Dayton, OH 45479
(513) 445-5000

President and Chief Operating Officer
Midland Ross Corporation (369)
20600 Chagrin Boulevard
Cleveland, OH 44122
(216) 491-8400

World Headquarters Purchases
Eaton Corporation (107)
100 Erie View Plaza
Cleveland, OH 44114
(216) 523-4388

Purchasing Department
Borden, Inc. (77)
180 East Broad Street, 31st Floor
Columbus, OH 43215
(614) 225-4466

Director of Purchases
Libbey-Owens-Ford Company (190)
811 Madison Avenue
P.O. Box 799
Toledo, OH 43695
(419) 247-3731

Purchasing Department
Dana Corporation (103)
P.O. Box 1000
Toledo, OH 43697
(419) 535-4753

Director, Purchases
TRW, Inc. (57)
23555 Euclid Avenue
Cleveland, OH 44117
(216) 383-3030

Purchasing Manager
Cincinnati Milacron, Inc. (373)
4701 Marburg Avenue
Cincinnati, OH 45209
(513) 841-8805

Manager, Administrative Services
Anchor Hocking Corporation (378)
109 North Broad Street
Lancaster, OH 43130
(614) 687-2057

Champion Spark Plug Company (352)
P.O. Box 910
Toledo, OH 43661-0001
(419) 535-2652

Corporate Purchasing
Sherwin Williams Company (170)
101 Prospect Avenue, N.W.
Cleveland, OH 44115
(216) 566-2561

Purchasing Department
Goodyear Tire & Rubber Company
   (35)
1144 East Market Street
Akron, OH 44316
(216) 796-2684

B. F. Goodrich Company (123)
500 South Main Street
Akron, OH 44318
(216) 374-2917

Purchasing Department
Procter & Gamble Company (22)
P.O. Box 599
Cincinnati, OH 45201
(513) 562-4010

Purchasing and Transportation
Owens Corning Fiberglas
   Corporation (110)
Fiberglass Tower
Toledo, OH 43659
(419) 248-8000

Director of Purchasing
Federated Department Stores
7 West 7th Street
Cincinnati, OH 45212
(513) 579-7521

Office Services Manager
Louisiana-Pacific Corporation (266)
1300 Southwest 5th Avenue
Portland, OR 97201
(503) 221-0800

Purchasing Manager
Williamette Industries, Inc.
Lebanon Plywood Division (285)
Albany, OR 97355
(503) 926-7771

Purchasing Department
Tektronix, Inc. (245)
P.O. Box 500
M/S 78-619
Beaverton, OR 97077
(503) 627-2702

Air Products & Chemicals, Inc. (205)
P.O. Box 538
Allentown, PA 18105
(215) 481-8731

Vice President, Purchasing
Koppers Company, Inc. (207)
801 Koppers Building
Pittsburgh, PA 15219
(412) 227-2773

Manager of Purchasing
Avco Lycoming Corporation
652 Oliver Street
Williamsport, PA 17701
(717) 327-7229

Purchasing Manager
Westinghouse Electric Corporation
   (32)
6 Gateway Center
Westinghouse Building
Pittsburgh, PA 15222
(412) 244-2000

Purchasing
U.S. Steel Corporation (15)
600 Grant Street, Room 427
Pittsburgh, PA 15230
(412) 433-2328

Director of Purchasing
USAIR
Greater Pittsburgh International
   Airport
Pittsburgh, PA 15231
(412) 262-7308

Manager of Procurement
Hammermill Paper Company (199)
P.O. Box 10050
Erie, PA 16533
(814) 456-8811

Coordinator, Procurement Procedures
Bethlehem Steel Corporation (70)
8th and Eaton Avenue, Martin Tower
Bethlehem, PA 18016
(215) 694-6279

Purchasing Manager
Smith Kline & French (121)
1500 Spring Garden Street
Philadelphia, PA 19101
(215) 751-4000

Purchasing Department
Scott Paper Company (130)
Scott Plaza
Philadelphia, PA 19113
(215) 522-5403

Purchasing Manager
Penwalt Corporation (299)
3 Parkway
Philadelphia, PA 19102
(215) 587-7260

PPG Industries, Inc. (88)
1 PPG Place
Pittsburgh, PA 15272
(412) 434-3630

Manager of Purchases
Scovill Manufacturing Company
Yale Avenue
P.O. Box 489
Lenoir City, TN 37771
(615) 986-7511

Director of Purchasing
Genesco, Inc. (208)
Genesco Park
Nashville, TN 37202
(615) 367-7175

Domestic Purchasing Manager
Exxon Company (2)
P.O. Box 2812
Houston, TX 77001
(713) 656-5565

Purchasing Manager
Marathon Oil Company
P.O. Box 3112
Houston, TX 77253
(713) 629-6600

Small Business Coordinator
LTV Company (43)
P.O. Box 225907
Dallas, TX 75265
(214) 266-3286

Purchasing Department
Texas Instruments, Inc. (75)
P.O. Box 660246, MS 3925
Dallas, TX 75266
(214) 995-7006

Purchasing Department
Tenneco Oil Company (118)
P.O. Box 2511
Houston, TX 77001
(713) 757-2131

Purchasing Director
Tandy Corp/Radio Shack
500 One Tandy Center
Fort Worth, TX 76102
(817) 390-3234

Purchasing Department
Big Three Industries (351)
P.O. Box 3047
Houston, TX 77253
(713) 868-0333

Purchasing Agent
Southland Corporation
2828 North Haskell Avenue
P.O. Box 719
Dallas, TX 75221
(214) 828-7374

Purchasing Services
Rockwell International (30)
P.O. Box 10462
Dallas, TX 75207
(214) 996-6365

Purchasing Coordinator
Pennzoil Company (167)
P.O. Box 2967
Houston, TX 77252-2967
(713) 546-4000

Manager of Purchasing
American Petrofina (157)
P.O. Box 2159
Dallas, TX 75221
(214) 750-2400

Director, Corporate Procurement
Figgie International (354)
1000 Virginia Center Parkway
Richmond, VA 23295
(804) 264-5730

Purchasing Department
Boeing Company (21)
P.O. Box 3707
Seattle, WA 98124
(206) 656-9462

Purchasing Department
Weyerhaeuser Company (68)
Corporate Headquarters, Mail Stop
    2630
Tacoma, WA 98477
(206) 924-2743

Purchasing Department
PACCAR (194)
P.O. Box 1518
Bellevue, WA 98009
(206) 455-7400

Administrator, Purchasing
Northwestern Mutual Life Insurance
  Company
720 East Wisconsin Avenue
Milwaukee, WI 53202
(414) 226-7300

Corporate Purchasing
Rexnord Corporation (293)
4501 West Greenfield
West Milwaukee, WI 53214
(414) 643-2011

Staff Vice President and Director of
  Purchasing
Kimberly Clark Corporation (94)
2100 Winchester Road
Neenah, WI 54956
(414) 721-2251

CALLING ON TECHNICAL PERSONNEL

An important and particularly effective strategy when calling on corporations, particularly if you offer a highly technical product or specialized service, is to bolster your presentation efforts by making contact with engineering or technical personnel. Morris says that "if the corporation purchasing manager is the 'bulls-eye' for small vendor companies seeking new business from Fortune 500 corporations, then the engineering and technical personnel who generate the work requirements provide the 'ammunition' needed to hit the target." However, he adds, contacting technical personnel "without going through the proper purchasing department channels could provide you with ammunition to shoot yourself in the foot."

Know the Corporation's Purchasing Department Type

Morris points out that there are three basic categories into which purchasing departments can be organized:

- *Centralized.*   One large purchasing department at corporate headquarters buys for all plants and facilities. Burlington Industries (141), for example, maintains a centralized purchasing department.
- *Semicentralized.*   The headquarters purchasing department may purchase all big-ticket items for the corporation and allow each plant to purchase its own small or specialized items. In this case, purchases by individual plants may be limited by total dollars spent, with approval needed from headquarters for any amount over the limit. Semi-

centralized corporations include Gould (233), Economics Laboratory (376), Hewlett-Packard (58), and Control Data (106).

- *Decentralized.* Each plant or facility purchases all of its materials, equipment, and services. A headquarters purchasing department may oversee individual locations, but the amount of its influence varies with each corporation. Singer (156), Eaton (107), Allegheny (171), International Multifoods (274), Brunswick (231), and Martin Marietta (85) are among the hundreds of corporations with decentralized purchasing programs.

Know the Corporation's Purchasing Policy

Virtually all corporations specify in writing that no personnel outside the purchasing department have the authority to commit the corporation to the purchase of materials or services from a supplier. This ensures proper coordination of their policies and procedures in working with vendors. Always ask for a copy of the corporate supplier guide (see page 209) if the corporation has one—and most do. It will explain the corporate purchasing philosophy, guidelines, and operating procedures.

Your first point of contact with a corporation should always be the appropriate purchasing department. If the corporation is decentralized, as a majority are, make an appointment with the appropriate plant or facility. Even if purchasing personnel are not technically oriented themselves, they will be able to help you identify needs within the corporation. Purchasing will have the final say, regardless of what connections you make with the technical staff, and it could make things difficult for a vendor that it feels is attempting to make an "end run."

If the corporation has a small business vendor coordinator, go through this person for your initial contact. To ignore the coordinator may diminish your marketing effectiveness. It is the responsibility of the coordinator to ensure that vendors have all the information they need to make a credible sales pitch. At such corporations as Harris (163), FMC (120), and Zenith (225), you may be pleasantly surprised at the assistance provided by the small vendor coordinator. The small business vendor coordinator can help you gain access to key engineering and technical personnel.

Does it help to make your capabilities known to others not in purchasing? John E. McCaffrey, Jr., director of administrative services at Amtrak, is responsible for writing and establishing supply specifications. Although

McCaffrey, a 12-year veteran, has no actual purchasing authority, he frequently receives brochures and capability statements from prospective vendors. "I pass along everything I get to the appropriate purchasing people. However, I do read what vendors send in, and if I happen to come across a particularly attractive package from a seemingly well-qualified vendor, I let purchasing know."

Discover Technical Needs

There are ways to find out the technical needs of a corporation without directly asking and without bypassing the purchasing department. Join appropriate local associations of engineers or other professionals, and listen to their discussions. Then, when you contact the purchasing department, you can say that you heard about a certain technical need through a social contact and you would like some advice on the proper channels to follow.

Another way to find out the technical needs of a corporation is to ask a purchasing staff member for an appointment to see the specifying engineer. This person is responsible for the specific materials used on a job, and he or she will often recommend to the purchasing department that a certain vendor be used. In high-technology areas especially, such "preselections" are often made very early in the procurement process.

The specifying engineer may even be assigned to the purchasing department. Asking to see him or her will show your interest in the project and, again, your willingness to work with the purchasing department "through the proper channels."

"Suppliers who take the initiative to analyze and evaluate needs and functions can uncover many opportunities for good payback," according to the Beech Aircraft Corporation manager of procurement. Corporations appreciate, and in many cases count on, the input of suppliers for engineering savings.

If you can find the names of the engineers on a particular project before you see the purchasing department, you will make a favorable impression for having done your homework and you may also gain key "inside" information. You can call the switchboard and ask in advance for the name of an engineer on a specific project, while not actually speaking to the engineer until you have checked with the purchasing department.

Once you have cleared with the purchasing department and have an appointment with the engineering or technical people, all of the previously supplied suggestions on marketing, documentation, and presentation are again applicable.

Play Both Ends against the Middle

Purchasing and technical personnel are complementary in function. As a vendor, you must satisfy the requirements of both to succeed in your selling efforts. Use purchasing to identify general needs and to make appointments with the appropriate technical people. Impress the technical people with your capabilities and understanding of their needs.

"Demonstrate that you recognize the importance and function of each department," says Morris, "and you'll end up with both on your side."

CHAPTER TEN

Determining Customer Needs, Providing Quality Assurance

*What great thing would you
attempt if you knew you could
not fail?*

ROBERT SCHULLER

Purchasing agents consider a variety of factors when making purchase decisions. To compete successfully for business, you must find out what the customer's needs are. Critical customer needs can be grouped according to quality standards, service, and price.

Standards of Quality

- Can you meet these standards with your current equipment/personnel?
- If your product greatly exceeds the standards, will your price be too high?
- Is your level of quality consistent over time?

Service Required

- Do you currently provide the appropriate services for this customer?
- Is your normal level of service sufficient, or will you need to allocate additional resources to provide the expected services to this customer?

Price

- Does this customer consider only price when making a purchase decision?
- Can you offer something more than your competitors are offering for the same price?
- Are the "extras" you offer—higher quality, better service—worth the increased price you charge?

You must always be digging to find out what buyers expect from suppliers in service levels, lead times, delivery schedules, and so forth.

177

You also need to know what help or exceptions they might be willing to give you in terms of technical assistance, financial assistance, and timing of payments.

"After you have acquired a customer," Vic Morris stresses, "communication becomes even more important." Keep in touch with the customer on a regular basis by giving him or her progress reports, and be available when the customer wants to meet with you. If at all possible, return customers' calls promptly.

Business excellence, according to Peters and Waterman's *In Search of Excellence,* comes from a constant emphasis, almost to the point of fanaticism, on staying "close to the customer." All companies preach this, but excellent companies do it. In this chapter we'll expand on ideas expressed earlier in Chapters 3, 4, 6, and 9.

Cost Reduction Program

An effective cost reduction program is one in which the vendor *always* strives to reduce costs without reducing quality. Seek out the advice of your employees on introducing new methods of production, improving materials handling, streamlining work flow, and locating new sources of suppliers. Across the board, purchasing agents agree that they expect vendors to continually be seeking new ways to reduce costs. Can the job be done with fewer parts? Will your product require less frequent maintenance? Will your product be easier to store and transport? Let customers know that you're working to help them. At Digital Equipment (55), purchasing agents are on constant alert to identify and retain vendors who do this. When you pass on any reduced costs, customers are appreciative and tend to want to keep working with you.

Conformance Standards and Innovation

You should know what your customers' standards are. It is better to know in advance what they are and whether you can meet them than to have your product rejected as substandard or unacceptable. This prior knowledge will save you money—namely, the money that you won't have to spend on reworking items or purchasing new equipment. More important, knowledge of conformance standards and of your ability to meet them will establish and enhance your firm's reputation.

A good way to indicate your propensity toward innovation is to ask your customers whether there is a product or service that they need or want. Many a profitable, innovative relationship between buyer and vendor started because the vendor asked that question. Indeed, many corporations, such as Amdahl (348), Stanadyne (472), and Boise Cascade (105), have initiated progressive programs that actively encourage vendor-initiated innovation. Is there a better way to service your customers? Find it and tell them about it.

Can you find new uses for an old product? How about instituting or improving your quality measurement program (see page 181). Do you see any potential for developing a new or improved distribution method? Are there new production methods that could lower costs while maintaining quality?

Security—A Growing Concern

Is your plant or place of business secure? Purchasing agents consider this important. The term *security* encompasses not only the physical security of your plant but also documents and any internal information that a customer shares with you. All of these should be protected.

Key security measures for your plant include the installation of a security system, the use of guards, the use of watchdogs, and the provision of good illumination at entrances and the surrounding areas after dark.

To safeguard documents, install a storage facility that will protect them from unauthorized persons, fire, and other hazards. Protecting the internal information of customers is particularly crucial, since the failure to do so may cause them not to trust you in the future.

Emergency Contingency Planning

If a customer fell victim to a fire or a flood, could your firm be flexible enough to meet that customer's emergency needs? Could you provide the customer with additional inventory? Provide space for storage? Fill a "rush order"? Provide special distribution?

By discussing such needs in advance with the customer, you will demonstrate your concern and provide the "something extra" that will make your firm stand out.

Quality Control Program

Certain types of products require uncommonly close adherence to specifications, which are normally clearly defined in the contract. A description of your quality control program tells buyers that you have a formal, documented system for evaluating your product or service according to predetermined standards.

A quality control program can be a point in your favor when your firm is producing on a contract that requires close adherence to specifications. The customer may wish to inspect the product at your plant before it is shipped or at his plant after it has been received.

If you don't have such a program, consider developing one if it suits your type of business. The balance of this chapter highlights and discusses a quality control and assurance plan, as developed by Vic Morris.

QUALITY CONTROL AND ASSURANCE FOR MANUFACTURERS AND DISTRIBUTORS

Assuring a purchasing agent that you have a system for quality control may not be enough. Unless that assurance is backed up with a written plan or a manual, you may not be considered for a contract. A quality assurance program demonstrates to purchasing agents that you consider quality to be vital and that you have taken the time to think through and prepare a real quality control system.

In the troubled economy of the early 1980s, price may have overridden quality as a deciding factor in selecting suppliers. Increasingly, however, purchasing managers are acknowledging that higher quality ultimately means lower costs for their corporations. In addition, increasing high quality foreign imports dictate a higher domestic quality level than ever existed before.

A prime responsibility of purchasing managers is to analyze all supplier qualifications and standards in detail. The purchasing manager's review of your written plan for quality assurance is the first step in documenting quality control. That review is often followed by an on-site visit to your plant or distribution warehouse to observe your quality assurance plan in action.

According to *Purchasing Magazine,* 80 percent of purchasing executives said that they made more trips in 1985 than they had made the year before. One study reveals that purchasing executives make an average of seven trips a year to check out existing or potential suppliers.

"Purchasing departments spend a great deal of time selecting the right suppliers for their raw material/big-ticket items," says Arthur E. Wiebe, vice president, LB & Associates, purchasing management consultants. On the next page is a sample vendor visitation report form. The items contained on the form are typical of the type of information that purchasing personnel are likely to seek when visiting your installation.

In Chapter 6 we looked at what information you needed to document your capabilities for presentation to a corporate buyer. If and when the buyer visits you on-site, you must present even greater detail about your operations.

VENDOR VISITATION REPORT

1. Company name _____
   Address _____
   Town _____ State _____ Zip _____
   Telephone _____

2. Purpose of trip _____
3. Principals, titles, and evaluation

   a. Manufacturing _____
   b. Marketing _____
   c. Administration _____
   d. Financial _____
   e. Logistics _____

4. Representatives

   a. _____
   b. _____
   c. _____

5. Volume of business _____
6. Principal products or services _____
7. Union and contract dates _____
8. Vendor key suppliers _____
9. Facilities (brief description) _____

   a. Building and size _____
   b. Shipping and receiving facilities _____
   c. Housekeeping: Poor _____ Good _____ Excellent _____

10. Equipment

    a. Type and condition _____
    b. Capable of future expansion: Yes _____ No _____

11. Quality assurance program: Yes _____ No _____
    Comments _____
12. Approved vendor for _____
13. Comments _____

Source: LB & Associates (adapted).

General Motors (1), Ingersoll-Rand (145), and Seagram (218) all make visits to small vendor plants. Here's what to expect:

- The inspection will most likely be conducted by a team that could include the purchasing agent, an engineer, and the corporation's own quality control person.
- The inspection team will probably look for quality control based on statistical process control techniques, not just finished goods inspection.
- The inspectors will want a demonstration of the policies that are implemented at the operating level, not just at final inspection. They will look for process controls, including proper training for workers, that reduce the likelihood of error.
- They may want to review scrap and rework records. Low scrap and rework levels are an indicator that quality is up.

Components of the Quality Assurance Plan

Here is a listing of the components of a complete quality assurance plan for manufacturers and distributors. Corporate visitors are apt to want to know about how you handle:

- Organization (as evidenced in the organization chart).
- Staff responsibilities.
- Documentation, records, and corrective action.
- Measuring and test equipment.
- Process control:
    Indication of inspection status.
    Customer-furnished material.
    Nonconforming material.
    Sampling inspections.
    Alternative inspection provisions.
    Receiving inspection.
    Customer evaluation.
    Segregation control.
    Drawing and change control.
    Purchasing and certification.
    Supporting documents.

Organization Chart.   Shows the lines of command and responsibility in your company (see Chapter 6) and illustrates the interrelated functions of different departments or personnel.

Staff Responsibilities. Specifies that all employees of the company are responsible for adherence to quality requirements and must be active participants in all quality programs. Also specifies the chain of command from the president through the quality manager and quality control inspectors.

Documentation, Records, and Corrective Action. Requires a specific quality control plan for each job. The size and complexity of the job will determine the detail needed. The completion of the quality assurance plan requires the development of detailed inspection sheets for each part, assembly, and unit. Since the inspection sheets are operating procedures for the quality inspectors, they must be clear, complete, and current.

Each inspection sheet includes basic contract identification data, specific drawing and drawing revision data, the name of the inspector, and the type of inspection. The body of the inspection sheet explains what procedure is to be done, any special testing or measuring restrictions, and approval/rejection criteria. The inspection sheet also specifies the test equipment necessary to perform required inspections.

If an item is rejected, a note is placed on the inspection sheet and a nonconformance report is completed that details the number and types of deficiencies found, their causes, and the steps that are being taken to correct them. The nonconformance report also describes the actions that have been taken to prevent recurrence of the problem.

Measuring and Test Equipment. Discusses intervals for calibration checks; measurement standards traceable to the National Bureau of Standards; the necessity of periodic review of the adequacy of standards; control over environmental conditions; calibration procedures; calibration sources; records showing calibration intervals, certification dates, and the results of the last calibration; calibration labeling; and government verification.

This section of the quality assurance plan also includes procedures for test equipment found to be out of tolerance—nothing works perfectly indefinitely. It's a solid demonstration of integrity to identify what's out of tolerance and why, how, and when test equipment was or will be properly adjusted.

Process Control. Parts of certain processes, such as plating, radiography, or heat treating, do not lend themselves to after-the-fact inspection. Thus quality assurance inspections are necessary while the work is being performed. This section of the quality assurance plan outlines procedures for work-in-process controls.

- *Indication of Inspection Status.*   Quality assurance inspections are performed during four phases—at receiving, in process, on the first item produced, and final—on materials and supplies used on jobs having a quality control requirement. An item is either accepted or rejected at each of these points.

    ''Accept'' tags provide the following information: item, job number, drawing number, lot number, type of inspection, quantity accepted for each inspection, date of inspection, and quality control inspector's initials or stamp.

    ''Reject'' tags indicate the cause of rejection, in addition to all of the information on the ''accept'' tag. A ''hold'' category describes pieces that have been neither accepted nor rejected. The tag indicates why a given item or lot has not been tagged as an accept or reject.

- *Customer-Furnished Material.*   Describes procedures used to inspect, identify, and protect material furnished by the customer. The accept or reject tags described in the previous section are used to identify the status of the inspected material.
- *Nonconforming Material.*   Describes procedures for identification, segregation, presentation, and disposition of nonconforming items. Such an item will remain in nonconforming storage until a decision has been made, in consultation with the customer, to offer it as is, to rework it, to repair it, or to scrap it.
- *Sampling Inspections.*   Establishes sampling inspection procedures for use when large quantities of like items are manufactured and the customer approves a sampling inspection.
- *Alternative Inspection Provisions.*   Specifies that the customer and an authorized vendor representative must approve all changes to inspection procedures and inspection equipment other than those specified in the initial contract.
- *Receiving Inspection.*   Describes procedure for quality inspection of all materials and supplies received by the company.
- *Customer Evaluation.*   Establishes procedures for review by all customers who request evaluation of the company quality assurance program. Specifies that requests will be honored.
- *Segregation Control.*   Ensures that all material requiring quality certification will be inspected, tagged, and placed in a segregated storage area.

- *Drawing and Change Control.* Specifies procedures to ensure that any old drawings are properly destroyed and that new drawings and changes are correctly logged and attached to drawings for the appropriate foreman or department head.
- *Purchasing and Certification.* Specifies the procedures for quality assurance of purchasing of material and services by the vendor.
- *Supporting Documents*
  Traveler/reject tag.
  Receiving inspection report.
  Nonconformance report.
  Nonconformance report supplement.
  Detailed inspection procedure and record.
  Instrument calibration forms.
  Certificate of compliance.
  Stores inventory log.
  Drawing revision/change record.
  Drawing control log.
  Operating procedures for precision measuring equipment.
  Checklist for evaluation of contractor's calibration system.

An aspect of quality assurance that may be overlooked is the appearance of your plant or warehouse and of your delivery vehicles. A product that has passed stringent quality control measurements but is delivered to the customer in a dirty truck makes a very poor first impression. Don't attempt a two-minute drill to improve the appearance of your plant and equipment just before you're being visited. Maintain them all the time. Well-kept facilities and equipment will indicate to customers that your quality assurance plan permeates every aspect of your company.

A typical quality assurance procedures manual can range from 25 to 85 pages. The types of products you produce and the size of your operation will determine how long your manual should be.

Quality assurance—it's vital both to have a realistic, specific plan and to implement that plan consistently. Quality control is the name of the game, and your plan will demonstrate that you play by the rules.

QUALITY CONTROL AND ASSURANCE FOR SERVICE FIRMS

Quality control has been considered the arena of manufacturing—measuring the quality of manufactured products against definable standards.

But companies providing *services* have more of a stake in developing a quality assurance program than do manufacturing companies because their outcomes are more difficult to measure. And the quality of your service is the basic factor separating you from the ever-burgeoning number of your competitors.

Developing a comprehensive quality assurance program for your service company, says Morris, will indicate to a potential client that you care about the quality of your service and that you realize the importance of controlling it from start to finish.

Developing an Overall Quality Assurance Program

The components of an effective service industry quality assurance program include:

- Appointing a quality assurance director or team.
- Developing a procedure for checking services in process.
- Monitoring time in an organized manner.
- Developing forms for internal communication and forms for communication with the client.
- Building flexibility into the program to meet the requirements of specific projects.

Appoint a Quality Assurance Director.　Depending on the size of your company and the number of projects that you handle at one time, you should appoint or assign a quality assurance director and involve others as part of a quality assurance project team. Quality assurance is often the responsibility of the project director. Good firms *always* take care of this task. The major job responsibility of the quality assurance director is to coordinate the overall schedule of work, to oversee all client communication, and to be responsible for the quality and timeliness of all deliverables.

A checklist of the quality assurance director's specific responsibilities could be included in your company's brochure. Once a contract has been received, outline the educational qualifications of all the people who will work on that project, as well as their responsibilities for specific aspects of the project.

Develop a Procedure for Checking Work in Process.　A procedure should be developed to check the work of the personnel involved in each project, not only as each deliverable is finished but also while work is in progress. In an architectural firm, for example, the quality assurance director should review the specs and plans for a building, develop a checklist of items to be included in each working drawing, handle communication with others affected by the building (such as the fire marshal), and monitor project activity for the duration of the project.

Monitor Time in an Organized Manner. Accounting for billed time must involve a well-developed system that allows you to monitor all personnel and their daily progress on tasks and subtasks. Several computer software programs are available for time management, but typed or handwritten forms are just as useful. Summary sheets detailing time billed to each task or subtask of the project should be made available to the quality assurance director each week. These will indicate whether the project is on track and will enable you to spot any problems quickly. It will also enable the quality assurance director to notify the customer well in advance of the deadline if a deliverable date must be delayed.

Develop Forms for Internal and External Communication. Forms allow concise communication. Proper internal distribution of forms will ensure that everyone on the project is aware of any changes in the scope of work. Some service companies develop intricate forms to impress clients. However, such forms may merely confuse clients. Use forms that communicate both the message and the intent easily.

Build Flexibility into Your Program. Your core program of quality assurance will remain the same for all projects; however, each project has its differences. Depending on the size and complexity of a project, you may opt to use a quality assurance director or a quality assurance team to handle quality control for the project. A quality assurance program should be developed for each project, incorporating the deliverables schedule, PERT chart, schedule of reporting, and forms that will be used according to the needs of the specific project.

Since a service may be difficult to measure, it is all the more important that you plan and outline your efforts to do so. You will have more flexibility than a manufacturer in both designing and implementing your plan, and a propensity toward innovation in quality control will stand you in good stead with potential and existing customers. Richard A. Connor, Jr., uses a powerful sentence with clients at the initial project meeting. Connor asks the client, "How will you and I know when the job has been done correctly?"

The accompanying outline presents the minimum information requirements for marketing to major corporations when you are calling on them or when their representatives are visiting you. It is a synthesis of the suggestions in Chapter 6, "Documenting Your Capabilities for Presentation," and the previous material in this chapter.

Whether yours is a manufacturing firm, a service firm, or anything in between, a sound quality control and assurance program will help keep large buyers happy!

MINIMUM INFORMATION REQUIREMENTS FOR MARKETING TO MAJOR CORPORATIONS: A QUICK SUMMARY

1. *Capability profile/statement/business plan*

   a. *Ownership.* Sole proprietorship, partnership, or corporation? List the major stockholders. Include an organization chart. State the market served.

   b. *Products/services.* Describe your firm's product or service clearly and completely.

   c. *Location(s).* List the address(es) and telephone numbers of your location(s).

   d. *Projects/activities.* Describe concisely recent jobs that your firm has undertaken on which you have performed well.

   e. *References* (*testimonials*). If you have received favorable letters commending your firm and the jobs you have done, include copies (but first get permission from the authors of the letters). If you have satisfied customers, ask them whether you may use their names as references for potential customers.

   f. *Description of your firm.* List the key members of your firm, their specialties, and their experience and state how long your firm has been in business.

   g. *Goals.* What are your goals for this specific customer? What product or service do you want to provide? What level of service will you provide?

2. *Technical capability*

   a. *Human.* The number of your skilled employees and their specialties, the experience of your skilled employees, and the number of your unskilled employees.

   b. *Equipment.* The number and types of machinery, capacities and ages.

3. *Quality*

   a. *Conformance standards.* If the customer has specifications that you must meet, explain your checks to determine adherence to specifications.

    b. *Guarantees/warranties.* Describe any guarantee for your product or service. Warranties should be checked with an attorney for wording to ensure that you are not getting in over your head. If you do warrant your product, outline the scope of the warranty.

    c. *Quality assurance program.* If your firm has an established program to monitor the quality of production, briefly describe the program and its benefits.

    d. *Measurement capability* (*testing and inspection*). Any equipment used for testing and inspecting should be itemized. State the tolerance range of the equipment.

4. *Facility and financial capability*

    a. *Manufacturing/assembly size and capacity.* State the size of your plant (square footage) and the daily output of your plant at maximum operating level.

    b. *Equipment list.* Type, capacity and quality.

    c. *Financial position.* Your balance sheet, your profit and loss statement, and information on your line of credit—if you have one.

5. *Price*

    a. *Specific costs.* Identify and itemize any initial charges and any charges for setup, development, engineering, tooling, special equipment, testing, materials, and machine rates.

    b. *Competitiveness.* What is your best price, best quality, and best delivery date?

    c. *Minimum deviation from customer requirements.* State your understanding of the customer's requirements and how you plan to meet them.

6. *Labor*

    a. *Availability of workers.* Skilled workers, semiskilled workers, and unskilled workers.

    b. *Hourly rates.* Those of your current employees, and of any additions to your work force that will be required for this job.

    c. *Union/nonunion.* Union, non-union? Is your firm in a right-to-work state?

7. *Security*

    a. *Confidentiality.* Guarantee that the customer's trade secrets, confidential information, and new product plans will not be divulged.

    b. *Plant security.* Describe your security measures for your plant, office, storage yard, and documents.

CHAPTER ELEVEN

Using Trade Shows to Bolster Marketing Efforts

All the world's a stage,
And all the men and women merely players.

WILLIAM SHAKESPEARE

One way to gain maximum marketing leverage for your time and resources is to exhibit at trade shows. A growing number of entrepreneurs have found that using trade shows as a marketing vehicle can provide an effective cost/benefit ratio.

Michelle Lusson, author of *Creative Wellness* (New York: Warner Books, 1987) and founder of Nimo Systems Limited, which offers seminars in stress, image, and health management, observes, "Our cost per new client through exhibiting at trade shows is lower than that of many of the other traditional marketing vehicles we've tried, such as direct mail, yellow pages advertising, and community seminars."

Exhibiting at trade shows has both advantages and disadvantages. "You can meet an awful lot of people in a short time," says Lusson, "but if you're exhibiting at the wrong trade show, or your marketing presentation needs polishing, you could end up wasting a lot of time and money."

BENEFITS ABOUND

Many benefits can be gained through trade show participation. For the small business vendor, trade shows provide contact with a large number of prospective buyers in a short time. Exhibitors can quickly find an audience that is prepared to do business, and since all of these contacts are generated in a few days, trade shows are a very effective use of time for the small business vendor. (See "Exhibiting at Trade Shows," page 200).

Trade show participation affords the opportunity to see potential competitors and the products or services they are offering. Keeping up with the competition is important, but is difficult for the small business owner who is involved in the details of running a business. Trade shows can also provide ideas for new products, services, or methods of distribution.

Trade shows offer the marketing entrepreneur an opportunity to polish presentation skills. Attending a trade show mandates professional contact and enables the entrepreneur to gain experience in dealing with prospective clients. Such interaction may reveal areas of a presentation that need clarification, products or services that are desired by prospective buyers, modifications that would enhance the demand for products or services, or the need to add completely new products or services to an existing line.

DIRECTORIES AVAILABLE

Several trade show directories are available for a small fee or through the local library.

For example, the *Directory of Conventions,* published annually by Successful Meetings, Inc., provides listings of conventions by geographic location. A key word index by industry group or interest is included for reference.

> Research Department
> *Directory of Conventions*
> Successful Meetings, Inc.
> 1518 Walnut Street
> Philadelphia, PA 19102
> (215) 546-3295

Trade Shows and Professional Exhibits Directory, edited by Robert J. Elster, gives detailed information on more than 2,100 scheduled exhibitions, trade shows, association conventions, and other sales events. It focuses on the United States but also includes many shows around the world. It is arranged by subject and gives types of audiences, anticipated attendance, and display prices.

> Gale Research Company
> Book Tower
> Detroit, MI 48226

National Trade and Professional Associations (NTPA) contains annual meeting or convention dates and locations for each association. The

1986 Directory of Conventions—Sample Pages

DIRECTORY OF CONVENTIONS - Geographic Section

A B C

ALABAMA

BIRMINGHAM

86 JUL 17 - 20   STATE EXH 1,800
HYATT HOTEL/CIVIC CENTER
AL NUMISMATIC SOC
MRS PURNIE MOORE , BOX 3601 BIRMINGHAM , AL 35211

86 SEP(T)   STATE EXH 150   UNIVERSITY INN
IL PROF SECRETARIES INTL
JOAN PADALINO
MORTIMER JORDAN HALL 117
UNIV STATION BIRMINGHAM , AL 35294

86 OCT 5 - 8   REGL 400   WYNFREY HOTEL
AL MS AMER WATER WORKS ASSN
J W ROBERTS , BOX C-110 BIRMINGHAM , AL 35283

*86 OCT 6 - 9   STATE EXH 2,000   HYATT HOTEL
SOC AMER FORESTERS
RICHARD ZABEL CONV MGR
5400 GROSVENOR LANE BETHESDA , MD 20814

*86 OCT 10 - 13   DIST EXH 750   CIVIC CENTER
MENS APPAREL CLUB BIRMINGHAM
JACK MANN , P O DRAWER 24M CINCINNATI , OH 45224

86 OCT 16 - 17   NATL 40
NATL ASSN BANK COST ANALYSIS WORKSHOPS
LINDA FELDMAN ADMIN COORD ,
BOX 27448 SAN FRANCISCO , CA 94127

*87 JAN 10 - 13   DIST EXH 750   CIVIC CENTER
MENS APPAREL CLUB BIRMINGHAM
JACK MANN , P O DRAWER 24M CINCINNATI , OH 45224

*87 MAR 26 - 29 STATE EXH 300 HYATT HOTEL/CIVIC CENTER
AL DIETETIC ASSN
JAN ROEBUCK PRES ,
3069 WHISPERING PINES CIR BIRMINGHAM , AL 35226

*87 MAR 26 - 29   STATE EXH 1,500
HYATT HOTEL/CIVIC CENTER
AL FOOD SERVICE EXPO
BETH GANN EXH CHRMN , BOX 1256 HUNTSVILLE , AL 35807

87 APR 9 - 11   STATE EXH 75   UNIVERSITY INN
AL SPEECH HEARING ASSN
DANIEL PHILLIPS ,
3800 RIDGEWAY DR
LAKESHORE HOSPITAL BIRMINGHAM , AL 35209

*87 APR 10 - 14   DIST EXH 750   CIVIC CENTER
MENS APPAREL CLUB BIRMINGHAM
JACK MANN , P O DRAWER 24M CINCINNATI , OH 45224

87 APR 11 - 13   STATE 800   WYNFREY HOTEL
AL PADARD ASSN AL
CAPT KENNETH MAE ,
1675 MONTCLAIR RD.STE 10B BIRMINGHAM , AL 35210

87 APR 23 - 25   STATE 1,000   WYNFREY HOTEL
AL MEDICAL ASSN
EMMETT WYATT , 19 S JACKSON MONTGOMERY , AL 36197

87 JUL(T)   STATE EXH 1,800
MRS PURNIE MOORE , BOX 3601 BIRMINGHAM , AL 35211

*87 OCT 10 - 13   DIST EXH 750   CIVIC CENTER
MENS APPAREL CLUB BIRMINGHAM
JACK MANN , P O DRAWER 24M CINCINNATI , OH 45224

DOTHAN

*86 OCT 11 - 25   DIST EXH 80,000   FAIRGROUNDS
NATL PEANUT FESTIVAL
JOHN T POWELL EXEC DIR ,
1691 ROSS CLARK CIR. SE DOTHAN , AL 36301

87 OCT 10 - 24   DIST EXH 80,000   FAIRGROUNDS
NATL PEANUT FESTIVAL
JOHN T POWELL EXEC DIR ,
1691 ROSS CLARK CIR. SE DOTHAN , AL 36301

GULF SHORES

*86 JUL 18 - 20   STATE 300   GULF STATE PARK
AL PRESS ASSN
BILL KELLER , BOX 1800 TUSCALOOSA , AL 35403

87 JUL 17 - 19   STATE 300   GULF STATE PARK
AL PRESS ASSN
BILL KELLER , BOX 1800 TUSCALOOSA , AL 35403

HUNTSVILLE

86 JUL 25 - 26   NATL 300   HILTON HOTEL
337TH INFANTRY REGIMENT 85TH DIV REUNION
BILL MITCHELL , 2332 21ST ST SW AKRON , OH 44314

*86 OCT 9 - 11   REGL 800   HILTON HOTEL
NATL COUNCIL TEACHERS MATH REG MTGS
MARNA J PETERSON DIR CONV SERV ,
1906 ASSOCIATION DR RESTON , VA 22091

87 MAR 19   STATE 700   HILTON HOTEL
AL ASSN LIFE UNDERWRITERS
JIM CUNNINGHAM EXEC VP ,
660 ADAMS AVE STE 254 MONTGOMERY , AL 36104

---

*87 JUN 2 - 4   NATL 550   MARRIOTT HOTEL
NATL CLASSIFICATION MANAGEMENT SOC
EUGENE J SUTO EXEC SEC ,
6116 ROSELAND DR ROCKVILLE , MD 20852

MOBILE

86 SEP 16 - 18   STATE 200   ADMIRAL SEMMES
AL CABLE TELEVISION ASSN
MARY JOHN GARRETT MARTIN EXEC DIR ,
2901 MOORCROFT DR MONTGOMERY , AL 36116

86 SEP(T)   STATE EXH 250   RIVERVIEW PLAZA
AL AMER INST ARCHITECTS
J R ORTEGA , BOX 237 MONTGOMERY , AL 36101

*86 OCT 12 - 15   REGL EXH 400   RIVERVIEW PLAZA
SOUTH VETERINARY MEDICAL ASSN
J T MERCER , 4185 CAMPUS STATION ATHENS , GA 30602

86 OCT(T)   NATL 350   RIVERVIEW PLAZA
NATL ASSN DEVELOP ORGANIZATIONS
ALICEANN WOHLBRUCK EXEC DIR ,
400 N CAPITOL ST NW ST372 WASHINGTON , DC 20001

86 NOV 17 - 19   NATL 150
AQUATIC PLANT CONTROL RESEARCH PROGRAM
W N RUSHING , BOX 631 VICKSBURG , MS 39180

*87 JAN 30 - FEB 1   STATE EXH 800   ADMIRAL SEMMES
AL NURSERYMEN ASSN
JUDY P COPELAND , BOX 9 AUBURN , AL 36831

87 FEB 11 - 12   REGL 135   HILTON HOTEL
SOUTHEAST SHIPPERS ADVISORY BOARD
HARRY CLARK GEN MGR ,
BOX 2623.O'NEAL STEEL INC BIRMINGHAM , AL 35202

87 FEB 27 - MAR 1   STATE 300   RIVERVIEW PLAZA
AL PRESS ASSN
BILL KELLER , BOX 1800 TUSCALOOSA , AL 35403

87 DEC(T)   NATL 500
INTERSTATE OIL COMPACT COMMISSION
W TIMOTHY DOWD EXEC DIR ,
BOX 53127 OKLAHOMA CITY , OK 73152

MONTGOMERY

86 OCT 3   STATE EXH 75   AUBURN UNIV
AL SPEECH HEARING ASSN
DANIEL PHILLIPS ,
3800 RIDGEWAY DR
LAKESHORE HOSPITAL BIRMINGHAM , AL 35209

*86 DEC 9 - 11   STATE 2,200   CIVIC CENTER
AL FARM BUREAU FED
DAVID SMART ADV PROM DIR ,
2108 EAST SOUTH BLVD MONTGOMERY , AL 36116

87 APR 30 - MAY 3   STATE 175   GOVERNOR'S HSE
AL DENTAL ASSISTANTS ASSN
R BROCK , 2506 POINCIANNA ST HUNTSVILLE , AL 35801

87 APR 30 - MAY 29 STATE EXH 1,200   GOVERNOR'S HSE
AL DENTAL ASSN
WAYNE MC MAHAN EXEC DIR ,
836 WASHINGTON AVE MONTGOMERY , AL 36104

87 OCT 7 - 10(T)   REGL 200
605TH ORDNANCE BATTALION ASSN REG MTG
HUBERT R HUNT SEC , 2830 ISLAND RD BRISTOL , VA 24201

POINT CLEAR

*86 AUG 10 - 13   STATE EXH 500   MARRIOTT HOTEL GRAND
LA ASSN REALTORS
CHARLES L FARRAR EXEC VP ,
BOX 14780 BATON ROUGE , LA 70898

*86 DEC 26 - 31   NATL 450   MARRIOTT HOTEL GRAND
NATL SCREW MACHINE PRODUCTS ASSN
FRANK T MC GINNIS EXEC VP ,
6700 WEST SNOWVILLE RD BRECKSVILLE , OH 44141

87 MAR 1 - 3   NATL EXH 400   MARRIOTT HOTEL GRAND
CATFISH FARMERS AMER
HUGH PURNELL EXEC VP , BOX 34 JACKSON , MS 39205

87 MAR 18 - 21   NATL 500   MARRIOTT HOTEL GRAND
NATL ASSN ACCOUNTANTS EXEC MTGS
JOHN C FREEMAN DIR MTGS ,
919 THIRD AVE NEW YORK CITY , NY 10022

87 MAR 29 - APR 1   NATL 500   MARRIOTT HOTEL GRAND
POWER TRANSMISSION DISTRS ASSN SPRING MTG
LINDA MC CHRYSTAL DIR ,
100 HIGGINS RD PARK RIDGE , IL 60068

87 APR 23 - 26   NATL 60   MARRIOTT HOTEL GRAND
AMER INNERSPRING MANUFACTURERS
DAVID C HULL EXEC DIR ,
1918 NORTH PARKWAY MEMPHIS , TN 38112

*87 MAY 3 - 6   NATL 300   MARRIOTT HOTEL GRAND
NATL ACCOUNTS MARKETING ASSN
ERNEST C BIGLOW JR EXEC DIR ,
50 E 41ST ST NEW YORK CITY , NY 10017

87 JUL 14 - 16   NATL 500   MARRIOTT HOTEL GRAND
NATL BROILER COUNCIL MTGS
IRMIE BELLMAN MTG COORD ,
1155 15TH ST. NW. STE 614 WASHINGTON , DC 20005

---

87 OCT 23 - 28   REGL 800   MARRIOTT HOTEL GRAND
AMER COLLEGE OBSTETRICIANS GYNECOLOGISTS DIST 7
JUDY G FIELDEN ASSOC DIR ,
600 MARYLAND AVE SW.#300E WASHINGTON , DC 20024

87 OCT(T)   NATL 80   MARRIOTT HOTEL GRAND
GYPSUM ASSN
A VICTOR ABNEE JR EXEC VP ,
1603 ORRINGTON AVE EVANSTON , IL 60201

UNIVERSITY

87 OCT 23 - 25   INTL 90   UNIV AL
INTERFRATERNITY CONGRESS
EXEC DIR , 8265 SOUTHWEST 114TH ST MIAMI , FL 33156

ALASKA

ANCHORAGE

*86 JUN 29 - JUL 2   NATL 500   CAPTAIN COOK
INTERSTATE OIL COMPACT COMMISSION
W TIMOTHY DOWD EXEC DIR ,
BOX 53127 OKLAHOMA CITY , OK 73152

86 JUL 27   STATE 1,000   SHEFFIELD HOUSE
AK KENNEL CLUB
RUTH H MARCY CORR SEC ,
BOX 100051 ANCHORAGE , AK 99516

86 AUG 15 - 16   STATE 100
HILTON HOTEL/SHERATON HOTEL
AK EDUC ASSN LEADERSHIP CONF
TRUDY RIBACCHI , 1411 W 33RD AVE ANCHORAGE , AK 99503

86 AUG 17 - 18   STATE 50   SHERATON HOTEL
AK EDUC ASSN BOARD DIRECTORS MTG
TRUDY RIBACCHI , 1411 W 33RD AVE ANCHORAGE , AK 99503

*86 SEP 28 - OCT 3   NATL EXH 2,000
EGAN CIVIC CONV CENTER
AMER SOC PHOTOGRAMMETRY
W D FRENCH EXEC DIR ,
210 LITTLE FALLS ST FALLS CHURCH , VA 22046

86 OCT 9 - 10   STATE 50   SHERATON HOTEL
AK EDUC ASSN BOARD DIRECTORS MTG
TRUDY RIBACCHI , 1411 W 33RD AVE ANCHORAGE , AK 99503

86 OCT 21 - 23   STATE EXH 325   SHERATON HOTEL
AK ASSN ELEM SECONDARY SCHOOL PRINCIPALS
DONALD L MAC KINNOH EXEC DIR ,
326 FOURTH ST, STE 211 JUNEAU , AK 99801

86 OCT 24 - 26   STATE 1,000
HILTON HOTEL/EGAN CONV CENTER
AK EDUC ASSN TEACHERS CONF
TRUDY RIBACCHI , 1411 W 33RD AVE ANCHORAGE , AK 99503

86 OCT 24 - 26   STATE 200   SHERATON HOTEL
AK SMALL SCHOOL CONF
DONALD L MAC KINNOH ,
326 FOURTH ST, STE 211 JUNEAU , AK 99811

*86 OCT 30 - NOV 6 REGL 150   CAPTAIN COOK
INTL NORTH PACIFIC FISHERIES COMMISSION
EVELYN FUNK ,
6640 NW MARINE DR VANCOUVER , BC V6T 1X2

86 NOV 6 - 9   STATE EXH 700   SHERATON HOTEL
AK EMERGENCY MEDICAL SERVICES
SECRETARY , 1135 W 8TH AVE, STE 7 ANCHORAGE , AK 99501

86 NOV 21 - 22   STATE 50   SHERATON HOTEL
AK EDUC ASSN BOARD DIRECTORS MTG
TRUDY RIBACCHI , 1411 W 33RD AVE ANCHORAGE , AK 99503

86 DEC 4 - 6   REGL 2,000   CAPTAIN COOK
NATL SCIENCE TEACHERS ASSN REG MTGS
ELLIE SNYDER DIR CONV ,
1742 CONNECTICUT AVE, NW WASHINGTON , DC 20009

86 DEC 11 - 12   DIST EXH 100   CAPTAIN COOK
ANCHORAGE SCHOOL DIST COUNCIL EDUC FACILITIES
PLANNING
GREG BRANCH , 4600 DEBARR ANCHORAGE , AK 99502

87 JAN 8   STATE 1,000   SHEFFIELD HOUSE
AK KENNEL CLUB
RUTH H MARCY CORR SEC ,
BOX 100051 ANCHORAGE , AK 99516

87 FEB 11 - 12   STATE EXH 500   SHERATON HOTEL
RESOURCE DEVELOP COUNCIL AK
PAULA EASLEY EXEC DIR ,
BOX 100516 ANCHORAGE , AK 99510

87 MAR 10 - 13   NATL 100
ROOFING INDUSTRY EDUC INST SEMINARS
LAURA OLSON ,
6851 S HOLLY CIRCLE,#100 ENGLEWOOD , CO 80112

87 APR 15 - 19   STATE EXH 200
AK AMER SOC MEDICAL TECHNOLOGY
NANCY O. DAVIS , 4730 1ST EAGLE RIVER , AK 99577

*87 MAY 14 - 16(T)   STATE 125
AK BENEVOLENT PROTECTIVE ORDER ELKS
EDWARD E CALLIHAN ,
2034 CRATAEGUS ANCHORAGE , AK 99508

(See Page C - in front of book - for an explanation of abbreviations and codes)
1

Reprinted with permission from *Successful Meetings* magazine. Copyright © 1986, Bill Communications, Inc.

1986 Directory of Conventions—Sample Pages

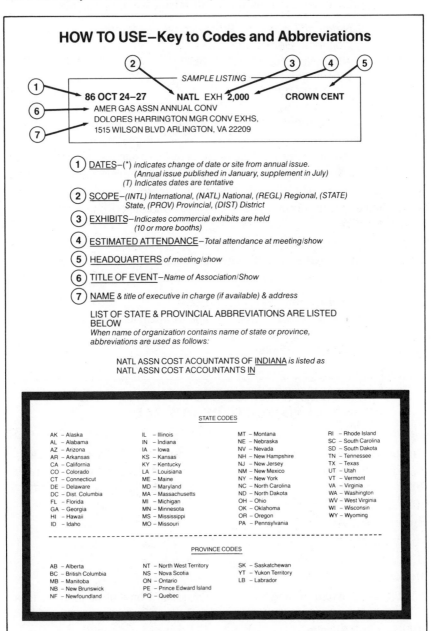

HOW TO USE–Key to Codes and Abbreviations

SAMPLE LISTING

86 OCT 24–27 **NATL** EXH **2,000** **CROWN CENT**
AMER GAS ASSN ANNUAL CONV
DOLORES HARRINGTON MGR CONV EXHS,
1515 WILSON BLVD ARLINGTON, VA 22209

(1) DATES–(*) *indicates change of date or site from annual issue.*
(Annual issue published in January, supplement in July)
(T) Indicates dates are tentative

(2) SCOPE–*(INTL) International, (NATL) National, (REGL) Regional, (STATE)*
State, (PROV) Provincial, (DIST) District

(3) EXHIBITS–*Indicates commercial exhibits are held*
(10 or more booths)

(4) ESTIMATED ATTENDANCE–*Total attendance at meeting/show*

(5) HEADQUARTERS *of meeting/show*

(6) TITLE OF EVENT–*Name of Association/Show*

(7) NAME *& title of executive in charge (if available) & address*

LIST OF STATE & PROVINCIAL ABBREVIATIONS ARE LISTED
BELOW
When name of organization contains name of state or province,
abbreviations are used as follows:

NATL ASSN COST ACOUNTANTS OF <u>INDIANA</u> *is listed as*
NATL ASSN COST ACCOUNTANTS <u>IN</u>

STATE CODES

AK – Alaska	IL – Illinois	MT – Montana	RI – Rhode Island
AL – Alabama	IN – Indiana	NE – Nebraska	SC – South Carolina
AZ – Arizona	IA – Iowa	NV – Nevada	SD – South Dakota
AR – Arkansas	KS – Kansas	NH – New Hampshire	TN – Tennessee
CA – California	KY – Kentucky	NJ – New Jersey	TX – Texas
CO – Colorado	LA – Louisiana	NM – New Mexico	UT – Utah
CT – Connecticut	ME – Maine	NY – New York	VT – Vermont
DE – Delaware	MD – Maryland	NC – North Carolina	VA – Virginia
DC – Dist. Columbia	MA – Massachusetts	ND – North Dakota	WA – Washington
FL – Florida	MI – Michigan	OH – Ohio	WV – West Virginia
GA – Georgia	MN – Minnesota	OK – Oklahoma	WI – Wisconsin
HI – Hawaii	MS – Mississippi	OR – Oregon	WY – Wyoming
ID – Idaho	MO – Missouri	PA – Pennsylvania	

PROVINCE CODES

AB – Alberta	NT – North West Territory	SK – Saskatchewan
BC – British Columbia	NS – Nova Scotia	YT – Yukon Territory
MB – Manitoba	ON – Ontario	LB – Labrador
NB – New Brunswick	PE – Prince Edward Island	
NF – Newfoundland	PQ – Quebec	

geographic, subject (key word), and budget indexes permit cross-referencing to appropriate associations for small business entrepreneurs.

National Trade and Professional Associations
Columbia Books, Inc.
1350 New York Avenue, N.W.
Washington, DC 20005-4780
(202) 737-3777

One of the associations listed, the International Association of Convention and Visitor Bureaus, P.O. Box 758, Champaign, IL 61820, is a good source of information, since there is at least one convention bureau in every state (see sampling below). Call your information operator to see whether there are any close to you. Another good source is the International Exhibitors Association, 5103 Backlick Road, Annandale, VA 22003.

The *Tradeshow Week Data Book,* published annually by the Tradeshow Bureau, features marketing and statistical data on over 5,000 trade shows. It can be obtained by writing:

Tradeshow Week Data Book
12233 West Olympic Boulevard, Suite #236
Los Angeles, CA 90064
(213) 826-5696

A STATE SAMPLING OF CONVENTION AND VISITORS BUREAUS

Alabama

Greater Birmingham Convention
and Visitors Bureau
2027 1st Avenue North
300 Commerce Center
Birmingham, AL 35203
(205) 252-9825

Alaska

Anchorage Convention and
Visitors Bureau
201 East 3rd Avenue
Anchorage, AK 99501
(907) 276-4118

Arizona

Phoenix and Valley of the Sun
Convention and Visitors Bureau
505 North 2nd Street, Suite 300
Phoenix, AZ 85004
(602) 254-6500

California

Pasadena Convention and Visitors
Bureau
171 South Los Robles
Pasadena, CA 91101
(818) 795-9311

San Diego Convention and
Visitors Bureau
1200 3rd Avenue, Suite 824
San Diego, CA 92101
(619) 232-3101

San Francisco Convention and
Visitors Bureau
201 3rd Street, #900
San Francisco, CA 94103
(415) 974-6900

Colorado
Denver and Colorado Convention
and Visitors Bureau
225 West Colfax Avenue
Denver, CO 80202
(303) 892-1112

Connecticut
Greater Hartford Convention and
Visitors Bureau, Inc.
1 Civic Center Plaza
Hartford, CT 06103
(203) 728-6789

District of Columbia
Washington Convention and
Visitors Association, Inc.
1575 Eye Street, N.W.
Washington, DC 20005
(202) 789-7000

Florida
Greater Miami Convention and
Visitors Bureau
4770 Biscayne Boulevard,
Penthouse A
Miami, FL 33137
(305) 573-4300

Tampa/Hillsborough Convention
and Visitors Association, Inc.
P.O. Box 519
Tampa, FL 33601
(813) 224-0091

Georgia
Atlanta Convention and Visitors
Bureau
233 Peachtree Street, N.E., Suite
#200
Atlanta, GA 30043
(404) 521-6600

Hawaii
Hawaii Visitors Bureau
2270 Kalakaua Avenue, Suite 801
Honolulu, HI 96815
(808) 923-1811

Illinois
Chicago Convention and Tourism
Bureau, Inc.
McCormick Place on the Lake
Chicago, IL 60616
(312) 225-5000

Indiana
Indianapolis Convention and
Visitors Association
1 Hoosier Dome, Suite 100
200 South Capitol Avenue
Indianapolis, IN 46225
(317) 639-4282

Iowa

Greater Des Moines Convention
and Visitors Bureau, Inc.
800 High Street
Des Moines, IA 50307
(515) 286-4960

Kansas

Wichita Convention and Visitors
Bureau
111 West Douglas, Suite 804
Wichita, KS 67202
(316) 265-2800

Kentucky

Greater Lexington Convention and
Visitors Bureau
430 West Vine Street, Suite 363
Lexington, KY 40507
(606) 233-1221

Louisville Convention and
Visitors Bureau
501 South 3rd Street
Louisville, KY 40202
(502) 584-2121

Louisiana

Greater New Orleans Tourist and
Convention Commission
1520 Sugar Bowl Drive
New Orleans, LA 70112
(504) 566-5011

Maine

Convention and Visitors Bureau
of Greater Portland
142 Free Street
Portland, ME 04101
(207) 772-4994

Maryland

Baltimore Convention Bureau
1 East Pratt Street, Suite 14
Baltimore, MD 21202
(301) 659-7300

Massachusetts

Greater Boston Convention and
Visitors Bureau
Prudential Plaza
P.O. Box 490
Boston, MA 02199
(617) 536-4100

Michigan

Metropolitan Detroit Convention
and Visitors Bureau
100 Renaissance Center,
Suite 1950
Detroit, MI 48243
(313) 259-4333

Minnesota

Minneapolis Convention and
Visitors Commission
15 South 5th Street
Minneapolis, MN 55402
(612) 348-4313

Mississippi

Jackson Convention and Visitors
Bureau
P.O. Box 1450
Jackson, MS 39205
(601) 960-1891

Missouri

Convention and Visitors Bureau
  of Greater Kansas City
1100 Main Street, Suite 2550
Kansas City, MO 64105
(816) 221-5242

St. Louis Convention and Visitors
  Commission
10 South Broadway, Suite 300
St. Louis, MO 63102
(314) 421-1023

Nebraska

Lincoln Convention and Visitors
  Bureau
1221 N Street, Suite 606
Lincoln, NE 68508
(402) 476-7511

Nevada

Las Vegas Convention and
  Visitors Authority
3150 Paradise Road
Las Vegas, NV 89109-9096
(702) 733-2323

New Jersey

Atlantic City Convention and
  Visitors Bureau
16 Central Pier
Atlantic City, NJ 08401
(609) 345-7536

New Mexico

Albuquerque Convention and
  Visitors Bureau, Inc.
202 Central Southeast, Suite 301
P.O. Box 26866
Albuquerque, NM 87102
(505) 243-3696

New York

Albany County Convention and
  Visitors Bureau
600 Broadway
Albany, NY 12207
(518) 434-1217

Buffalo Area Chamber of
  Commerce
Convention and Tourism
  Division
107 Delaware Avenue
Buffalo, NY 14202
(716) 849-6609

New York Convention and
  Visitors Bureau
2 Columbus Circle
New York, NY 10019
(212) 397-8200

North Carolina

Charlotte Convention and Visitors
  Bureau, Inc.
1 Independence Center, Suite
  1290
Charlotte, NC 28246
(704) 334-CCVB

Winston-Salem Convention and
  Visitors Bureau
Greater Winston-Salem Chamber
  of Commerce
500 North 5th Street
P.O. Box 1408
Winston-Salem, NC 27102-1408
(919) 725-2361

Ohio
Greater Cincinnati Convention
  and Visitors Bureau
200 West 5th Street
Cincinnati, OH 45202
(513) 621-2142

Convention and Visitors Bureau
  of Greater Cleveland
1301 East 6th Street
Cleveland, OH 44114
(216) 621-4110

Oklahoma
Oklahoma City Convention and
  Tourism Bureau
4 Santa Fe Plaza
Oklahoma City, OK 73102
(405) 278-8912

Tulsa Convention and Visitors
  Bureau
616 South Boston
Tulsa, OK 74119
(918) 585-7201

Oregon
Greater Portland Convention and
  Visitors Association, Inc.
26 Southwest Salmon
Portland, OR 97204-3299
(503) 222-2223

Pennsylvania
Philadelphia Convention and
  Visitors Bureau
3 Penn Center Plaza
Philadelphia, PA 19102
(215) 636-3300

Pittsburgh Convention and
  Visitors Bureau
4 Gateway Center
Pittsburgh, PA 15222
(412) 281-7711

Rhode Island
Greater Providence Convention
  and Visitors Bureau
Commerce Center
30 Exchange Terrace
Providence, RI 02903
(401) 274-1636

South Carolina
Charleston/Trident Convention
  and Visitors Bureau
P.O. Box 975
Charleston, SC 29402
(803) 723-7641

South Dakota
Rapid City Convention and
   Visitors Bureau
P.O. Box 747
Rapid City, SD 57709
(605) 343-1744

Tennessee
Chattanooga Area Convention and
   Visitors Bureau
1001 Market Street
Chattanooga, TN 37402
(615) 756-2121

Memphis Convention and Visitors
   Bureau
203 Beale Street, Suite 305
Memphis, TN 38103
(901) 526-1919

Convention and Visitors Division
Nashville Area Chamber of
   Commerce
161 4th Avenue, North
Nashville, TN 37219
(615) 259-3900

Texas
Dallas Convention and Visitors
   Bureau
1507 Pacific Avenue
Dallas, TX 75201
(214) 954-1410

Greater Houston Convention and
   Visitors Council
3300 Main Street
Houston, TX 77002
(713) 523-5050

San Antonio Convention and
   Visitors Bureau
P.O. Box 2277
San Antonio, TX 78298
(512) 270-8700

Utah
Salt Lake City Convention and
   Visitors Bureau
180 South West Temple
Salt Lake City, UT 84101-1493
(801) 521-2822

Virginia
Metropolitan Richmond
   Convention and Visitors Bureau
300 East Main Street, Suite 100
Richmond, VA 23219
(804) 782-2777

Virginia Beach Convention
   Bureau
P.O. Box 136
Virginia Beach, VA 23458
(804) 428-8000

Washington
Seattle/King County Convention
   and Visitors Bureau
1815 7th Avenue
Seattle, WA 98101
(206) 447-4200

West Virginia
Charleston Convention and
   Visitors Bureau
200 Civic Center Drive
Charleston, WV 25301
(304) 344-5075

Wisconsin
Green Bay Area Visitors and
   Convention Bureau, Inc.
1901 South Oneida Street
P.O. Box 10596
Green Bay, WI 54307-0596
(414) 447-4200

Greater Milwaukee Convention
   and Visitors Bureau
756 North Milwaukee Street
Milwaukee, WI 53202
(414) 273-3950

KEY PERIODICALS

In addition to all of the directories cited above, here are a few key periodicals that offer important information on trade shows.

Tradeshow Week lists trade shows scheduled for the week six months in advance. Included in the listing are the location, contact name, address, phone number, projected square footage of exhibit space, number of booths, number of exhibiting companies, and professional attendance expected.

> Tradeshow Week, Inc.
> 12233 West Olympic Boulevard, Suite #236
> Los Angeles, CA 90064
> (213) 826-5696

Industrial Distribution provides its readers with information on scheduled trade shows, including the dates, locations, and a phone number.

> Industrial Distribution
> Technical Publishing Company
> 875 3rd Avenue
> New York, NY 10022
> (212) 605-9400

Special Events Reports is an international newsletter on events, festivals and promotions which is published biweekly.

> Special Event Reports, Inc.
> 213 West Institute Place, Suite #303
> Chicago, IL 60610
> (312) 944-1727

The *Newsletter Yearbook Directory* can be used to locate additional publication sources for trade fairs.

Newsletter Clearinghouse
44 West Market Street
P.O. Box 311
Rhinebeck, NY
(914) 876-2081

ASSOCIATION CONVENTION INFORMATION

The American Society of Association Executives produces a calendar of various programs of affiliated societies that may provide information on relevant trade shows and meetings.

American Society of Association
Executives
1575 Eye Street, N.W.
Washington, DC 20005
(202) 626-2773

FEDERAL AND STATE AGENCY INFORMATION

The Small Business Administration, the Minority Business Development Agency (U.S. Department of Commerce), the Department of Transportation, and other federal agencies, as well as state agencies (see Chapter 13), periodically sponsor trade fairs to bring together small and/or small disadvantaged enterpreneurs and representatives of government procurement offices. Similar opportunities for expanding the pool of small business suppliers may exist at the local government level. To obtain announcements of forthcoming fairs, contact the National Minority Supplier Development Council, Inc., 1412 Broadway, 11th Floor, New York, NY 10018 (212-944-2430). Or you can write to the sponsor directly.

Minority Small Business—Capital
  Ownership Development
U.S. Small Business
  Administration
1441 L Street, N.W., Room 602
Washington, DC 20416
Minority Business Development
  Agency

U.S. Department of Commerce
14th Street and Constitution
  Avenue
Washington, DC 20230
Minority Procurement Office
U.S. Department of
  Transportation
400 7th Street, S.W.
Washington, DC 20590

Other minority and small business trade groups promote the interests of small minority businesses that are seeking markets in the private sector (see Chapter 13). For example, the National Association of Women Business Owners and the U.S. Hispanic Chamber of Commerce, sponsor commercial gatherings to foster the interchange between small firms and corporate America as well as federal, state, and local governments. These groups are listed in *National Trade and Professional Associations.*

Regional Purchasing Magazines

Review the list of 30 regional purchasing periodicals provided in Chapter 8. These publications, all of which are affiliates of the National Association of Purchasing Management, are targeted at purchasing personnel and highlight forthcoming trade shows within the respective region and in adjoining regions. Not surprisingly, most small business entrepreneurs are unaware of these shows and of the opportunities that attending them affords.

EXHIBITING AT TRADE SHOWS

The cost of exhibiting can range anywhere from $800 to $1,200 in rental fees per 80 square feet of booth space, with an additional cost of $3,000–$4,000 for a professionally designed exhibit (which hopefully will be reused). "The small business entrepreneur who has never exhibited before needs to do his or her homework before attempting such a venture," said an excutive with a Boston-based trade show management company. "A lot of 'amateur' exhibitors make a horrible showing the first time out because they have no idea of the level of preparation and professionalism required to be successful at the show."

Here are some rules for good "boothmanship" offered by marketing consultant David Voracek:

- Do not smoke, eat, or drink while in the booth.
- Avoid chitchat with others on your staff, or you'll miss the prospects.
- Dress conservatively, and skip the after-shave and perfumes.
- Never sit down unless you're with a client.
- Keep your hands out of your pockets, and keep your body language "approachable."
- Get to bed early enough to be fresh for booth duty every day.

Joe Jeff Goldblatt, President of the Wonder Company adds that the average booth visit is less than one minute! You or your representative are producing a live commercial. You must be concise, direct, and engaging.

Exhibiting at Trade Shows, published by the Dartnell Corporation, 4660 Ravenswood Avenue, Chicago, IL 60640, provides excellent step-by-step information for both first-time and veteran exhibitors. "Designing a Trade Fair Stand," an article by Bruce Bendow and Gareth Jones in the April 1985 issue of *International Trade Forum,* can help you to develop or select a suitable design for a trade fair stand or exhibit.

International Trade Forum
UNCTAD/GATT
Palais des Nations
1211 Geneva 10, Switzerland

Secondary benefits accrue to the trade show exhibitor. "It's a great way to scan the product and service offerings of competitors," says Lusson, "and you can do some instant market research by varying your presentation or accenting different products and services and seeing how well these go over."

Exhibiting is not for everyone, however. On the downside, you and/or members of your staff may spend two or three days at the show; counting preparation and postshow activities, participation in a trade show can easily tie up at least 10–12 person-days. In addition to the cost of the show and related expenses, work at the office continues. Why, then, do trade shows continue to be so popular among small business entrepreneurs? Jeff Stevens, marketing representative for Phoenix Radiology in Chatsworth, California, comments, "Where else are you going to meet so many potential targets in such a short time? And why worry about the problems back at the office? There'll always be problems, and when you get back, you'll take care of them just like you always do."

Industrial psychologist Allen Konopacki, president of Incomm International, in Chicago, suggests giving trade show salespeople specific goals for each day. For example: "Come up with three prospects who can buy $150,000 worth of equipment." This enables salespeople to focus their activities and avoid meaningless contacts within an otherwise potentially disorienting environment.

A MODERN-DAY PHENOMENON

Trade shows have become something of a phenomenon. Joanne Tritsch, director of research and development at Successful Meetings/Databank, reports that over 1,200 exhibits and trade shows and over 21,000 association-based conventions and exhibitions have been scheduled for the coming year. "It really doesn't matter what you're offering," says Tritsch, "the odds are there's a trade show that's right for you."

Convinced that trade shows might be for you? If so, a good first step would be to attend one, with a new perspective. Critically examine which booths attract your eye and why. Stevens says, "Note the type of signs and displays being used, the handouts and other promotional materials, and the dress, demeanor, and accessibility of those working the booth." Also, ask exhibitors what their experiences have been and what benefits they are deriving, or hope to derive, from the present show.

Also, get the name of the show management group and ask for a copy of the exhibitor instructions and guidelines. Most trade shows have them, and they represent a valuable free source of information. Finally, call several local graphic arts services and audiovisual suppliers to determine what it would cost to develop the kind of exhibit you wish to present.

A LOW-COST ALTERNATIVE

Visiting a trade show is, of course, less costly than exhibiting in it. Plan your time at the show carefully, visiting the firms that you would like as customers. Maximize your use of your time by visiting the press or information area and obtaining a list of exhibitors and their locations. Talk with the exhibitors who could be likely customers for you, but don't come on too strong since they're the ones who are exhibiting— not you. Simply leave your business card.

If there is time and the corporate reps are not too busy, obtain the names, addresses, and phone numbers of the small business vendor coordinator or the appropriate purchasing agent. Try to procure copies of vendor guides for use in identifying potential customers for your firm. You may not be able to get all of this information as a visitor. However, the contact you've made is still valuable.

Once back in your office, be sure to follow up on whatever contacts or information you've developed. The contacts you've met also met 200 other people at the show, so your follow-up must be swift, informative, and professional.

Here's a quick summary of the benefits that you can derive from trade shows:

- Demonstrate new products.
- Find new customers.
- Take orders.
- Develop mailing list.
- Promote the company image.
- Determine what competitors are doing.

If you haven't considered trade shows before, don't overlook the significant marketing opportunities that they can offer. Goldblatt advises regarding the trade show as a chance to appear in the Olympics of your industry. They're an investment that can pay off in a big way. Corporate America meets at trade shows—you should be there too.

CHAPTER TWELVE

Corporations That Go the Extra Mile

*Efforts and courage are
not enough without purpose
and direction.*

JOHN F. KENNEDY

In this chapter we take a look at uncommon efforts made by some corporations to attract and assist small vendors, highlighting Control Data Corporation (106).

"Business as usual—stick with vendors who are large and reliable and have built a good reputation." That advice has become axiomatic. However, it has been flouted by Control Data Corporation of Bloomington, Minnesota. Control Data's credo is "Business *not* as usual." Leslie Rhatican examined Control Data Corporation's aggressive program to seek out and use small and disadvantaged businesses. What follows is based on Rhatican's findings.

Right up front, Control Data's small vendor guide says:

> Control Data believes that there is a compelling need for the business sector to take the initiative and provide leadership in addressing major societal needs as an integral part of their businesses, in partnership with government and other sectors.

Control Data feels that addressing these societal needs as an integral business strategy can generate profits as well as improve society. The Control Data action plan to conduct "Business-*not*-as-usual" was instituted in 1973, and it has grown to encompass procurement, training, and financing activities.

Control Data has established an aggressive small business purchasing program. The purchasing function is decentralized into over 35 facilities located throughout the country. Basic supplies and services are purchased within a local or regional area. However, products and services that are used at more than one location can still be purchased under a regional or national agreement through the corporate procurement staff.

Control Data has produced a pamphlet identifying the goods and services it seeks and a directory of its purchasing facilities. The firm's needs are broken down into two broad areas: (1) manufacturing and production; and (2) service, administration, and nonproduction. The directory keys the firm's purchasing facilities according to these two designations so that vendors can identify appropriate potential buyers.

LAYING IT ON THE LINE

Each Control Data division is charged with the responsibility for seeking out and using small vendors. To encourage such efforts, quarterly reports are filed, indicating:

1. The small and small disadvantaged vendors being used.
2. Dollar goals and commitments.
3. The number of prospective vendors that have been identified, interviewed, and visited.
4. The percentage of commitments with identified vendors.

Local purchasing managers and buyers maintain responsibility for ensuring that the Control Data small business purchasing program is actively pursued.

The corporate procurement office provides training courses to buyers so that they fully understand corporate policy and procedure. This office also promotes intradivision competition for procurement from small disadvantaged businesses, with plaques awarded for meeting a facility's goal and an awards ceremony for the top 10 facilities.

The corporate procurement office provides direction, assistance, and encouragement to aspiring vendors. Control Data maintains a Small Business Advocate Office to serve as troubleshooter for any problems that vendors may encounter.

FREE TRAINING COURSES

To create a healthier climate for small vendors, Control Data has developed a network of more than 100 Education Centers. Located in principal cities throughout the nation, these centers provide responsive and affordable training and use Control Data's PLATO computer-based education system.

The courses are specifically tailored to the needs of both the small business entrepreneur and his or her empoyees. Management courses range from how to establish and manage a small business, to accounting, selling, purchasing, and government regulations. Individualized employee courses focus not only on technical skills but also on basics, such as reading and mathematics. The PLATO terminals are linked to a central computer and provide a one-on-one teaching atmosphere enabling self-pacing by the student.

Another aspect of training is provided through Control Data Business Advisors, Inc. Business Advisors acts as a consulting organization to small businesses in need of specialized management assistance. A computerized skills bank identifies Control Data employees who are available to provide consulting services on a project basis. Also the skills bank identifies available experts in many specialized fields from leading universities and research centers.

Clients of Business Advisors, Inc. can receive professional management assistance in the following areas: financial analysis and planning; marketing and sales; technology management; manufacturing and processing; communications, advertising, public relations, and sales promotion; personnel and human resource development; operations development; and strategic and business planning.

FINANCING AT COMPETITIVE RATES

Control Data's "business-not-as-usual" philosophy is also applied to the critical area of financing. Control Data has established several sources to provide financing for small and small disadvantaged firms at competitive rates.

Commercial Credit Business Loans, Inc. provides revolving loans secured by either accounts receivable or inventory; term loans secured by machinery and equipment, real estate, or other fixed assets; and package loans that are available through any combination of receivables, inventory, and fixed assets. It also offers short-term capital loans for seasonal enterprises.

Commercial Credit Financial Corporation is authorized to issue loans guaranteed by the Small Business Administration. The maximum loan amount guaranteed under the Small Business Administration loan program is $500,000. Interest rates vary with the prime rate, and maturities average approximately seven years. Commercial Credit Financial Corporation will make loans to finance new companies, to refinance young and growing companies, to assist in the purchase of equipment and the expansion of facilities, and to provide operating capital for established small companies

Commercial Credit/McCullagh Leasing, Inc. provides an effective means for conserving working capital for vendors through fixed-asset financing. Equipment that can be financed or leased ranges from standard capital investments to a variety of specialized commercial equipment.

Control Data Capital Corporation is a licensed Small Business Investment Company that provides long-term investment capital to small firms. The Capital Corporation fund is capitalized to make equity investments in the $100,000–$500,000 range.

Control Data Community Ventures Fund, Inc. is licensed by the Small Business Administration as a Minority Enterprise Small Business Investment Company to provide long-term financing for small business persons whose participation in the free enterprise system is hampered by social or economic disadvantages. The fund is specifically designed for enterprises with at least 51 percent minority ownership.

Finally, Control Data Financial and Human Resources Fund, Inc. is a "high-risk" fund that provides seed money to assist the start-up of technologically oriented small businesses.

MAKING THE "NOT USUAL" USUAL

These Control Data programs were not instituted overnight, reminds Rhatican. Many major obstacles had to be overcome during their development. Buyers had to be educated to use small suppliers and small disadvantaged suppliers. Established purchasing patterns had to be irrevocably altered, and suppliers had to be identified and qualified. Control Data engineering and quality assurance personnel worked with some firms for up to nine years to assure their qualification.

WHAT ELSE ARE CORPORATIONS DOING?

Most major corporations have good intentions with regard to awarding contracts to small vendors. However, not all purchasing managers realize that the length of the corporate procurement cycle—the time from initial marketing contact to actual contract award—effectively eliminates many small firms from contention for new contracts.

At a national purchasing conference, one corporate purchasing executive admitted that the average length of the procurement cycle at his company was 24 months. He said that most large corporations were burdened by contracting procedures that made the procurement cycle a hardship for many small vendors. Here are some of the ways in which corporate procurement procedures have been modified so as to be more responsive to small business vendors.

1. Corporations such as Control Data (106), Pfizer (91), and McDonnell Douglas (29) determine, on a long-term basis, which contracts will be limited to small and small minority business. In this way, there is ample time to outline qualifications, specifications, and other desirables for the small vendors months in advance.

2. Some contracts are earmarked to be sole-source, nonbid proposals, or competitive bids for small business vendors. Job size has a lot to do with this determination, along with knowledge of capable vendors with whom the purchasing department is already acquainted. From their list of eligible vendors, some corporations develop a list of qualified vendors for each contract—well before contract announcement or proposal solicitation, so that less time is wasted in qualifying eligible vendors.

3. The largest portion of time in the procurement cycle is spent in determining whether or not a group of small vendors actually qualifies to perform a particular job. Some corporations cut down the number of unqualified proposals submitted by providing small vendors with a checklist of what they need and don't need to qualify for specific contracts. Also, in recent years procurement processing time has been cut by streamlining the forms and other documentation required from small business vendors.

4. Corporations such as Todd Shipyards (462) set priorities for small business procurement and establish time frames for job announcements, bid or proposal deadlines, and contract award announcements.

5. Many corporations are striving for better communication with small vendors. Better communication means that less time is required to convey contract needs and that there are fewer misunderstandings leading to delays in the procurement process. Progressive corporations have installed a procurement spokesperson to deal with small vendors exclusively, usually the small business coordinator. Thus time-consuming communications between the wrong parties are often eliminated.

6. Increasingly, corporations are providing all contract information and specifications in one package to avoid costly revisions and time delays for vendors.

7. Some corporations maintain candor with small vendors, advising them as soon as possible when their proposals or bids fail to meet qualification standards. This policy frees up everybody's time. It gives vendors a chance to move on and concentrate on other opportunities. Also when

you've been told in timely fashion why you didn't receive a contract award, you'll tend to think more highly of, and respect, the corporation to which you've made a bid.

EFFECTIVE SUPPLIERS GUIDES

An important feature that makes such companies as Control Data so attractive to small vendors is a well-written, readily available suppliers guide. Dianne Walbrecker reviewed a sampling of suppliers guides.

The Grumman Corporation (131) brochure for prospective vendors includes photographs, buying responsibilities, and direct-dial numbers of all buyers. Northrop Corporation (71) sends a monthly newsletter, *Small Business Purchasing,* to all vendors—established or potential— on its mailing list. Pfizer (91) sends out a brochure listing its product needs, plant locations, and telephone numbers. Gulf Oil Corporation sends a vendor application form in response to queries from potential vendors.

A concise, informative suppliers guide is a crucial tool for any product or service vendor aiming to sell to the Fortune 500. If you are unfamiliar with the policies and procedures of a corporation, getting hold of its suppliers guide will enable you to give a better presentation once you've determined a need you can fulfill.

The business ethics policy, often included in the suppliers guide, is usually broad in scope, stating that buyers are instructed to deal with all suppliers in a fair and impartial manner and that purchasing personnel should neither seek nor accept gifts. Several suppliers guides also mention that purchases are made on the basis of quality, service, and price.

Some corporations prepare special guidelines on minority purchasing policies. Other corporations simply state in the suppliers guide that they will help "develop minority vendors into useful and competitive suppliers of goods and services equivalent in quality to those available elsewhere." Statements on minority purchasing range from a declaration that "the corporation does not discriminate" to a commitment to seek out and use minority vendors.

Some suppliers guides address the subject of "end runs"—to technical staff—around the purchasing department. If these are not allowed, this is usually stated in the suppliers guide.

Corporations that are committed to using small vendors make suppliers guides readily available by mail from purchasing departments and display them in waiting areas on-site.

WHY SHOULD WE BUY FROM YOU?

One corporation poses the above question to potential vendors in its suppliers guide. It also asks "what distinguishes your company and your products/services from your competitors?" and presents the following questionnaire as a checklist for vendors:

Have you presented a new idea to us lately?

What is your best idea to reduce our cost?

Do you have products or services that will increase our productivity? How?

Will your organization provide technical services to us?

Are your complete capabilities known to us? Are we using them?

Do you tell us promptly of new products or of new ways to use existing ones?

What is your approach to quality? Do you know the consistency of the product you ship us—or just think you do—or assume it is OK unless you receive complaints?

What are you doing to improve the consistency of your product quality?

Are you willing to certify your shipments to us as meeting quality standards?

Have you established a record of "delivery reliability" with us?

Is every shipment of your product within agreed-to tolerances, properly packaged and marked with the proper code number, having the exact count, and shipped to the proper destination?

Do you always ship only the quantity ordered? (No overage unless within the agreed-to size.)

Do you always ship on the specified date—and not before, unless the purchase order permits early shipment?

Do you always ship as instructed by us?

What specific ideas can you offer to minimize transportation costs on items we buy from you?

Will you hold prices longer for more business?

Terms are a part of price. We pay on time. Are your quoted prices on the basis of our prompt payment?

Have you developed a "Volume Discount" program with us?

Do you participate in our "Committed Stock" program?

Are you interested in consignment inventory on or near our premises? Vendor stocking, on your premises, may offer opportunities for additional volume.

Have you reviewed your lead time requirements with us? Shorter lead times may give you a competitive advantage.

After reviewing a suppliers guide, you may decide that you do not have the products or services in need. Thus you have saved yourself valuable time.

Many suppliers guides include a vendor questionnaire (see next page). This indicates to you that the suppliers guide is the first step in the procurement process and not merely a delaying tactic. The vendor questionnaire is important and should be filled out as completely and accurately as possible.

There is absolutely no point and no advantage in beefing up your credentials on application forms. I've seen small vendors who added 50 percent to their plant's square footage, "doubled" the number of their employees, and added several years to how long they had been in business. These tactics never work in the long run. Integrity does. The purchasing agents with whom you deal have "seen it all." Your best chance is to maintain 100 percent honesty—*really*.

Many corporations, such as Philip Morris (27) and McDonnell Douglas (29), produce a directory of potential vendors that is distributed to all buyers throughout the corporation. The corporation's vendor application forms provide the information for such directories. This document serves as a "ready reference" when a new source or new materials are required. McDonnell Douglas publishes a directory of vendors quarterly.

Not all corporations, however, have developed suppliers guides, and some that have don't distribute them in a timely manner. In May 1986, I requested a suppliers guide from Motorola (66), National Semiconductor (266), Bell and Howell (371), Abbott Laboratories (116), and Cummins Engine (174), and eight months later I had still not received any reply from them.

Here is a review of items commonly found in suppliers guides:

- Business ethics policy.
- Small vendor purchasing policy, including specific goals, if applicable.
- Items and services purchased by plant or buying center.
- Names, addresses, and phone numbers or specific purchasing managers, including their areas of responsibility.
- Best time of day or week to see buyers.
- Location of plants (if purchasing is decentralized).
- Background on the company.
- What the company expects of its supplier; special qualifications required of vendor for specific products/services.
- Vendor questionnaire.

VENDOR QUESTIONNAIRE

Your company's name _____

Address _____ Phone (___) _____

City _____ State _____ Zip _____

Names of principals and partners _____

_____

Contact person and title _____

Describe type of goods or services provided (list SIC numbers if known)

_____

_____

Gross annual sales $_____ Number of employees _____

Years in business _____

_____ Sole proprietorship _____ Partnership _____ Corporation

Is the company a manufacturers' representative? _____ Yes _____ No

(If yes, list product lines carried) _____

_____

_____

Geographic service area _____

Ownership: (1) U.S. citizens? _____ Yes _____ No

              If no, permanent U.S. visas? _____

           (2) 51% minority owned? _____ Yes _____ No

Are you presently doing business with us? _____

Have you done so in the past? _____ (If yes, please complete the following.)

Division, Facility, City	Buyer's Name and Phone	Specific Product or Service
_____	_____	_____
_____	_____	_____
_____	_____	_____

Please list three company credit references:

Company Name	Contact Person	Address and Phone
_____	_____	_____
_____	_____	_____
_____	_____	_____

Please list three of your major clients:

Company Name	Contact Person	Address and Phone	Specific Product or Service
_____	_____	_____	_____
_____	_____	_____	_____
_____	_____	_____	_____

Give any other information you feel pertinent _____

_____

Submitted by (name): _____ Title _____ Date _____

Sample Pages from Honeywell's Corporate Supplier/Vendor Guide

HONEYWELL FACT BOOK 1985

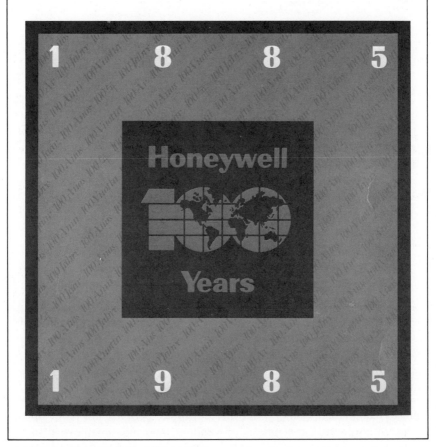

Reprinted with permission from Honeywell, Inc.

Contents

Cover:

To help celebrate Honeywell's 100th birthday — and symbolize the global bond of Honeywell employees — a centennial poster printed in the native language of most countries where Honeywell does business was distributed to company offices around the world. The poster commemorates Honeywell's 100 years of business in Spanish, Portuguese, French, Italian, Japanese, Dutch, Finnish, Swedish, German, and English. The 100 year logo, printed in the center of the poster, was also presented to employees in the form of lapel pins.

Reprinted with permission from Honeywell, Inc.

In summary, an effective suppliers guide spells out corporate commitment to using small vendors, outlines corporate policies and procedures, discusses corporate expectations of vendors, and may enable you to be a part of the vendor roster. A suppliers guide can pack a lot of information into a small amount of space, saving both you and the corporation purchasing department time and money. Isn't that what it's all about?

Honeywell Guide to Products and Services

"Does Honeywell make central nervous systems for intelligent buildings or set-back thermostats for heat pumps?"

Find the answer fast with this guide to Honeywell products and services.

The *Honeywell Guide to Products and Services* is a pocket reference that lists Honeywell's major products and services, organized by customers' lines of business. Honeywell products and services are divided further by the company's three basic product groups: Computers, Communications and Controls. Division abbreviations and phone numbers also are listed.

You can "localize" this guide too. Simply use the space provided to list the names and phone numbers of local division contacts.

We're One Honeywell, an international company serving a world of markets. For more information on our products and services, call:

Telemarketing Center's
Product Info Line
(800) 328-5111, ext. 99
or HVN 870-2026

Or call divisional headquarters, with numbers listed in this guide.

Reprinted with permission from Honeywell, Inc.

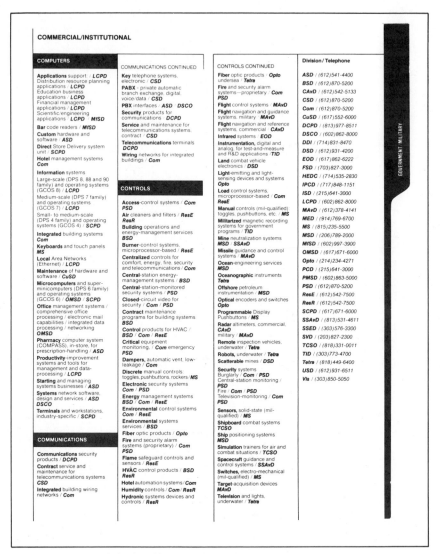

Reprinted with permission from Honeywell, Inc.

CORPORATE INITIATIVES TO USE MINORITY VENDORS

There is growing interest among some corporations in instituting minority purchasing programs, for a variety of reasons—compliance with federal law for government prime contractors, social responsibility, improved community relations, and a broadened supplier base.

Goal setting is necessary in the development and implementation of a minority purchasing program. Dr. Larry C. Giunipero, of Florida State University, did a study that identifies the required elements of an effective minority purchasing program:

- Gaining support from top corporate management—both verbal support and the issuance of a formal policy.
- Assigning responsibility for coordinating the program to one individual.
- Establishing the program within a framework in which corporate, operating unit, and individual purchasing agent goals are set and buyers are appraised on how well they have satisfied minority vendor goals.
- Developing techniques to locate minority vendors.
- Monitoring and reviewing minority purchasing progress by including minority purchasing goals as a factor in performance appraisals, by reporting minority purchasing progress on a regular basis, and by having several levels of top management participate in the review of minority purchasing progress.

Dr. Giunipero based his conclusions on 190 responses to questionnaires mailed to 504 manufacturing companies, including 390 firms listed in the Fortune 1000. The specific policies and procedures that a major corporation uses in developing a minority purchasing program is determined by its industry, the types of products it purchases, and its purchasing structure. Automobile manufacturers, computer manufacturers, pharmaceutical companies, and aerospace manufacturers have traditionally demonstrated leadership in this area.

The common denominator of successful minority purchasing programs is that quantifiable goals are set and performance is then matched against these goals. Each purchasing agent acknowledges the corporate commitment to a minority purchasing program and his or her required participation in the program. Purchasing agents are given training to help them understand the goals and purposes of the program and the techniques needed for success.

The minority purchasing program coordinator or someone with a similar title has responsibility for monitoring the program, which may include offering assistance to purchasing agents and compiling reports on purchasing performance for distribution to all of the company's units. Hundreds of firms, among them Monsanto (53), Polaroid (257), Hughes Tool (265),

Perkin Elmer (256), Prime Computer (366), Raytheon (60), and Ex-Cell-O (287), now have special minority purchasing coordinators.

What is the easiest way to determine whether a corporation has instituted a minority vendor purchasing program? Ask it. Those that have don't keep it a secret.

AN INSIDE LOOK AT CORPORATE USE OF MINORITY VENDORS

Here's a look at what a handful of corporations do, or don't do, to facilitate the use of minority vendors. This section makes no attempt to be judgmental—rather, it attempts to provide a realistic portrait of some typical Fortune 500 corporations.

International Multifoods (274)

International Multifoods' director of corporate recruiting and placement has responsibility for all of the firm's minority relations—minority purchasing as well as minority personnel recruitment. Observation of Multifoods' use of minority vendors and its outreach activities leads one to believe that there is no proactive or formal minority vendor utilization program. However, International Multifoods does participate in the Minnesota Minority Purchasing Council and it has a written corporate policy and top-management commitment to use minority vendors—as long as such use does not adversely affect profitability.

Each Multifoods plant operates as a profit center, and purchasing is decentralized. Corporate representatives have knowledge of sources for identifying minority vendors but observe that there are few minority vendors in the grain business. They seek vendors who offer reliable delivery and handle transactions in a professional, businesslike manner.

Economics Laboratory, Inc. (376)

Economics Laboratory has a formal policy and top-management support for minority vendor utilization; however, it has no full-time program. Essentially, the corporate purchasing policy is procurement of quality goods at lowest cost. If this can be accomplished using minority vendors, all the better.

Economics Laboratory will make an extra effort to do business with minority vendors as long as the corporation's profitability criteria are met, and it has three major reasons for doing so:

- On government contracts, its use of minority vendors is mandated by federal legislation.
- It feels responsible to the community at large.
- It believes in increasing the number of reliable vendors.

The corporate purchasing manager routinely submits vendor information to local plant purchasing managers and monitors their vendor usage. The corporate purchasing manager reports directly to the vice president for purchasing, and these two persons are charged with minority vendor procurement responsibility.

Economics Laboratory currently uses minority vendors for less than 1 percent of its purchases. The company participates in the Minnesota Minority Purchasing Council, trade fairs, and the Minnesota Economic Development Association. It also provides free space for the Minnesota Hispanic Chamber of Commerce, and it has conducted in-house trade fairs with members of this group. Economics Laboratory sponsors an annual purchasing conference that addresses, among many other issues, the use of minority vendors.

About 65–70 percent of Economics Laboratory's needs are for chemical cleaning products and packaging goods, in varieties and quantities that seem to preclude many minority firms from bidding. Economics Laboratory uses minority vendors for ancillary services, including travel, messenger, office supplies, trucking, architecture, and engineering. Most of Economics Laboratory's procurement is generated through corporate headquarters, which maintains control over support services, rather than through field production plants.

Vendors wishing to market here should make planned follow-ups after initiating contacts. Only a small number of the minority vendors Economics Laboratory representatives met through the Minnesota Minority Purchasing Council trade fairs ever followed up.

Zenith Radio Corporation (225)

Zenith Radio Corporation has had a formal minority vendor utilization program since the early 1970s. That program is now administered by the director of equal opportunity and administrative services. A company-sponsored minority economic development committee includes the vice president or purchasing manager from each corporate facility. Each facility sets its own annual goals for minority vendor utilization, while progress is reviewed by the committee on a quarterly basis. A monthly report on minority vendor utilization is circulated to all purchasing managers, buyers, and committee members. The committee also receives top-management support; all managers have been given minority utilization goals and objectives.

Zenith maintains its essential purchasing function at headquarters, while manufacturing is done in about 15 facilities throughout the country, including a number in the Sun Belt region. Movement of many of Zenith's manufacturing facilities to the South and to Mexico led to the decline of its Chicago-area vendor network. The company seeks to establish a similar network in the South.

There have been difficulties with using minority vendors. Technological changes within high-tech products, including solid-state composition, resulted in reduced numbers of component parts. Many minority vendors produced picture tubes and transistors that are no longer needed. In addition, increased technological complexity, enhanced quality-control systems, and increased belt tightening have resulted in greater vertical integration in the development of Zenith's products.

Zenith wants vendors who have researched the company so that their sales calls will be well targeted to its needs. The minority coordinator's office is willing to work with vendors to improve their marketing presentation and facilitate their ability to effectively call on the company's purchasing office.

Teledyne, Inc. (122)

Teledyne has over 100 divisions, and each division maintains its own minority vendor procurement information. Thus the various Teledyne divisions must be contacted individually to learn of their minority vendor utilization.

In contacting specific Teledyne divisions, one encounters numerous delays and other bureaucratic measures. Corporations determined to be unresponsive to minority vendor procurement can use elaborate "corporate runaround" systems to all but guarantee no useful exchange of information.

Todd Pacific Shipyards Corporation (462)

The small business administrator at Todd Pacific Shipyards maintains a wealth of information regarding Todd's utilization of small vendors and minority vendors.

Todd publishes a small business quarterly for purchasing personnel. This newsletter highlights the activities of Todd's purchasing department in identifying and working with vendors. Of particular interest is the buyer performance log, which details on a yearly basis, the performance of each Todd buyer in procuring goods and services from small and minority businesses. The dollar figures and number of the contract awards initiated by each buyer are prominently displayed on the buyers' performance roster. The newsletter also contains information on upcoming events, new suppliers, small business, new minority trade associations, and Todd purchasing agents. Todd appears to maintain an aggressive small/minority business utilization program.

Vendors seeking to market to Todd should first contact the small business administrator to make an appointment. During the in-person interview, the vendor should provide a description of operations, including products and services, plant location, capability, production capacity, equipment, and quality control. Vendors must also complete a vendor registration form, which requests basic information about the company. Todd Shipyards then provides vendors with the name of the appropriate company buyer. Vendors should write or call the company buyer and maintain follow-up. The buyer may ask the vendor to come in or to call back by a future date. The Todd small business administrator wants to be kept informed of all vendor progress with buyers.

Todd's objective is to give small disadvantaged and female-owned business enterprises the maximum practical opportunity to participate in company contracts. The company views minority business development as an opportunity to fulfill its responsibility as a good corporate citizen for the benefit of shareholders, employees, consumers, and society.

Northrop Corporation (71)

Northrop's corporate philosophy includes an expressed obligation to give disadvantaged vendors a fair and equitable opportunity to participate in solicitations. All suppliers must produce a quality product or service that is competitively priced and provided on schedule. Strict quality control standards must be established and maintained. Northrop awards many contracts to distributors rather than original assemblers or manufacturers of products. While the procurement department has no preferential list of vendors, it frequently seeks solicitations from all qualified suppliers.

Northrop publishes a variety of reports and pamphlets for minority vendors. The *Small Business Report* is a quarterly publication whose front page lists the names and direct-dial phone numbers of all small

business officers at Northrop's divisions. The balance of the publication contains stories on how Northrop and its suppliers together overcame complex production, engineering, and business problems.

Northrop also publishes a booklet titled *How to Become a Northrop Team Member*. This booklet encourages prospective suppliers to contact the buying staff to discuss opportunities with Northrop and furnishes helpful information about buyers, sellers, general procurement, quality standards, bid solicitation, buyer source lists, company programs, and professional affiliations, as well as definitions of terms. The booklet also contains the names and direct-dial phone numbers of Northrop's divisional small business officers and a sample listing of items being solicited.

Northrop's divisional purchasing departments are organized on a commodity basis. Each buying staff member is assigned responsibility for a particular family of commodities. Northrop asks vendors to complete a supplier capability questionnaire, a three-page document that includes questions on certification of vendor status—that is, small business, minority business, female-owned business, large business, or nonprofit concern.

Much of Northrop's business involves contracts with the federal government, and the company is keenly aware of the need to identify and use minority vendors.

Martin Marietta Corporation (85)

Martin Marietta initiated a minority vendor utilization program in the mid-70s. However, it has no expressed or written corporate-wide policy on minority vendor utilization. Individual divisions establish their own policies. Martin Marietta maintains decentralized purchasing through its aerospace, chemical, aluminum, aggregate, data systems, and energy divisions. These six divisions, which comprise a total of 250 facilities, are constantly looking for minority vendors. That quest has both top-management support and the active involvement of headquarters purchasing, which conducts audits on the percentage of business done with minority vendors.

There are no formal incentive programs for purchasing agents, but recognition is offered. The corporation maintains its own directory of minority vendors, "Reach Out," originally developed by the Aerospace Division, which is the most active division in identifying and using minority vendors.

Minority vendors can more effectively market to Martin Marietta by improving their management systems and quality control, and by being competitive in terms of price, quality, and service.

Figgie International (359)

The director of corporate procurement and small/minority business coordinator for Figgie International Corporation observes that there is now an open-door policy at Figgie for all prospective vendors. If a minority vendor has the capabilities and is competitive, he or she gets the work. Previously, Figgie had problems when it tried to establish corporate goals for minority vendor utilization. When corporate sales fell off in the early 1980s, there was no staff to maintain the close monitoring that was necessary to ensure a concerted effort.

In 1982, at a meeting of divisional purchasing managers the corporation provided some instruction on how to react to and use minority vendors. Figgie has no formal incentives for purchasing agents to contract with minority vendors, and it has no figures on or estimates of the dollar value of the contracts awarded to minority vendors.

Figgie could use better vendor evaluation data, though it appears responsive and committed. It recognizes that the spin-off benefits of using minority vendors—the positive public relations that this could generate as well as the fulfillment of social responsibility—may sometimes outweigh any extra costs.

Figgie cites price, quality, delivery, and competitiveness as important components of the successful vendor marketing presentation. It also considers personal contact to be of great importance. Figgie does not want to lead a supplier on if there does not appear to be the potential for a good fit. It would rather spend some time initially with a would-be supplier to see whether he or she can handle the responsibilities. A vendor must have a good track record as well as solid quality control and maintenance capabilities.

Figgie seeks to offer more contracts to fewer suppliers, thereby establishing more involved relationships. Figgie is also interested in working with nearby vendors and suggests that such vendors invite corporate purchasing agents for on-site visits.

IN SUMMARY

It would not be accurate to say that the trend among Fortune 500 corporations is toward increased assistance to small or small minority business vendors. Changes in the political, technological, social, and economic environments continue to alter the nature of the relationships between corporate purchasing departments and the vendors that are seeking to do business with them. Nevertheless, the commitment to small vendor purchasing of some corporations, such as Control Data, Todd Shipyards, and Northrop, is certainly inspiring.

CHAPTER THIRTEEN

Small Business Vendor Support Groups

*All great developments of ideas
come modestly and silently to
fruition, without blare of
trumpets or pomp or praise.*

JOHN WANAMAKER

This chapter will explore some small business associations and advocacy groups that many successful entrepreneurs have joined and found supportive of their marketing efforts. The chapter will also examine the purchasing councils that have been established specifically to aid small disadvantaged entrepreneurs.

Joining any of the organizations profiled below will not, in and of itself, increase your effectiveness in marketing to Fortune 500 corporations. However, since each of these organizations provides specific benefits, is widely known, and generates significant economic and political influence, becoming a member of one or more of them can add to your overall visibility and credibility and help support a highly professional image.

> Chamber of Commerce of the United States
> 1615 H Street, N.W.
> Washington, DC 20062
> (202) 659-6000

The Chamber of Commerce of the United States is organized on the local, state, and national levels. On the *national level*, it works to develop local and state chambers of commerce and represents national business interests to the federal government.

State chambers of commerce coordinate local chamber programs and represent the state business community to the state government. Information on small business programs in a state is available through the state Chamber of Commerce.

Local chambers of commerce serve the local business community

with programs in economic development, community and human resources, and public affairs. Such programs may include:

- Small business development.
- Group and individual counseling on small business problems.
- Group courses and seminars on management led by professionals
  or practitioners.
- Start-up assistance, equity capital programs.

The Small Business Programs Office of the U.S. Chamber of Commerce
serves as a central clearinghouse for information on getting started in
business, expanding your business overseas, and managing your business.
Two valuable information sources published by the U.S. Chamber are:

- *Information Resources Guide*—lists U.S. Chamber publications,
  guides, filmstrips, and slide shows for small business.
- *The State and Local Chamber List*—provides a complete listing of
  the state and local chambers that have small business and export
  assistance programs.

You can also consult with the U.S. Chamber staff specialists who
provide information, opinions, and analysis for small business. Call (301)
468-5128 and ask for the U.S. Chamber staff specialists' brochure. With
that brochure, you can select the appropriate specialist to help you.

> National Federation of Independent Business (NFIB)
> 150 West 20th Avenue
> San Mateo, CA 94403 (headquarters)
> (415) 341-7441
>
> 600 Maryland Avenue, S.W., Suite 700
> Washington, DC 20024
> (202) 554-9000

The NFIB represents more than 500,000 business owners in the legisla-
tures as well as with federal and state agencies and is the nation's largest
organization representing small and independent businesses. NFIB also
offers information on free enterprise, entrepreneurship, and small business; provides surveys on economic trends, studies on a broad range of
information pertinent to businesses, and entrepreneurial educational materials; and lobbies for small business members on particular issues.

NFIB publications include:

- *NFIB Mandate*—explains the legislative actions of NFIB lobbyists;
  sent monthly to members.

- *How Congress Voted*—describes the trends of voting in Congress and provides a rundown, by state, of the voting on NFIB issues by members of Congress; printed for each congressional term.
- *NFIB Legislative Priorities*—published before each session of Congress to expound the position of NFIB on issues related to small business.
- *Action Report*—reports on positions taken by the NFIB; comes out after each session of Congress.

National Small Business United (NSBU)
1155 15th Street, N.W. Suite 710
Washington, DC 20005
(202) 293-8830

The NSBU is a membership-based association of business owners representing all types of business. It presents the point of view of small businesses to all levels of government, and it develops programs on issues of national policy that are of concern to the small business community.

Key services of the NSBU include providing members with a monthly newsletter and other materials that keep them up-to-date on issues affecting their businesses. A program alerting members to federal contracting opportunities through the Bidder's Early Alert Message system may be renewed.

National Association of Manufacturers (NAM)
1776 F Street, N.W.
Washington, DC 20006
(202) 637-3046

NAM, a group widely recognized by large corporations, has 13,000 member manufacturing firms, over 75 percent of which have fewer than 500 employees. The member firms of NAM account for 80 percent of the nation's industrial capacity. NAM is a strong voice for the manufacturing community in Washington. It provides members with an opportunity to participate in the public policy process through membership on its 14 policy committees. Major subject areas of these policy committees include:

- Resources and technology—energy, the environment, innovation, natural resources.
- International economic affairs—international investment, finance, and trade.

- Industrial relations—labor relations, human resources, employee benefits, loss prevention and control.
- Government regulation, competition, and small manufacturing.
- Taxation and fiscal policy.

NAM services include a roster of 100 subject specialists—legislative specialists, lawyers, communications advisers, public affairs experts, and so on—who help members with questions and problems. The NAM *Member Service Guide* provides the names and telephone numbers of these specialists. In addition, *Enterprise,* NAM's monthly magazine, focuses on emerging issues and provides articles written by industry experts and national figures.

> National Association of Women Business Owners (NAWBO)
> 600 South Federal Street, Suite 400
> Chicago, IL 60605
> (312) 922-0465

The National Association of Women Business Owners has 27 local chapters and 2,400 members nationwide. NAWBO helps female business owners to expand their operations and represents the business interests of women to the federal and state governments.

NAWBO services include providing counseling and technical assistance at the local level, primarily through networking with local members; holding monthly programs at the local chapters that address the problems of female business owners; and sponsoring an annual national conference that provides management and technical assistance training through workshops and seminars.

> Small Business United (SBU)
> 69 Hickory Drive
> Waltham, MA 02154
> (617) 890-9070

SBU is a network of regional small business organizations, representing these organizations and the concerns of small business before lawmakers. SBU works regularly with congressional and executive branch officials in Washington and the field. SBU offers no direct services to small business in particular; such services are offered by its member organizations, which are listed below.

SBU's member organizations work at the regional level to serve the needs of small business. These organizations are diverse in their orientation and in the services they provide. The services may include management assistance, educational programs, troubleshooting for common business problems, counseling, regional networking information, and the promotion of regional small business interests.

The member organizations of SBU may offer publications that provide key regional information. Here is a listing of these organizations:

Smaller Business Association
of New England
69 Hickory Drive
Waltham, MA 02154
(617) 890-9070
(800) 368-6803

Smaller Manufacturers' Council
339 Boulevard of the Allies
Pittsburgh, PA 15222
(412) 391-1622
Serves western
Pennsylvania, eastern Ohio,
and northern West Virginia.

Independent Business Association
of Wisconsin
415 East Washington Avenue
East Madison, WI 53703
(608) 251-5546

Council of Smaller Enterprise
690 Huntington Building
Cleveland, OH 44115
(216) 621-3300
Serves Greater Cleveland and
the surrounding region.

Small Business Association
of Michigan
490 West South Street
Kalamazoo, MI 49007
(616) 342-2400

Texas Association of
Small Business Councils
Greater Chamber of Commerce
P.O. Box 1628
San Antonio, TX 78296
(512) 366-0099

Independent Business Association
of Illinois
8565 West Dempster, Suite 200
Niles, IL 60648
(312) 692-7306

Ohio Small Business Council
Ohio Chamber of Commerce
35 East Gay Street
Columbus, OH 43215
(614) 228-4201

STATE AND REGIONAL SMALL BUSINESS ORGANIZATIONS

These organizations deal with the problems and concerns of small business focused at the state level or, in some cases, the regional level. Many of their members face the same problems that you face in marketing to the Fortune 500.

Associated Industries of Kentucky
200 West Chestnut Street
Louisville, KY 40202
(502) 587-0769

Associated Industries of
  Oklahoma
429 Northeast 50th Street
Suite 206
Oklahoma City, OK 73105
(405) 524-7686

Associated Oregon Industries
P.O. Box 12519
Salem, OR 97309
(503) 588-0050

Association of Washington
  Business
P.O. Box 658
Olympia, WA 98507
(206) 943-1600

Business Council of Georgia
575 North Omni Street
Atlanta, GA 30335
(404) 223-2264

Business Council of New York
  State
152 Washington Avenue
Albany, NY 12210
(518) 465-7511

Central Florida Small Business
  Association
P.O. Box 30533
Orlando, FL 32862-0533
(305) 859-5013

Chicago Association of
  Commerce and Industry
130 South Michigan Avenue
Chicago, IL 60603
(312) 786-0111

Colorado Association of
  Commerce and Industry
1390 Logan Street, Suite 308
Denver, CO 80203
(303) 831-7411

Columbus Area Chamber of
  Commerce
37 North High Street
Columbus, OH 43215
(614) 221-1321

Connecticut Business and Industry
  Association
370 Asylum Street
Hartford, CT 06103
(203) 547-1661

Florida Federation of Independent
  Business
P.O. Box 8871
Jacksonville, FL 32239
(904) 725-3980

German-American Business
  Association of California
15125 Burbank Boulevard
Van Nuys, CA 91411
(213) 873-1395
(818) 787-4565

Grand Rapids Area Chamber of
Commerce
17 Fountain Street, N.W.
Grand Rapids, MI 49503
(616) 459-7221

Greater Cincinnati Chamber of
Commerce
120 West 5th Street
Cincinnati, OH 45202
(513) 579-3149

Greater Fort Wayne Chamber of
Commerce
826 Ewing Street
Fort Wayne, IN 46802
(219) 424-1435

Greater Minneapolis Chamber of
Commerce
15 South 5th Street
Minneapolis, MN 55402
(612) 370-9155

Greater Springfield Chamber of
Commerce
3 South Old Capitol Plaza
Springfield, IL 62701
(217) 525-1173

Greater Washington Ibero-
American Chamber of
Commerce
2100 M Street, N.W., Suite 607
Washington, DC 20037
(202) 296-0335

Hawaii Business League
1177 Kapiolani Boulevard, Suite
201
Honolulu, HI 96814
(808) 533-6819

Idaho Association of Commerce
and Industry
P.O. Box 389
Boise, ID 83701
(208) 343-1849

Illinois Manufacturers Association
175 West Jackson Boulevard
Chicago, IL 60604
(312) 922-6575

Illinois Petroleum Marketers
Association
P.O. Box 1508
Springfield, IL 62705
(217) 544-4609

Illinois Retail Merchants
Association
36 South Wabash
Chicago, IL 60603
(312) 726-4600

Illinois Small Businessmen's
Association
407 South Dearborn
Chicago, IL 60605
(312) 427-0207

Illinois State Chamber of
  Commerce
20 North Wacker Drive, Suite
  1960
Chicago, IL 60606
(312) 372-7373

Independent Business Association
  of Minnesota
7800 Dupont Avenue, South
Minneapolis, MN 55420
(612) 881-1331

Independent Business Association
  of Washington
1644 116th Street, N.E.
Bellevue, WA 98004
(206) 453-8621

Independent Business Council
1980 Kettering Tower
Dayton, OH 45423
(513) 226-1444

Indiana State Chamber of
  Commerce
1 North Capitol, Suite 200
Indianapolis, IN 46204
(317) 634-6407

Iowa Association of Business and
  Industry
706 Employers Mutual Building
717 Mulberry
Des Moines, IA 50309
(515) 244-6149

Iowa Small Business Employers
P.O. Box 437
Mason City, IA 50401
(515) 424-3187

Kansas Chamber of Commerce
  and Industry
500 First National Tower
Topeka, KS 66603
(913) 357-6321

Long Island Association of
  Commerce and Industry
80 Hauppauge Road
Commack, NY 11725
(516) 499-4400

Massachusetts Businessmen's
  Association
135 Wood Road
Braintree, MA 02184
(617) 848-4950

Michigan Retailers' Association
221 North Pine Street
Lansing, MI 48933
(517) 372-5656

Michigan State Chamber of
  Commerce
Business and Trade Center, Suite
  400
200 North Washington Square
Lansing, MI 48933
(517) 371-2100

Mid-Continent Small Business
  United
1608 Holmes Street
Kansas City, MO 64108
(816) 842-6454

Minnesota Association of
  Commerce and Industry
300 Hanover Building
480 Cedar Street
St. Paul, MN 55101
(612) 292-4650

Missouri Chamber of Commerce
Missouri Center for Free
  Enterprise
P.O. Box 149
428 East Capitol Avenue
Jefferson City, MO 65102
(314) 634-3511

Missouri Merchants' and
  Manufacturers' Association
910 Clayton Road, Suite 322
St. Louis, MO 63011
(314) 458-2051

National Federation of
  Independent Business—
  Colorado
1391 North Speer Boulevard,
  Suite 470
Denver, CO 80204
(303) 534-1631

National Federation of
  Independent Business—Indiana
5726 Professional Circle, Suite
  #205-F
Indianapolis, IN 46241
(317) 241-1118

National Federation of
  Independent Business—Iowa
820 1st Street, Suite 200
West Des Moines, IA 50265
(515) 255-9190

National Federation of
  Independent Business—Kansas
10039 Mastin Drive
Shawnee Mission, KS 66212
(913) 888-2235

National Federation of
  Independent Business—
  Missouri
111 Madison
P.O. Box 1543
Jefferson City, MO 65101
(314) 634-7660

National Federation of
  Independent Business—
  Nebraska
525 South 13th Street, Suite 3
Lincoln, NE 68508
(402) 474-3570

National Federation of
  Independent Business—New
  York
8 Elk Street
Albany, NY 12207
(518) 434-1262

National Federation of
  Independent Business—
  Washington
711 South Capitol Way, Suites
  #201-9
Olympia, WA 98501
(206) 786-8675

Nebraska Association of
  Commerce and Industry
1008 Terminal Building
P.O. Box 95128
Lincoln, NE 68509
(402) 474-4422

New England Business
  Association
P.O. Box 535
Plaistow, NH 03865
(603) 382-4711

New Jersey Coalition of Small
  Business Organizations
% Concorde Chemical Company
17th and Federal Streets
Camden, NJ 08105
(609) 966-1526

Ohio Chamber of Commerce
17 South High Street, 8th Floor
Columbus, OH 43215
(614) 228-4201

Ohio Manufacturers Association
100 East Broad Street
Columbus, OH 43215
(614) 224-5111

Oregon's Small Business Council
P.O. Box 455
Salem, OR 97308
(503) 585-5846

St. Paul Area Chamber of
  Commerce
701 North Central Tower
445 Minnesota Street
St. Paul, MN 55101
(612) 222-5561

Seattle Chamber of Commerce
1200 One Union Square
Seattle, WA 98101
(206) 447-7285

Small Business Advocates, Inc.
1270 Chemeketa Street, N.E.
Salem, OR 97301
(503) 370-7019

Small Business Association of
  Michigan
Legislative Office
530 West Ionia Street
Lansing, MI 48933
(517) 484-2277

Small Business Association of the
  Southeast
% Hyatt and Rhoads
2200 Peachtree Center
Harris Tower
Atlanta, GA 30303
(404) 659-6600

Tennessee Small Business
  Roundtable
% Brookmeade Hardware
6006 Bressland Road
Nashville, TN 37205
(615) 256-0450

Texas Association of Business
6900 Fannin, Suite 240
Houston, TX 77030-3880
(713) 790-1010

Toledo Area Small Business
Association
218 Huron Street
Toledo, OH 43604
(419) 255-1726

Utah Council of Small Business
10 South Main, Suite 210
Salt Lake City, UT 84101
(801) 322-1338

Wisconsin Association of
Manufacturers and Commerce
Madison Legislative Office
30 West Misslin, Suite 302
Madison, WI 53703
(608) 255-2312

Women in Business
815 Moraga Drive
Los Angeles, CA 90049
(213) 476-8429

INDUSTRY SUPPORT GROUPS

The following industry-based associations also provide support service to member firms. For a more complete list, consult the *NTPA Directory*.

Textile Mill Products
Industrial Fabrics Association
International
345 Cedar Building, Suite 450
St. Paul, MN 55101
(612) 222-2508

Lumber and Wood Products
International Woodworkers
of America
1622 North Lombard Street
Portland, OR 97217
(503) 285-5281

Chemical and Allied Products
Chemical Manufacturers
Association
2501 M Street, N.W.
Washington, DC 20037
(202) 887-1100

Machinery, except Electrical
Farm Equipment Manufacturers
Association
243 North Lindberg Boulevard
St. Louis, MO 63141
(314) 991-0702

National Machine Tool
Builders Association
7901 Westpark Drive
McLean, VA 22102
(703) 893-2900

National Tooling and Machining
Association
9300 Livingston Road
Fort Washington, MD 20744
(301) 248-6200

*Electrical and Electronic
   Equipment*
Motor and Equipment
   Manufacturers Association
P.O. Box 439
Teaneck, NJ 07666
(201) 836-9500

Electronic Industries Association
2001 Eye Street, N.W.
Washington, DC 20006
(202) 457-4900

National Electrical Manufacturers
   Association
2101 L Street, N.W., Suite 300
Washington, DC 20037
(202) 457-8400

Instruments and Related Products
Scientific Apparatus Makers
   Association
1101 16th Street, N.W., Suite 300
Washington, DC 20036
(202) 223-1360

Manufacturers Agents National
   Association
P.O. Box 3167
Laguna Hills, CA 92653
(714) 859-4040

Wholesale Trade: Durable Goods
Automotive Service Industry
   Association
444 North Michigan Avenue
Chicago, IL 60611
(312) 836-1300

National Tire Dealers and
   Retreaders Association, Inc.
1250 Eye Street, N.W., Suite 400
Washington, DC 20005
(202) 789-2300

National Hardwood Lumber
   Association
Box 34518
Memphis, TN 38184-0518
(901) 377-1818

NAVA—International
   Communications Industry
   Association
3150 Spring Street
Fairfax, VA 22031
(703) 273-7200

Construction
Associated General Contractors of
   America
1957 E Street, N.W.
Washington, DC 20006
(202) 393-2040

Associated Builders and
   Contractors, Inc.
729 15th Street, N.W.
Washington, DC 20005
(202) 637-8800

Special Trade Contractors
Air Conditioning Contractors of
   America
1228 17th Street, N.W.
Washington, DC 20036
(202) 296-7610

American Society of Plumbing
Engineers
15233 Ventura Boulevard
Sherman Oaks, CA 91403
(213) 783-4845

National Electrical Contractors
Association
7315 Wisconsin Avenue
Washington, DC 20814
(202) 657-3110

National Insulation Contractors
Association
1025 Vermont Avenue, N.W.,
Suite #410
Washington, DC 20005
(202) 783-6277

THE SMALL BUSINESS ADMINISTRATION

The U.S. Small Business Administration (SBA) offers several fine management, certification and procurement assistance programs at the *district* and *regional* levels. Addresses and phone numbers are provided in your local telephone directory. *Procurement center representatives* work full-time to identify small business subcontracting opportunities with corporations handling federal contracts, particularly Department of Defense contracts (see page 6). Representatives of *SCORE* (the Service Corps of Retired Executives), operating under the direction of SBA district offices, offer one-on-one assistance to small business entrepreneurs, for extended time periods if necessary.

MINORITY ASSOCIATIONS

A number of minority associations offer services that can be helpful to small vendors seeking to market to major corporations or to serve as subcontractors on federal procurement contracts. *National Trade and Professional Associations of the United States and Canada* (NTPA) lists over 30 such associations. Among them are:

American Association of Minority
Enterprise Small Business
Investment Companies
915 15th Street, N.W., 7th Floor
Washington, DC 20005
(202) 347-8600

National Association of Black
Accountants
1010 Vermont Avenue, N.W.,
Suite 901
Washington, DC 20005
(202) 783-7151

National Association of Minority
Contractors
1603 Rhode Island Avenue, N.W.
Washington, DC 20018
(202) 347-8259

National Business League
4324 Georgia Avenue, N.W.
Washington, DC 20011
(202) 829-5900

DIRECTORY LISTINGS

While many Fortune 500 corporations recognize that doing business with minority and small disadvantaged businesses is a good way to strengthen the economy, demonstrate social responsibility, and aid disadvantaged groups in achieving economic parity, even among those ready and willing to participate, this familiar question is heard: "Where can one find viable small business enterprises?" To answer this question, the small business utilization officers at the corporate headquarters as well as purchasing agents often look to directories and data banks that provide information on vendors. The following are a few places where minority and small disadvantaged businesses can be listed.

The *Small Business Administration,* 1441 L Street, N.W., Washington, DC 20416, (202) 653-6365, publishes and distributes an annual directory that designates firms found to be socially or economically disadvantaged.

Try Us and *Guide to Minority Directories* are two directories published by the National Minority Business Campaign, 65 22nd Avenue, N.E., Minneapolis, MN 55418. *Try Us* lists several thousand minority business enterprises arranged by product and service areas. It also provides the names of the president and previous clients, the amount of sales, and plant square footage. The *Guide to Minority Directories* contains an extensive list of minority business directories published by various groups throughout the country.

The *Garrett Park Press,* located in Garrett Park, MD 20766, (301) 946-2553, publishes information and directories on minority individuals and businesses. One of its directories lists thousands of minority managers and executives in business and industry. Another provides the names of institutions and programs that offer special employment and business opportunities for minorities.

In cities of 100,000 people or more, the *local Chamber of Commerce* usually publishes a directory of businesses, often with a special section listing minority business enterprises. One call will determine whether your local chamber lists minority and small disadvantaged business enterprises.

MINORITY SMALL BUSINESS DEFINED

An important distinction in the world of corporate procurement programs is "minority business," companies that have at least 51 percent minority ownership. The Small Business Administration defines minorities as those groups whose members are socially or economically disadvantaged. The regulations governing the practical application of that definition are complicated, and various criteria are used.

Social disadvantage has to do with membership in one of several different racial or ethnic categories as defined by regulation. It is determined on a case-by-case basis for those individuals who feel that they are socially disadvantaged (e.g., the physically handicapped). Economic disadvantage has to do with the barriers that social disadvantage has placed in the way of an individual's participation in business and employment.

For further clarification, call any Small Business Administration office and ask for its minority business representative. The Minority Business Development Agency of the Department of Commerce can also be of assistance in this area.

REGIONAL MINORITY PURCHASING COUNCILS

The manager of corporate purchasing for Norton Company (277) says he has found the answer to that nagging question, "Where can I find qualified minority vendors and suppliers?" In his view, "One of the best ways for minority firms and large corporations to discover each other is through the Regional Minority Purchasing Councils." He is not alone in his thinking. One purchaser at Burlington Industries (141) says, "I think the Regional Councils enhance the scope of the national minority vendor network and they do it in an efficient, effective way." The purchasing director of a Tennessee-based corporation is an active participant in his local purchasing council and recommends its services to other purchasing directors.

The 43 Regional Minority Purchasing Councils located across the country differ in some respects—services offered, membership dues, and government sponsorship—but they all share one goal. That goal is to bring corporate purchasing agents together with representatives of small disadvantaged businesses, in both formal and informal settings, to foster the development of long-term, mutually beneficial business relationships. Dianne Walbrecker examined the services and activity of several councils around the nation. Here is a look at the councils that she and William Holleran visited.

Tidewater Regional Minority Purchasing Council

Amid the bustling redevelopment of the Norfolk, Virginia, waterside sits a yellow brick building that houses the two-room office of the Tidewater Regional Minority Purchasing Council. No money here is spent on frills.

The director is open and friendly. His job is to locate small disadvantaged businesses, certify through on-site visits that they are at least 51 percent minority owned and operated, bring in new corporate members, and facilitate linkages between the corporate members and the small disadvantaged businesses whenever possible. He holds 11 meetings a year, usually at corporate locations so as to hold down costs, and minority vendors are invited to make presentations at these meetings. The last meeting was attended by representatives of 22 corporations, including 8 from the ranks of the Fortune 500, and four minority vendors gave formal presentations.

Major corporations and nearby city governments send bids to the director, which he then sends to small disadvantaged businesses that he believes can compete for the jobs. As many as 54 bid referrals pass his desk each day. Frequently, a corporate purchasing agent will ask for the name of a small disadvantaged business to do a certain job. The director knows what businesses he has on file and can give the purchasing agent two or three names immediately.

Funding assistance from the Department of Commerce enables the council to keep dues low; corporate members pay $150 for the first year and $300 per year after that. Small disadvantaged businesses pay a fee of $25 per year to belong. The 86 member corporations include Amoco (11), Bendix, Chesapeake and Potomac Telephone Company, and Sears Roebuck & Co.

The benefits of corporate membership include a yearly directory of small disadvantaged businesses in the area, monthly meetings, a newsletter, an annual luncheon, and, perhaps most important, the freedom to call for referrals at any time.

Small disadvantaged businesses receive an annual directory of the corporate members that lists the services and equipment needed by each corporate member.

Beyond providing linkages, the director's responsibility is to increase awareness of the factors that have stood in the way of both corporations and small disadvantaged businesses. "You wouldn't believe how many purchasing agents just pick up the phone and use the supplier they've been using for years."

Houston Business Council

The Houston Business Council accepts no government funds—membership dues pay for the operation. In addition to publishing minidirectories of its 96 corporate and 840 small disadvantaged members, the Houston Business Council uses a computerized system called the Vendor Information System. The system includes information on the products and services of over 1,100 vendors in the Houston area and also stores corporate information, such as the commodities that corporations buy and the name and phone number of the appropriate purchasing contact person. Among the numerous corporate members of the Houston Business Council are Exxon (2) and Big Three Industries (351).

The council recruits volunteers to advise minority business owners in such areas as marketing and long-range strategy, and it arranges educational seminars, workshops, and quarterly membership meetings. It also holds the nation's largest trade fair and sponsors golf and tennis tournaments where corporate purchasing agents and small disadvantaged business owners can get together in an informal atmosphere conducive to the personal contact that brings contracts.

With over 6,000 referrals per year, the Houston Business Council plays a significant role in the marketing program of its small vendor members.

Chicago Regional Minority Purchasing Council

The Chicago Regional Minority Purchasing Council is funded entirely by its 70 corporate members, including a large contingent of Fortune 500 corporations, and by its 317 small disadvantaged business members. The fees paid by corporations range from $2,000 to $5,000 a year, depending on the level of their minority purchasing. Small disadvantaged members are charged a $50 application fee and voluntary dues of $125 per year. The council's director says, "The Chicago council is a joint venture of minority and majority firms, each expected to contribute to the council's support."

Services provided by the Chicago Regional Minority Purchasing Council include product luncheons, organized by purchasing categories, at which vendors speak directly to appropriate purchasing agents; educational programs that focus on marketing, public relations, and advertising in particular; referrals providing corporate members with the entire list of small disadvantaged businesses in the category that they are seeking; business opportunity fairs; a directory of members; and golf outings.

Los Angeles and Southern California Purchasing Council

The Los Angeles and Southern California Purchasing Council was started in 1975 and is now funded entirely through membership dues.

Over 100 corporations pay $3,000 per year, if they are headquartered in Los Angeles. Regional corporate offices pay half that amount. There is no charge to the over 2,350 small disadvantaged business owners who have joined.

"Small disadvantaged business owners are quite frequently excellent technicians who just miss on the marketing side," reports the director. "So we provide sales training courses taught by salespeople from the ranks of our corporate members."

Of the corporate members, the director says, "All we're asking them to do is change their attitude about using minority businesses. In addition, the corporations have the opportunity to develop additional suppliers and to provide an atmosphere of economic advantage to the entire community."

Middle Tennessee Regional Minority Purchasing Council

The Middle Tennessee Regional Minority Purchasing Council has played a significant role in helping vendors to market successfully to major corporations. Since 1979, corporate members of the council have increased their purchases from minority vendors by over 300 percent. In 1983, corporations voluntarily reported to the council a total of $49.8 million worth of goods and services purchased from minority vendors.

The council publishes a quarterly newsletter and provides corporate and vendor directories, trade fairs, monthly meetings, and sales training courses. The director believes that its most important activity is to encourage direct involvement in the council by purchasing managers and small disadvantaged business owners.

Both corporate and minority members sit in on planning meetings and serve on the numerous committees required to develop and implement the various activities of the council. The chairman of a Trade Fair Committee was an executive of Southwestern-Great American Opportunities, Inc., and the vice chairman was from South Central Bell. "Working together for a common goal and for the increased economic stability and prosperity of this region is a great way for members to have a direct say in their council, and for both corporate members and members to get the most benefit," notes the director.

Regional Minority Purchasing Councils across the country allow corporate and minority members a chance to work together and thus increase awareness of their respective opportunities and problems. Through meetings, trade fairs, and other activities, corporations can increase their supplier base as well as contribute to the overall economic growth of their area. To find the regional office in your area, write National Minority Supplier Development Council, Inc., 1412 Broadway, 11th Floor, New York, NY 10018, or call (212) 944-2430.

STATE SUPPORT

State offices for small business affairs often serve as a contact point for referral to other programs (see Chapter 7), but a majority of these offices offer training programs or seminars and many of them offer one-on-one counseling to small businesses. Over half of the state offices for small business offices are specifically targeted to firms owned by minorities or minorities and women.

Thirty-eight states have programs to help small and small disadvantaged businesses cut through the red tape and confusion of dealing with state agency procurement procedures. In some states, free publications such as "How to Do Business with the State of XYZ" are offered. In other states, the procurement assistance office answers procurement questions over the phone or in person. Arkansas, Florida, Iowa, Ohio, and Tennessee have established toll-free numbers for questions about procurement and marketing assistance.

Permit information clearinghouses are available in 15 states. These serve as a reference point for businesses needing information about federal, state, and local licensing and permit requirements.

Thirteen states have a business ombudsman, and Kentucky has a minority business ombudsman. These ombudsmen handle specific complaints about state agencies from small businesses.

Small Business Development Centers (SBDCs) have been established in 26 states. These centers offer personalized assistance to small businesses. States that have an SBDC network usually offer individualized counseling by students under supervision of their university professors. Seminars and workshops are also an important part of the services offered by SBDCs. Located within universities and colleges throughout the state, SBDCs often reach small businesses that would otherwise not request assistance.

CHAPTER FOURTEEN

Mastering the Nuances, Handling the Problems

*Work and play are two
words used to describe
the same thing under
differing conditions.*

MARK TWAIN

When you submit a bid to a purchaser, competing with other vendors who are seeking the same contract, you are participating in a "game of chance." For your firm to "win" in this competition, your bid must be superior to those of the other vendors. To win, you must often go beyond the standard requirements and offer the extra edge that will set you apart. Generally speaking, that extra edge is not price related.

"Promise the highest quality product that *you can deliver,*" advises Vic Morris, "using current employees and equipment." If the buyer has specification requirements, make sure you can equal or exceed them. Then accurately assess your scheduling and delivery abilities. Don't promise what you can't deliver in an attempt to secure the contract. This is the quickest route back to marketing to other small businesses or to the government.

WHAT'S YOUR UNIT BREAK-EVEN POINT?

To carefully estimate a fair and competitive price that will enable your firm to profit from a contract, Leslie Rhatican suggests performing a break-even analysis. The following will help you find your break-even price.

To determine the costs of production, first distinguish fixed costs from variable costs. Fixed costs generally do not vary with changes in the number of units produced or sold. For example, the cost of renting a factory does not change because production increases from one shift to two shifts a day or because twice as much of product X is sold. Rent may increase over time, but not because the factory has doubled production or revenue.

Total variable costs change directly with changes in the number of units produced or sold. The wages for a second shift and the cost of twice as much paper and dyes are extra costs that occur when production is doubled. Variable costs per unit are constant, that is, twice as many workers and twice as much material produce twice as much of product X. Total cost is the sum of all fixed and variable costs.

Total revenue is derived by multiplying price by quantity. If 10,000 units of product X are sold at $10 per unit, the total revenue equals $100,000. Profits are whatever is left of the $100,000 after all expenses have been paid. Losses occur if there are costs left to be paid after revenue has been used up.

The graph below illustrates the relationship between costs, revenue, profits, and losses in determining the break-even point. Knowing the number of units necessary to break even is important in setting the price. If it is determined that a product priced at $100 per unit has a variable cost of $60 per unit, then the contribution per unit to fixed costs is $40. With total fixed costs of $120,000, the break-even point in *units* is determined as follows:

$$\text{Break-even point} = \frac{\text{Fixed costs}}{\text{Per unit contribution to fixed costs}}$$

$$\text{Break-even point} = \frac{\$120,000}{\$40/\text{Unit}} = 3,000 \text{ units}$$

Break-Even Analysis

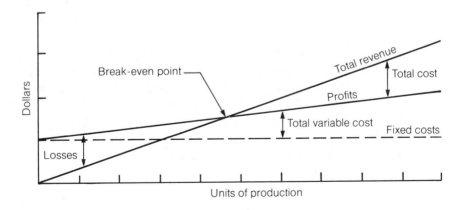

In other words, with a $40 per unit contribution to fixed costs (hence a $40 gross profit margin per unit), 3,000 units must be sold to break even. Above the break-even point of 3,000 units, in this example, the per unit contribution to fixed costs goes to profits. For example, sales of 3,001 units yield a profit of $40. Each unit sold above 3,000 adds another $40 to profits.

To calculate the break-even point in terms of dollar sales volume, multiply the break-even point in units by the price per unit. In the example above, the break-even point in terms of dollar sales volume would be 3,000 (units) times $100 (price per unit), or $300,000.

$$3,000 \text{ units} \times \$100 \text{ price/unit} = \$300,000$$

SERVICE PROVISION

Your bid price should also take into consideration the cost of providing service. If you can guarantee your service in your bid, that is a big plus.

In recent years, product liability has become a major legal issue. The manufacturers of component parts, like the manufacturers of end products, can be sued. Vic Morris advises stating in your bid whether or not you assume responsibility for product liability. If you do, be sure that your insurance covers it.

THE MID-PROJECT SLUMP

You will make a very important point in your favor if, somewhere in your bid, you assure that your firm will maintain a continuous or increasing level of performance.

A curious phenomenon sometimes occurs within firms that have achieved at least a moderate level of success. Erroneous notions about contract requirements or potential problems may occur when the entrepreneur lets down his or her "guard" (see page 255). You have to work hard to win new customers, and you have to work hard to keep them. Avoiding the mid-project slump is taxing, but it may also be rewarding, because it often means that you've successfully avoided the project deadline crunch.

Typical Project Activity Chart

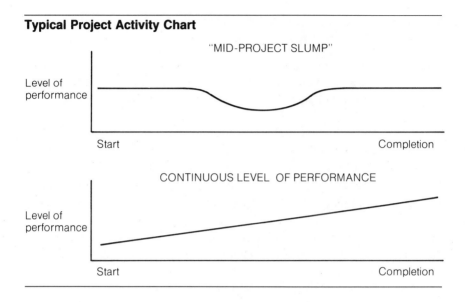

DON'T SHORTCHANGE YOUR NEED FOR LEGAL ASSISTANCE

All 500 of the Fortune 500 employ full-time legal specialists, and many of the Fortune 500 maintain elaborately layered legal departments. There will be times when you should use an attorney skilled in general contract and business law, and such times will occur more often as your revenues increase. Contacting an attorney *before* a contract or bid is signed can prevent problems.

A small business attorney can provide advice on such matters as corporate structure, sales and bid contracts, leases, government regulations and ordinances, employment contracts, tax laws, and labor laws. Trying to handle these items by yourself can be more costly in the long run. Remember the Fram Oil Filter commercial where the mechanic says, "You can pay me now or you can pay me later"? The same principle applies here.

To locate a qualified small business attorney, ask your local banker, accountant, or insurance agent for suggestions, or contact a local law school (some provide legal services using their third-year students). Small Business Administration district offices may also be able to offer suggestions.

CONTRACT LAW ENFORCEMENT—
A QUICK SUMMARY

Existing government regulation of monopolistic and unfair trade practices directly affects and benefits small business. While the various acts summarized below may not become household words to you, they do merit brief mention.

The U.S. Department of Justice enforces the Sherman Antitrust Act, which outlaws monopolies and other types of business combinations formed to restrain trade or commerce. The Clayton Act was designed to prohibit practices that might substantially lessen competition or tend to create a monopoly. The Robinson-Patman Act, an amendment to the Clayton Act, gives the Federal Trade Commission authority to eliminate quantity discounts and prohibit promotional allowances except on an equal basis. All three of these acts are enforced by the U.S. Department of Justice.

The Federal Trade Commission, a U.S. government agency, prohibits unfair methods of competition and unfair and deceptive acts and practices in commerce. Such corporations as Hewlett Packard (58) and 3M (47) state their compliance procedures in the supplier guides that they've developed. The Federal Trade Commission has identified certain types of activities as unfair business practices. These include:

- Making false and inaccurate statements about competitors' products and/or their business.
- Selling rebuilt, secondhand, or old articles as new.
- Simulating trade names or labels of competitors and affixing them to your own product.
- Bribing customers or employees to obtain patronage.
- Buying up supplies to hamper competitors.
- Stifling or eliminating competition.

While the above activities are labeled unfair, the Federal Trade Commission considers the following activities to be outright unlawful:

- Price-fixing.
- Exclusive deals.
- False and deceptive advertising.
- Price discrimination.
- Payment of brokerage to buyers.

ALL CONTRACTS ARE NEGOTIABLE

Between the time you make a bid (or a request to bid) on a contract let by a major corporation and the time you actually win the contract award, a substantial amount of negotiating may occur. This entails face-to-face exchanges between buyers and sellers. Discussion and communication of the terms and methods by which the contract will be fulfilled are a prerequisite to a mutually favorable business transaction.

The first step in becoming a skilled negotiator is to do your homework. Dr. Chester A. Karrass, Gerald I. Nierenberg, Herb Cohen, Neil Rackham, and other top negotiators and negotiation trainers agree that the best negotiators are well prepared and have done lots of homework before entering into the negotiation process.

First, establish your objectives. Why are you seeking a particular contract? The answer may be obvious, but ask yourself this question nevertheless. Will your bid price produce a profit for your company? How will you meet or exceed the contract requirements? These are the types of questions that you are likely to be asked at any point in the process of calling on and triumphantly marketing to the Fortune 500.

Second, examine your capabilities. For example, what advantages do you have over your competitors, particularly in the areas of technology, production, manufacturing, scheduling, or other performance factors? What are your financial needs to complete this contract? Will you need outside financing? Will you seek assistance from the buyer, or can you carry all of the costs internally? What are your cash flow requirements for the duration of the contract?

TACTICAL DECISIONS

Effective negotiators also make tactical decisions before entering into the negotiation process. Will you negotiate as an individual, or will you use a team? This will depend largely on the importance of the negotiation, the time available, and the skills required to successfully close the deal. When selecting a negotiating team, says Vic Morris, "be certain that each member has a specific function." Each member of the negotiating team should know the agreed-upon strategy and objectives, have a specialty, and demonstrate his or her confidence. Everyone is there to be a productive member of the team—clear up any internal disagreements well in advance of the negotiation.

There are advantages to using a single negotiator. They include the following:

- Prevents a "divide and conquer" strategy by opponents.
- Demonstrates that the negotiator has complete responsibility.
- Avoids a weakened position resulting from differences of opinion among team members.
- Facilitates on-the-spot decision making, particularly in the area of granting or receiving concessions.

Another component of negotiation strategy is to determine in advance what you really want to get from the negotiation and for what you will settle. Purchasing agents are more receptive now than ever before to your ideas on improving their operations. Your good ideas are negotiating tools.

In many ways, negotiation is like a poker game in that you don't really reveal the cards until after you have won. Thus, when first starting to negotiate, it is not wise to reveal the exact terms that you want; instead, reveal them slowly, much as you would add cards to your hand in a poker game until you have a "winning hand."

At the beginning of a negotiation, both the buyer and the seller will usually state what they are ostensibly seeking. Each will find the position of the other to be somewhat unreasonable. Throughout the course of the negotiation, each side will make counterproposals and concessions until, hopefully, mutually agreeable positions have been reached. Thus it is wise not to reveal what you really want but instead to ask for more than you want, recognizing that the resulting compromises will eventually come close to your initial unrevealed position.

LISTEN AND REBUT

Negotiation trainer Neil Rackham observes that the best negotiators carefully listen to the points presented by the other side. Then they attack those points, indicating that they understood what the other side said, that they agree in part with some of the points made, but that they disagree with "X, Y, and Z" and "here is why." This is far more successful, believes Rackham, than politely listening to what the other side says and then launching into what you want to say without addressing what the other side has just said.

The best negotiators choose words and tone of voice carefully. It is often difficult to do this, but try to pose questions in a way that does not offend. Good negotiators have notes prepared and take notes during the negotiations. In his book *You Can Negotiate Anything,* Herb Cohen humorously points out that one of the best tactics for assuring a successful negotiation is to find out in advance the time constraints or deadline that your opponent is facing. Cohen observes that people tend to be a lot more agreeable when facing a deadline. However, don't let your opponent know that you know his or her deadline.

The purchasing agents from Fortune 500 companies negotiate far more often than you and with better results. If they're part of a top purchasing department, such as that of Union Carbide (39), General Foods (38), or Monsanto (53), then they've received top training. Also, all purchasing agents are privy to the excellent array of audiovisual training materials available through the National Association of Purchasing Management.

"Do not go gentle into that good night." You need to bone up on negotiating!

YOUR BOTTOM LINE

Your bid should reflect complete cost information. Before entering into the negotiation you will have determined your "bottom-line bid," under which you cannot go, because to do so would cause your firm to lose money on the contract. Therefore, rather than cut or lower the price when faced with a difficult negotiation, modify service or delivery terms that you can readily offer cost effectively (see page 176).

Be ready to present a counterproposal—most small business entrepreneurs overlook this or don't even know that one should be prepared. During negotiations, it may be difficult to accurately assess the impact of suggested positions. Anticipate these before negotiating so that you know what the net effect of an alternative will be. For example, dividing a job into three consecutive tasks may serve the client better and be more manageable for you. In advance of the negotiation proceedings, determine what the effects of dividing one big job into three would be from management, production, administrative, and cost standpoints. The small business vendor who comes to the negotiating table with effective counterproposals has a feather in his or her cap.

STANDING OUT FROM THE CROWD

One purchasing representative for FMC Corporation (123) indicated several areas in which small vendors needed to improve in dealing with corporate purchasing departments, including understanding the corporate procurement cycle, maintaining nonadverse relationships when faced with delays, financing large jobs, and computing job costs, particularly overhead costs.

Some small vendors, confronted with their first opportunity to do business with a Fortune 500 corporation, make the mistake of underbidding—either because they have not properly computed internal costs or, in hopes of winning the contract to get a foot in the door that will lead to ''profitable'' contracts. Either reason for underbidding is dangerous and may lead to disastrous results, such as furnishing lower quality and slower delivery than were agreed upon.

Low bidding can wreak havoc on your cash flow, necessitate refinancing, and result in profit margins that are slim or nonexistent. The client will not be the only dissatisfied party. Low bidding tends to affect your own employees—engendering low morale, loss of employee confidence, and even burnout. If you're forced to make a low bid in order to win, abandon ship—there will be other voyages.

It is hard to sit here and advise you not to take marginal jobs, especially when your plant or office is underutilized, you have a payroll to meet, and you ''just know'' that this contract will lead to great things. Yet the battered dream of many an entrepreneur can be traced to low bidding.

HOW ONE FIRM AVOIDS CONTRACT DIFFICULTIES

Italicized below are ways in which small vendors and contractors frequently run into trouble. Each of these is followed by a description of how one contractor in the Rocky Mountain area, which we'll call CMR, avoids that particular difficulty.

1. *Failure to read with meticulous care the solicitation and its attachments and the specifications.* CMR carefully reviews all of the materials contained in a request for a proposal or a solicitation. It maintains familiarity with purchasing and procurement procedures, specifications, material allocation, delivery and supply expectations, and related matters. It obtains appropriate counsel when needed for advice on such matters as bidder's rights and obligations, appeal procedures, termination, and default actions. CMR is cognizant of the resources required for contract administration and of the extensive documentation that is needed to successfully manage contracts.

2. *Excessive optimism in assessing the task, the risk, and in-house capabilities.* CMR takes a realistic approach in determining whether

it has the overall capability, both technical and financial, to perform on selected projects. Delays in the receipt of goods and supplies from subcontractors, for example, could cause considerable setbacks during contract performance. CMR takes these factors into consideration when it prepares bids and when it is awarded contracts. It approaches each solicitation critically and proceeds only after generating substantial evidence that the firm can successfully execute the contract.

3. *Bidding on unreliable purchase descriptions or specifications.* When needed, CMR immediately calls or writes for clarifications of unclear purchase or specification information. CMR strives to ensure that any and all copies of the latest revisions to specifications are obtained before it submits a bid.

4. *Bidding based on estimations, not factual cost data.*   Many firms prepare cost estimates based on what they think will get the job. CMR prepares cost estimates on a per bid basis, neither relying on previously prepared bids nor assuming that standard cost estimates or "ballpark" figures will be sufficient. Key factors that are considered in any of CMR's bids include:

- Subcontractor and equipment vendor costs.
- Overhead and overhead rates.
- Learning curves for labor and salaried personnel.
- Estimate of person-days required.
- Availability of client-furnished materials and equipment.
- Labor and salary rates and predictable changes.
- Profit potential.

5. *Bidding under time pressure.*   CMR maintains long-term monitoring and tracking on all significant business opportunities. It forgoes bidding on attractive solicitations when the deadline is not sufficient to prepare a thoroughly researched, double-checked bid. It also avoids projects that call for an unrealistic time frame.

6. *Accepting assignments beyond the state of the art.*   Corporations occasionally request creative and exploratory procurements that are negotiated with performance specifications. In such cases, the end products may be prototypes or test and evaluation models. While CMR is eager to conduct this type of project and has done so successfully in the past, its highly capable, technically oriented staff carefully analyzes solicitations of this kind to determine whether the projects are, in fact, feasible.

7. *Failure to take remedial action.*   CMR maintains a legal staff and appropriate resources that are sufficient to appeal claims against

WHY DIDN'T WE GET THE JOB?: A SELF-ANALYSIS

When you visited a potential buyer, were you or your salespeople:

Prepared? Knowledgeable of the customer's needs?
Knowledgeable of your product or service?
Dealing with the "right" person?
Capable of successfully completing the job you were seeking?

Were you available when your customer tried to reach you?

Did you return his or her calls promptly?
Did you keep the customer informed of progress *and* problems?
Did you deliver on time?
Were your reports comprehensive and well prepared?

Consider the impression that your office or plant makes on a visitor:

Is the office or plant clean?
Are supplies stored conveniently yet out of the way?
Do your employees conduct themselves as "professionals"?
Would a fresh painting or cleaning improve the visitor's impression?

Remember: First impressions are lasting impressions.

If too many defects caused a problem on previous contracts, examine all of the following areas to identify the defects, eliminate them, and prevent a recurrence of the problem:

Were defects caused by human or machine error?
How do you handle the responsibility for defects?
  Don't assign *blame*.
  Give *authority* to deal with the problem.
What is your frequency rate, the total number of defects compared to the total number of items produced?
Does your quality control program prevent defective items from leaving your shop? If not, what can you do to solve this problem?
Did you tell the customer about your corrective actions?

With hidden and underlying problems, you must "look in the mirror" and be honest with yourself. Was the problem:

Yourself—trying to do too much yourself?
  Working 16-hour days, not delegating to others?
  Were you "on top" of this job, or were you busy doing other things?
Your employees?
Your equipment—wrong for the job?
Your schedule—unreasonable and impossible?

the firm that CMR believes were made in error. This is an important strength for small contractors.

ENTREPRENEURS CAN LOSE PERSPECTIVE

Even entrepreneurs that handle bidding and contracting as well as CMR does, are prone to fall in love with what got them "there," what made them successful, or what seems to work. Here is a look at some mistaken notions of business owners and managers that can reduce the gains achieved from earlier successes. Among these mistaken notions are the notion that industry trends are predictable, that costs will stay the same or rise at a constant rate, that competition is insignificant, that skilled labor will not be a problem, and that what worked before will work again.

The Notion that Industry Trends Are Predictable

Given the exponential technological changes that have been witnessed in recent years and the exponential technological advances that can be expected in future years, there will be few industries whose trends can be reasonably predicted beyond a few years. Here are examples of changes that helped foster dramatic shifts in the economy, thereby throwing "off course" what were thought to be industry "trends":

- *Improved Phone Communications Systems.*   Trend alteration: Greater reliance on conference calls, lesser frequency of small on-site conferences.
- *Proliferation of Photocopy Equipment.*   Trend alteration: Despite comprehensive, updated copyright laws, thousands of authors and publishers across the country are denied royalties because of overuse of office copiers to reproduce articles, pamphlets, and other published materials.
- *Music Synthesizers.*   Trend alteration: In a few short years, 80 percent of all the music we hear may originate from computers, not musicians. The jobs of studio musicians are now in jeopardy.
- *Developments in Footwear.*   Trend alteration: The full-line, "everything for everyone" shoe store is being replaced by stores that carry athletic shoes only, women's shoes only, men's shoes only, sandals and beach footwear, or shoes for camping, hiking, and rough terrain.

Technological change, social trends, or environmental factors can often undermine the objectives of the business and leave the entrepreneur wondering, "What went wrong?"

The Notion that Costs Will Stay the Same or Rise at a Constant Rate

In the past ten years, we have seen the cost of energy and phone service more than triple. The minimum wage has risen several times and is due to go higher yet. Existing government regulations are now costing the average businessperson as much as 15 percent of his or her time, while the dollar costs of those regulations are as yet uncalculated.

Inflation may have cooled off, but it will be back, and maybe worse than before. In the coming years, the cost of water will rise dramatically. Other items whose costs may rise beyond the predictable rate include office supplies, business insurance, and employee benefit packages.

With profit margins staying the same or declining slightly and operating costs inching ever upward, mammoth increases in business volume will be necessary to sustain viability.

The Notion that Competition Is Insignificant

It's amazing to note the number of successful small business vendors who, when asked about the effects of competition, respond, "They're insignificant," and when asked about what their competitors are doing, respond, "They're not up to much." Yet the advent of just-in-time delivery, electronic networks, and material requirements planning; shifts in lifestyle, appetites, and demands; and new findings in such areas as health and safety signify that the competitive edge of a business can be wiped out literally overnight.

If Fortune 500 CEOs in transportation, steel, business machines, and so on maintain a keen awareness of the moves of their competitors and of the market share that each of these competitors possesses, why not take a cue from the top? Why do small business vendors consistently fail to take into consideration the actions, promotions, products, and strategies of their competitors?

The Notion that Skilled Labor Will Not Be a Problem

The shortage of clerical workers is now apparent in all major U.S. cities. Significant shortages of all types of skilled labor can be expected in the coming years, as we move from the age of industry to the age of information. Shortcomings in our educational system have already prompted such Fortune 500 firms as General Electric (10) and Procter & Gamble (22) to offer remedial reading courses to their employees. Remedial reading! There are 27 million Americans who can't read this sentence and another 31 million who can, but with difficulty. As my assistant, Louis Baron, says, "That's 25 percent of America."

For the small vendor, labor will always be a problem, as some employees use the small business experience as a springboard to obtaining other positions or to starting their own firms. Also, the cost of attracting and maintaining good employees is a much greater percentage of total costs for the small vendor than it is for a major corporation that merely debits corporate "development" expense.

The Notion that What Worked Before Will Work Again

This erroneous notion represents the greatest area of potential trouble for the small vendor, as what worked before may not have anything to do with current or future business requirements. Paradoxically, among the business owners that have been successful, many never comprehend why they achieved success or what they must do to sustain that success.

In professional services, success is often a function of the uneven distribution of competitors within a geographic area. For smaller manufacturers, success is often based on the fact that product sales in their particular market niche are not sufficient to attract larger manufacturers. For example, you can independently mix, bottle, distribute, and make profit from consumer or industrial cleaning compounds until your sales in a specific geographic area begin to cut into the market of the corporate giants. Once that happens, any success that you have achieved over a number of years may be wiped out in a matter of months as the larger distributors undercut your price and mass-distribute their products in your territory. Since you cannot meet their price and you cannot sustain a positive cash flow with a reduced level of activity, you go under.

Past successes have only limited meaning for the future, and the best defense, as always, is to stay flexible and roll with the punches.

CHAPTER FIFTEEN

Improving Your Financial Image

Do what you can,
with what you have,
where you are.

THEODORE ROOSEVELT

Your financial image goes a long way toward enhancing your market efforts. All other things being equal, a vendor that appears to be on a firm financial footing is more attractive to purchasing agents than one that is not. In a study recently conducted by *Purchasing,* 60.6 percent of buyers of originally manufactured components, materials, and supplies mentioned that financial stability is a concern when choosing a supplier.

According to Cahners Publishing Company, the cost of making a sale to a new customer is nearly $1,500 and climbing. Your financial status most definitely affects your ability to market.

Let's first take a look at potential sources of funds. Where can you get money to operate and effectively market your business to major corporations?

If your company is a sole proprietorship:

Personal funds of the proprietor.

Bank loans.

Loans from individuals.

Loans from or guaranteed by a government agency.

Loans from other businesses.

The amount of the loans and the interest rates will be determined by:

Track record of the proprietor.

Size of inventory.

Rate of inventory turnover.

Market potential.

Profit potential.

If your company is a partnership: All of the above and

Contributions by each partner to the capital of the business.

Loans from partners.

If your company is a corporation: All of the sources available to a proprietorship and

Initial stockholders.

Equities—selling additional stock, common or preferred.

Industrial revenue bonds.

SPELL OUT YOUR FUNDING NEEDS

There is a paradox confronting successful small firms: the larger the contracts won, the less likely it is that such a firm will be able to sufficiently stock the required inventories and raw materials.

The funding of sufficient inventories is largely a generic problem. Any small firm that undertakes a large project or handles an unusually large amount of business experiences financing problems. Only in the ideal setting, unfortunately, where a small business receives an equal volume of work each month and accounts receivable and payable are in perfect harmony, can a large inventory of raw materials be financed primarily through internal cash flow. Corporations and financial institutions sensitive to this problem can be hard to find.

What are the alternatives? You could try using front-loaded contract billing, obtaining a revolving line of credit, and maintaining a strong working capital position.

When you set out to borrow money for your company, advises Leslie Rhatican, it is important to know what kind of financial assistance you'll need from a bank or other lending institutions. When making the decision to borrow, there are two important concerns to consider: What will the funds be used for? What is the source of money for repayment? Short-term loans are usually repaid from the liquidation of the current assets they have financed. Long-term loans are usually repaid from earnings.

Dealing with banks requires planning and forethought. Try to establish an ongoing business relationship with your bank. Visit your banker, or a banker, and establish rapport *before* you need a loan. The banker

---

RAISING CAPITAL

Short-term bank loans

Used for:

Financing accounts receivable 30 to 60 days.
Building a seasonal inventory over a period of five to six months.

Banks lend this money as:

Unsecured loans—you do not have to put up collateral; the bank relies on your credit reputation.
Secured loans—you pledge some or all of your assets.

Long-term loans

Used for:

Start-up, growth, and maintenance.
Financing plant, equipment, other fixed assets.

Banks lend this money as:

Secured loans—you offer a first or second position on fixed assets, and possibly personal assets as well.

Equity capital

Money you get by selling a partial interest in your company.

You take people into your business who are willing to risk their money on it in return for a share of the profits.
You don't repay equity money (you may buy out shares).

---

will then know you and your business, and will thus be more favorably disposed to grant you a loan when you actually need one.

A good guide for raising money is *Small Business Guide to Borrowing Money,* by Richard Rubin and Philip Goldbery (New York: McGraw-Hill, 1980). This book is designed to help you to avoid the pitfalls of borrowing money and to obtain the fastest and best financing. Appendixes include a sample packet of materials to present to a lender and lists of venture capital and small business investment companies.

FINANCIAL STATEMENTS AND YOUR IMAGE

Financial statements are prepared from accounting records to aid management in analyzing the performance of the business. They are also examined

---

QUICK TIPS FOR DEALING WITH BANKS

Show loyalty by dealing with one bank:

Savings.
Checking accounts.
Loans.

To enhance your chances of receiving a loan:

Prepare a loan proposal—include:
Amount of capital needed.
Type of loan—long- or short-term.
Terms: secured, unsecured.
Desired interest rate.
Proposed payback schedule.

Clearly explain the purpose of the loan.

Present company financial statements:
Cash flow and pro forma projections.
Balance sheets and income statements for past three years.
Collateral.
Inventory.
Fixed assets.
Life insurance.
Listing and aging of accounts receivable.

Provide related nonfinancial information:
Business strategy.
Data on company's industry.
Company's position in the industry.
List trade suppliers for references.

Other factors:

Repay loans on time.
Make yourself known to bank officers, well before you need a loan.
Bring in business for the bank.
Ask—the bank can't help you if it doesn't know your needs.

---

by purchasing agents when they are evaluating your firm as a prospective vendor.

Are your financial statements audited by a certified public accountant (CPA)? This process serves as notice that these statements meet certain accounting tests and standards. Auditing lends credibility and professionalism, and the winners have it done.

"What are audited statements?" you ask. Price Waterhouse, one of the Big Eight in accounting, defines them as documents presenting your company's financial data in a periodic, consistent, and acceptable fashion. They are very important for marketing purposes because they present your company to outsiders in a "professional and current manner reflecting your progressive and professional organization." Audited statements are your statements. A CPA firm merely attests that "in its opinion, the financial statements present fairly the operations of your company for a given period of time, and the financial condition of your company at a given point in time."

Many others besides purchasing agents are favorably influenced by firms with audited financial statements. Price Waterhouse cites five instances in which having audited statements can be beneficial.

1. *Banks.* Lending institutions are in business to make money, just like you. They do this by lending money to sound investments. They seek to determine the ability of borrowers to repay in accordance with the terms of the loan. A bank can reduce its risk by being selective among borrowers, provided it has enough competent data to make the decision. In the end, if a decision comes down to two apparently similar companies, one of which has audited statements, a bank will probably place more confidence in the audited numbers because a professional independent agent was involved in reviewing their makeup.

2. *Bonding Companies.* Those in the construction business know the importance of the bonding company. The larger your bonding capacity, the larger the jobs on which you can bid. Your financial statements play a significant part in getting the bonding capacity you desire, and the reliability of these statements weigh heavily in the eyes of the bonding agent.

3. *State Requirements.* Incorporated businesses in several states must file, on a yearly basis, a certificate of condition. In some states, if a company's assets are over a certain amount, an independent auditor's statement is required.

4. *Selling Business and Going Public.* If you ever sell your business outright, or sell shares of the business, you must present a history of the firm to the potential investors—the Securities and Exchange Commission requires a five-year audited summary. Most buyers look askance at unaudited data.

5. *Creditor Requirements.* Often your suppliers may request financial information before extending credit. Depending on the size of the order and past experience, a supplier may require audited financial statements as opposed to in-house statements.

One basic objective of financial statements, according to Price Waterhouse, is to provide information useful for making economic decisions. The regular audited financial statement is a measurement of the period-by-period progress of an enterprise toward its overall goals. Periodic audits of a company's financial statements ensure that the data being used are reliable and accurate.

WHAT DO AUDITS INVOLVE?

The focus of the auditor's examination is the financial statements of the company at their year-end date. The auditor must examine these financial statements as well as the underlying data, accounting records, and accounting systems that support them.

The audit manager, through meetings with management, discusses operations for the period, reviews interim operating statements, and acquires basic information about the company in order to formulate a plan of attack for the examination.

Next, an audit team visits the company and tests its accounting records and its method of recording transactions. The Price Waterhouse examination generally entails a study and evaluation of internal controls. The key questions are: What are the internal controls, and why are they necessary? The auditor reviews the transactions to see whether they are properly recorded and executed within the existing system of procedures and controls.

After the auditor is satisfied that the internal accounting controls and procedures are working correctly, he or she examines the year-end statements. Through the use of third-party confirmations, the auditor can obtain independent support of cash balances (from banks), accounts receivable (from customers), and notes and accounts payable (from creditors). Through physical testing and observation, the auditor can determine the reasonableness of inventories and fixed assets.

The auditor concludes the examination and issues one of several types of reports:

1. *Unqualified*—you pass with no problem!
2. *Qualified opinion*—there were inconsistencies, uncertainties, or limitations in the scope of the audit.
3. *Adverse opinion*—your financial statements deviate materially from generally accepted accounting procedure, or there is inadequate disclosure.

4. *Disclaimer of opinion*—there were obstacles limiting the auditor's ability to render an opinion.

Price Waterhouse emphasizes that the audit process must involve your full cooperation so as to facilitate a thorough examination and so that all the necessary facts supporting the financial statements are disclosed. Having an audit sounds scary, but it is actually a routine event with firms that successfully market to the Fortune 500.

The results of an audit can be more substantial than the auditor's report itself. Through the auditor's experience and knowledge, he or she can suggest tax planning and saving techniques and ideas for increasing the efficiency of company personnel.

ACCENTING THE POSITIVE

Especially when you have had some lean years (and who hasn't?), your financial image should be presented as favorably as possible. If your

---

HORIZONTAL TREND ANALYSIS

Base year equals 100 percent; subsequent years are shown as percentages of the base-year figures. Example:

Balance Sheet

	Base Year	2nd Year	3rd Year
Total assets:	100%	105%	104%
Current	100	102	108
Fixed	100	98	99
Other	100	107	110
Total liabilities:	100	106	105
Short-term	100	102	101
Long-term	100	101	103
Net worth	100	101	104

Income Statement

	Base Year	2nd Year	3rd Year
Sales	100%	104%	109%
Cost of goods sold	100	102	111
Gross profit	100	102	98
Operating expenses	100	102	102
Net profit before taxes	100	101	100

VERTICAL TREND ANALYSIS

Total assets and total sales equal 100 percent, and the component entries
are listed as percentage portions of those totals. Example:

Balance Sheet

		Base Year	2nd Year	3rd Year
Total assets (100%):		100%	100%	100%
Current	(Sums to 100%) {	14	11	8
Fixed		52	54	54
Other		34	35	38
Total liabilities:		106	104	101
Short-term	(Sums to 100%) {	36	33	32
Long-term		70	71	69
Net worth		−6	−4	−1

Income Statement

		Base Year	2nd Year	3rd Year
Sales (100%)		100%	100%	100%
Cost of goods sold	(Sums to 100%) {	79	79	80
Gross profit		21	21	20
Operating expenses		20	18	18
Net profit before taxes		1	3	2

---

firm has had a steady rate of growth or an improving cash position,
even if you have a long way to go before you can show a profit, emphasize
the positive aspects of this improvement. Horizontal and vertical trend
analysis are techniques that can be used to present your financial image
favorably. The accompanying box shows a sample horizontal trend analysis for balance sheets and income statements.

With a horizontal trend analysis, you set all components of your
balance sheet equal to 100 percent in the base year. Then, for succeeding
years, you show how the amount for each component compares to that
component's base-year amount. For example, if the amount for a component did not change, that component would remain at 100 percent. The
same approach can be applied to the components of your income statement.

With vertical trend analysis for balance sheets, the figure for each
year's total assets is set equal to 100 percent. Other balance sheet components are then expressed as percentages of the total assets. For income
statements, vertical trend analysis works the same way, using sales in
place of assets.

IMPROVING YOUR CREDIT RATING

Many small businesses that could successfully market to Fortune 500 corporations never even try because of a poor credit rating. Let's focus on steps to improve your credit rating, and take a look at what the credit bureaus examine in determining your credit rating.

Suppose you've been in business for a few years but have had trouble in meeting accounts payable only lately. How can you keep your suppliers and creditors happy and give your company the appearance of financial solvency?

Contact Your Suppliers

The best way to reestablish a good credit rating with suppliers is to enclose a personal letter to each one with the next payment due. The letter should explain the reasons for slow payment in the past and offer a brief synopsis of your present operations. It should also thank the supplier for exhibiting patience and support, if applicable, with the assurance that every effort is being made, and will continue to be made, toward full payment and the development of a solid working relationship.

It is best to deal honestly with suppliers, avoiding commitments that cannot be met. When in doubt, follow the path of integrity. In the short run, you may take some knocks. In the long run, you'll always come out ahead. After you have been in business for longer than one to two years, if your relationship with your suppliers has been honest, they can be used as valuable sources of short-term financing via the extension of trade credit.

What the Credit Bureaus Seek

Dun & Bradstreet, one of the world's largest credit rating agencies, examines the following areas when making a credit evaluation:

- What are the character, reputation, and management ability of the principals? Are the principals conservative or venturesome? Do they seem intelligent? Do they have high living standards?
- Is the credit requested unreasonable or unusual for this type of business?
- What is the business location like, and what is the condition of the neighborhood?

- Is credit information readily furnished, and are the answers given direct and concise?
- Do the principals have other enterprises? Do these enterprises enhance the credit risk?
- How does the highest credit line extended to a customer compare with the present request under current business conditions?
- Is the business insurance adequate? Has a safety check been made to reduce fire hazards and other disasters?

In addition, cash, accounts receivable, and inventory are investigated in detail. Specific information sought can include the following:

Cash

- Is your money deposited with a bank that also carries your outstanding loans? In such a case, the money deposited is usually encumbered directly to the extent of those loans.
- How much of the available cash is earmarked for immediate payment of wages, dividends, bonuses, loans due, and purchase commitments or for expansion programs?
- If there are unusually large cash balances, are there indications of inefficient use of capital?
- If there are unusually low cash balances, will assets, such as accounts receivable or inventories, have to be pledged for losses to the disadvantage of general creditors?

Accounts receivable

- What portion of the receivables may be classed as "good," what portion can be counted on for payment when due, and what portion are "bad"?
- Which accounts are past due, and why?
- What is the credit standing of each substantial past-due account and of each unusually large current account? Does the information on sales jibe with the information on past-due accounts?
- Have some accounts been sold or assigned, without being so indicated?

Inventory

- Are inventories kept under control by means of accurate and detailed records?
- Have goods received on consignment been included in inventory?
- Are slow-moving, obsolete items regularly eliminated from the inventory accounts?

- In consideration of seasonal changes or other factors, is the estimated liquidity of inventory sufficient?

Supplier Credit Checks

Many suppliers undertake their own credit evaluation. In evaluating the credit of your firm, suppliers may:

- Look for and analyze distress signals, such as partial payment being made or notes being offered in payment.
- Check in advance to find out what guarantees or securities are available should the circumstances suggest that these are needed.
- Examine your business hazards, personnel, sponsors, and links to other enterprises.
- Check outside mortgages, liens, or control on the management by other creditors or interested parties.
- Check to see whether your industry is subject to unusual price-cutting and excessive risks and whether you have tie-ins with any other companies that are likely to affect the risk.
- Obtain the facts of any bankruptcies or receiverships mentioned in your credit applications.
- Check to find out whether others have ever had to institute legal action for collection.
- Search the public records for judgments and other liens that may not have been mentioned in the customary sources of credit information.
- Determine whether there is any contest by insurance companies or underwriters about fire losses.

Honesty Is the Best Policy

It is better to show some financial weaknesses if that is the case, and maintain integrity. Stated another way, when it comes to favorably influencing creditors and credit bureaus, honesty *is* the best policy.

COLLECTING ON THE OVERDUE ACCOUNT

One way to bolster your financial position is to maintain a professionally aggressive program for receiving funds due to you. There is no surefire method for effectively collecting overdue accounts. Large firms often have a full-time collection department. As owner or manager of a small firm you must generally rely on your bookkeeper or yourself. Three aspects of collection are discussed below:

> General collection policies, including recontract agreements.
> Planning once a payment is overdue.
> Strategies for collection.

General Collection Policies

Mutually agreeable payment terms should be established in writing, prior to the start of each contract, regardless of the size and importance of the customer.

Clients having a poor track record of payment should be required to pay an initial portion of the fee immediately, make progress payments on a specified basis, and complete all payments within 30 days of contract completion. Of course, as a small business vendor, you may not have this kind of control with Fortune 500 corporations.

Use of the telephone for collection correspondence is acceptable if the telephone call is documented with a brief follow-up letter. The letter can be as simple as this:

Date

Dear _____:

    This is to confirm our phone conversation on _(date)_ regarding the _(amount)_ overdue to XYZ Company and the payment plan that was established, _(terms)_.

Sincerely,

(Signature)

A copy of the letter should be sent to your attorney, who, as previously indicated, should be permanently retained for legal advice and counsel.

Planning Once a Payment Is Overdue

AT&T (8) offers this advice. Once a payment is overdue, prior to calling, check to see whether:

1. Your company is at fault.
2. Any previous collection steps were taken.
3. You have the name of the person who can authorize payment.

You are now ready to call; the following steps are recommended:

1. Identify yourself, your firm, and the reason for the call.
2. Make a strategic pause (the customer will then automatically speak).
3. Determine why payment wasn't made.
4. Set up a new payment plan.
5. Send a new letter confirming the conversation directly after the call.
6. Record all notes.
7. Wait for the next payment under the new payment plan.

Strategies for Collection

If the above polite procedures have not resulted in payment, then, depending on the amount due, your past history with the customer, the potential for future contracts, and so forth, other strategies should be considered.

Segment overdue bills into three classifications:

1. Customers that you *do* wish to retain. Negotiation and flexibility are important here.
2. Customers that you *may* wish to retain. Negotiation and flexibility are important; however, it is also important to be firm and to establish your billing requirements.
3. Customers that you *do not* wish to retain. Getting paid is your only consideration. Use all of the means at your disposal to accomplish this. Then consider the following traditional collection strategies.

- *Calling often and calling loud.* If you let the customer know that you want your money, your bill may be among those that get paid on time.
- *Turning the account over to a reputable collection agency.* Generally, the earlier the amount is collected, the larger your share. When an agency has been assigned collections after the 10th day, it charges a higher percentage. The agency's fees may seem costly, but the monies collected by the agency may be crucial in maintaining a positive cash flow.
- *Consulting the client's attorney.* For large amounts, litigation may be justifiable on a cost basis. Also, the mere threat of lawsuit can

sometimes be an effective strategy, though that threat is not likely to make any Fortune 500 corporation quiver.

Often the best approach involves a combination of all three strategies. Unfortunately, when it comes to collecting on overdue accounts, it is "the squeaky wheel that gets the grease."

CHAPTER SIXTEEN

A Vendor's Golden Rules

Enlightened men living in a
democracy readily discover that
nothing can confine them, hold
them, or force them to be
content with their present lot.

ALEXIS DE TOCQUEVILLE

Don't hope for excellence,'' says Zoltan Merszei, president and chief operating officer of Occidental Petroleum Corporation (19). "Demand it, of yourself and others." The *excellence* of Peters and Waterman's *In Search of Excellence* is not just a buzzword used in corporate literature but a belief system that views staying close to the customer—being attuned to the customer's wants and needs—as the best path to a strong, healthy business.

Flexibility is another essential element of successful competition in our dynamic, technologically driven society. The Chinese had developed a fairly sophisticated method for printing books in A.D. 600; 855 years later, the German inventor Gutenberg began printing his 42-line Bible at Mainz. Today, however, gut-wrenching, world-changing, technology breakthroughs are soon superseded by even greater breakthroughs. It has been observed that as recently as 60 years ago, technological advance occurred in 25-year cycles. By the 70s and 80s, the technology cycle had decreased to under 10 years, according to some estimates.

Before this century is over, the technology cycle may well be less than two years. Such rapid change will have a profound effect on the ability of individuals to keep pace in society. The rapidity of technological change also forebodes the coming of an ever-increasing array of opportunities for bold, innovative entrepreneurs. "Develop a vision of what is to come in the world," says Merszei; "that is the ultimate assurance of success."

One of the fastest ways to accelerate at a rate in which you effectively penetrate the Fortune 500 market is to *identify the 10 or perhaps 15 people that you must know and then meet them.* Who are the 10 people that you must know? They are different for everyone, but they generally include the head of your industry's association, a banker, a few directors of a few target corporations, certainly a handful of key purchasing agents at target corporations, perhaps a management consultant or adviser, a Small Business Administration management assistance officer, a good graphics and design professional, and assorted others based on the specifics of your product or service offering.

What is it you wish to be known for? If you are *known for something*—providing superior service, being the best producer of your product in the world, and so on—the key 10 or 15 people with whom you make contact will have an easier time remembering you and your company, and what you stand for.

Read what your targets read. This was mentioned previously. However, its importance cannot be overstated. When you read what your targets read, you begin to develop the ability to tap into the mind-set of those who can reward your firm with contracts.

Tie short-run objectives to long-run goals. Professor Donald W. Huffmire believes that this is particularly essential for small vendors. When you take on new tasks, do you carefully assess the downstream potential? Do you carefully assess a contract's potential for both maintaining your company's working capital requirements and adding to the experience, track record, and capabilities of the company?

In the early years of a business, when the prime objective is survival, this type of consideration would be a luxury. However, at some point in the growth and development of your company, any contract you undertake should be carefully assessed for both its long- and short-term contribution to the overall objectives of the company.

Look for opportunities in adversity. Some 50 years ago, Dale Carnegie taught this to the students who had enrolled in his course to develop greater self-confidence. So, too, can the entrepreneur develop a greater sense of business confidence by looking behind, above, beyond, and through adversity for the opportunity created as a by-product. The great architect Frank Lloyd Wright once said, "Limitations have always been the best friends of architecture." Wright used adverse environments (e.g., ground prone to earthquakes, waterfalls, restricted space) to design some of the most enduring buildings of the 20th century.

Develop the habit of looking for opportunities in adversity. Every entrepreneur who has been in business for longer than a month knows that adversity and entrepreneurship go hand in hand. Those who accept adversity as defeat are defeated. Those who see adversity as a normal occurrence within the life of a business survive. And those who view adversity as the flip side of opportunity succeed.

Simplify! Simplify! Simplify! Henry David Thoreau said it best over 140 years ago. Our lives and our businesses are "simply cluttered" with too many activities, and too many slips of paper, that simply don't support us. The golden rule for the entrepreneur is to stay with the 20 percent of our activities that yield 80 percent of the results and to drop the rest.

Always *act with integrity*. Truly, nothing will produce greater long-term results, or greater peace of mind.

Finally, *burn the past*. Learn from your experiences—from what went wrong and what went right—but invest in the future. You and your company are not just an extension of what came before today, because you have the ability to create. What products or services do you want to be offering a year from now? Three years from now? What profit level do you want to realize on the contracts you undertake? What do you want your image to be in the marketplace?

If you view your business and your marketing efforts as being inexorably tied to what came before, then all you have ever been is all you will ever be. How does the small vendor who has never had a Fortune 500 contract finally get one? Or examining the larger question, how do losers ever win? By going where they have never gone before. By doing what they fear. By doing what winners do.

> *The future doesn't belong
> to the fainthearted. It
> belongs to the brave.*
>
> RONALD REAGAN

GLOSSARY

Advertising.   Any paid form of nonpersonal presentation of ideas, goods, or services by an identified sponsor. Advertising is the main form of mass selling.

Auditing.   An examination of financial statements, underlying data, accounting records, and accounting systems to determine whether a company's financial statements are in accordance with generally accepted accounting procedures.

Bidding. The process of formally indicating interest in contracting with another party to perform a specific task or set of tasks. The bid generally includes an itemized cost and fee schedule.

Business cycle. A definable pattern of changes in business activity that is periodically repeated. Particular cycles do not correspond to any accounting period.

Business name. A registered business name, usually on a "doing business as . . ." (DBA) form with the local government. Part of the business licensing process, preventing any other business from using that same name for a similar business in the same locality.

Business plan. The strategy or game plan of a business. Includes a review of all the components of the business and of their contribution toward its objectives.

Buyer. An individual charged with the responsibility for identifying, analyzing, and selecting goods and services.

Capability statement. A written description of the background, experience, and current activities of a business that demonstrates its effectiveness in offering specified goods or services.

Capital assets. See *Fixed assets.*

Carrying costs. The costs associated with holding inventory, such as interest charges on funds invested in inventory and storage and devaluation costs.

Cash. A broad classification of easily transferred negotiable assets, such as coin, paper money, checks, money orders, and money on deposit in banks.

Cash cycle. The length of time between the purchase of raw materials and the collection of accounts receivable generated in the sale of the final product.

Centralized commodity management (CCM). A purchasing program whereby a commodity manager buys specified items for all plants and divisions.

Certified purchasing manager (CPM). An accreditation awarded by the National Association of Purchasing Management to individuals who have satisfied certain minimum requirements and who have demonstrated a high level of professional competence and integrity.

Clayton Act. A federal law that prohibits certain practices in commerce that lessen competition or tend to create a monopoly. This law also exempts labor unions and farm cooperatives from the provisions of the Sherman Antitrust Act.

Client-centered marketing. The continuing process of developing and enhancing advocate-oriented relationships with receptive people who are or can be useful to you in using, retaining, and referring you and your services.

Clipping bureau. A business whose chief function is to supply article reprints and information on a predetermined topic.

Collections. The systematic process of obtaining money due to a business.

Communication. Transmitting a message from a sender or source to a receiver.

Consumer market. All of the individuals and dwelling units that buy or acquire goods and services for personal consumption.

Consumerism. An organized movement of citizens and government to enhance the rights and power of buyers in relation to sellers.

Corporation. A business that has been granted a charter recognizing it as a separate entity having its own rights, privileges, and liabilities distinct from those of its members.

Credit. With suppliers, a trade courtesy enabling one to receive goods to be paid for later. With bankers, a financial reputation for being able to meet obligations.

Cues. Stimuli that elicit responses.

Customer. The only element crucial to the existence of a business. A person or group with potentially unmet needs.

Customer service. Satisfying and helping consumers by various means, such as offering technical assistance, handling grievances, providing information, and making substitutions.

Direct mail. A form of advertising in which a message is sent to preselected targets.

Distribution channel. The set of parties that assist in transferring particular goods or services from the producer to the consumer.

Distributor. An element or party in the distribution channel that transfers items of value between other parties in the channel.

Documentation. Written materials that support claims as to specific or general capabilities. May include proofs, photos, testimonials, references, and other supporting evidence.

Downtime. A disruption in routine operations in which a machine, department, or factory is inactive during normal hours.

Entrepreneur. An individual who conceives of, converts, or makes available a product or service that fulfills a need in the marketplace.

Equity. The net worth of a business, consisting of capital stocks, capital or paid-in surplus, earned surplus or retained earnings, and possibly certain net worth reserves.

Escrow. The property, money, or assets that are placed in the hands of a third party for release to a grantee only upon the fulfillment of a condition.

Factoring. A method of financing accounts receivable wherein a firm sells its accounts receivable (generally without recourse) to a financial institution (the factor).

Fixed assets. Assets of a business that are of a relatively permanent nature and are necessary for functioning, such as buildings, furniture, and equipment.

Fixed costs. Costs that do not vary with changes in output, such as rents, salaries, and interest on long-term loans.

FOB (free on board). This refers to the point at which title of goods transfers from the producer to the buyer. "FOB-origin" means that title is transferred when the goods leave the loading dock of the producer and that the shipping costs are paid by the buyer.

Forecasting. The art of anticipating what amount of revenue will be generated in a given time period or what buyers are likely to do under a given set of conditions.

Fortune 500. Major U.S. industrial corporation, as ranked by *Fortune* magazine, with sales (in 1985) of over $400 million.

FTC (Federal Trade Commission). An independent administrative agency that assists in the enforcement of the Clayton Act and other laws for maintaining free, competitive enterprise in support of the American economic system.

Geographic segmentation. Subdividing a market into such units as continents, nations, states, regions, counties, cities, or neighborhoods.

Good faith. Acting in the sincere belief that the accomplishment intended is not unlawful or harmful to another.

Goodwill. The intangible assets of a firm, whose value is established by the amount of the price paid for the going concern above and beyond its book value.

Image. The sum total of the perceptions that your customers, clients, and others have about you and your business.

Implied warranty. A guarantee that arises from contract law and implies that goods for sale are reasonably fit for their ordinary and intended purpose.

Inventory. The total of items of tangible personal property that (1) are held for sale in the ordinary course of business or (2) are in the process of production of goods or services that will be available for sale.

Job cost. The aggregate cost of the direct labor and material costs and the indirect manufacturing costs that are associated with a specific order or job.

Just-in-time (JIT). A program for eliminating waste by assembling the minimum resources required to add value to a product. Although often typified by low inventories or stockless production, it is not an inventory program per se.

Leveraging. The process of identifying and capitalizing on the smallest number of actions that produce the largest number/amount of results.

Life-of-the-program. A working arrangement whereby one vendor is used exclusively to supply a product for as long as a corporation produces a certain end product.

Line and staff.   A descriptive term that defines the structure of an organization. Line personnel have direct authority and responsibility for output, while staff personnel contribute indirectly to production and usually advise line personnel.

Line of credit.   An arrangement whereby a financial institution commits itself to lend up to a specified maximum amount of funds during a specified period.

Liquidity.   A measure of a firm's cash position and of its ability to meet maturing obligations.

Maintenance repair and overhaul (MRO).   A purchasing category for goods or services that preserve or enhance capital assets and resources.

Major corporation.   As used in this book, a company employing over 500 people that has an established purchasing department and regular product/service needs.

Market.   The set of existing and prospective users of a product or service.

Market penetration.   A systematic campaign to increase sales in the current markets of an existing product or service.

Market segment.   A distinct or definable subset of a target market.

Marketing.   The process of planning and executing the conception, pricing, promotion, and distribution of ideas, goods, and services to create exchanges that satisfy individual and organizational objectives.

Marketing information system.   A network of people, equipment, and procedures to collect, organize, analyze, evaluate, and distribute timely, relevant, and accurate information used by marketing decision makers.

Marketing management.   The analysis, planning, implementation, and control of programs designed to create, build, and maintain mutually beneficial exchanges with target buyers for the purpose of achieving organizational objectives.

Marketing plan.   The "hard-copy" end product of the marketing planning process.

Marketing planning.   The continuing process of auditing the company and its markets to identify opportunities and problems; establishing priorities; setting goals; allocating and organizing the resources required to accomplish those goals; and scheduling, achieving, and monitoring results.

Marketing research.   The systematic collection, analysis, and reporting of data to provide information for marketing decision making.

Marketing segmentation.   A marketing strategy conceived to produce a product or service that embodies characteristics preferred by a small part of the total market for the product or service.

Marketing strategy.   The marketing logic by which a business seeks to achieve its marketing objectives.

Material requirements planning (MRP). A systematic approach to purchasing that involves forecasting needs, identifying sources, establishing delivery schedules, and monitoring programs.

Minority businesses. Businesses whose owners are deemed, usually on the basis of government-produced criteria, "socially and/or economically disadvantaged."

News release. An announcement of community, state, national, or international interest that is distributed to print media by the organization for which and about which the release has been written.

Niche. An identifiable market or market segment that can be readily and prosperously penetrated.

Organization chart. A linear direction of responsibility and authority within a company or an institution.

Overhead. All the costs of business other than the costs of direct labor and materials, including such items as maintenance, supervision, utility costs, and depreciation.

Owners' equity. Those assets that are left over after all creditors have been paid off. The two sources of equity are owner investment and prior earnings from profitable operations.

Patent. The licensing of property rights to an individual or a corporation for exclusive use and protection of a product or process.

Payback period. The length of time that is required for the net revenues of an investment to return the cost of the investment.

Personal selling. A professional marketing effort involving face-to-face communication and feedback, with the goal of making a sale or inducing a favorable attitude toward a company and its products or services.

Physical distribution. The tasks involved in planning, implementing, and controlling the physical flows of materials and final goods from points of origin to points of use to meet the needs of customers at a profit.

Procurement. A contract award that secures the delivery of specific goods or the performance of specified services.

Product. Products or services that satisfy a want or need and can be offered to a market for acquisition, use, consumption, or adoption.

Product differentiation. Presenting a product so that it is perceived by customers as unique or as somewhat distinctive from other available products.

Product line. A group of products that are closely related because they satisfy a class of needs, are used together, are sold to the same customer groups, are marketed through the same type of outlet, or fall within given price ranges. Can also mean the full range of the products marketed by a company.

Product mix. The set of all product lines and items that a particular seller offers for sale to buyers.

Promotion. The act of furthering the growth and development of a business by generating the exposure of goods or services to a target market.

Proposal. A document designed to describe a firm's ability to perform a specific task by indicating that the firm has the facilities, human resources, management experience, and track record to assure the successful completion of that task.

Prospecting. Seeking potential buyers or customers; identifying and contacting likely candidates for the purchase of your goods or services.

Purchasing agent. As used in this book, a general term connoting any employed individual whose job responsibility involves buying goods or services.

Purchasing department. The portion of a company that is charged with the task of buying goods and services; supplies and commodities; and maintenance, repair, and overhaul.

Purchasing manager. One who supervises, trains, and develops buyers and assistant purchasing managers while maintaining some direct buying responsibilities.

Qualifiable vendor. A supplier of goods or services who may be able to competently fulfill corporate needs.

Qualified vendor. A supplier of goods or services who is able to competently fulfill corporate needs.

Reputation. The perception of value and integrity that is created by serving customers.

Robinson-Patman Act. An amendment to the Clayton Act giving the FTC jurisdiction to eliminate quantity discounts; to prohibit promotional allowances, except on an equal basis; and to forbid brokerage allowances, except to independent brokers.

Sales management. Operations and activities involved in the planning, directing, and controlling of sales activities.

Sales territories. Market allocations, based on geography, line of business, or other criteria, that facilitate the sales management function.

Security clearance. A certification or other form of inspection signifying that measures have been taken to ensure that an individual or a company does not pose an identifiable risk, particularly the risk of espionage or sabotage.

Selling. The exchange of goods, services, or ideas between two parties.

Setup. The time and activity required to establish an environment conducive to production.

Sherman Antitrust Act. The initial law passed by the U.S. Congress to preserve competition in the "free market" system by outlawing monopolies and other combinations to restrain trade or commerce.

Size standards. Measurements of business size that determine whether a business is "small" by the definitions of the Small Business Administration, which are usually based on the particular type of business, the number of employees, or gross annual sales.

Social responsibility. The concept of a corporate conduct that demonstrates concern for and participation in the surrounding community and society in general.

Sole source. Soliciting and using only one vendor to supply predetermined products or services.

Sourcing. As in "identifying new services." Can be for goods or services or for the vendors that supply them.

Standard. Basic limits or grade ranges in the form of uniform specifications to which particular manufactured goods may conform and uniform classes into which products may or must be sorted or assigned.

Standard Industrial Classification (SIC). A U.S. Bureau of the Census classification of industries based on the products they make or the operations they perform.

Standardization. A process whereby uniformity and conformity are sought.

Statistical process control. A quantitative tool for enhancing quality control that relies on probability theory and random sampling techniques.

Supplier. One who fulfills product or service needs.

Supplier certified. Responsibility for inspection rests solely with the vendor. A working arrangement between buyers and vendors.

Target market. The portion of the total market that a company has elected to serve.

Target marketing. Focusing marketing efforts on one or more segments within a total market.

Tax number. A number assigned to a business by a state revenue department that enables the business to buy goods wholesale without paying sales tax on them.

Test marketing. Selecting one or more markets in which to introduce a new product or service and a marketing program so as to observe and assess performance and to determine what revisions are needed, if any.

Trade association. An organization established to benefit members of the same trade by informing them about issues and developments within the organization and about how changes outside the organization will affect them.

Trade credit. Interfirm debt arising through credit sales and recorded as an account receivable by the seller and as an account payable by the buyer.

Trade show. A commercial or industrial gathering over a concentrated time period in which sellers at preassigned stations present goods and services for possible sale to prospective buyers.

Trademark. A graphic symbol, device, or slogan that identifies a business and provides legal protection and whose use is restricted to its owners.

Uniform Commercial Code. A comprehensive code of practices that has been established to simplify, clarify, and modernize the law governing commercial transactions; to permit the continued expansion of commercial practices through custom, usage, and agreement of the parties; and to make uniform the commercial law of the various jurisdictions.

Value analysis. An approach to cost reduction in which components are carefully studied to determine whether they can be redesigned or standardized or made by cheaper methods of production.

Vendor. As used in this book, synonymous with *supplier;* one who fulfills product or service needs.

Working capital. A measure of a firm's short-term assets—cash, short-term securities, accounts receivable, and inventories—and of its ability to meet short-term obligations.

INDEX